Teaching Women's History

I0084270

Teaching Women's History: Breaking Barriers and Undoing Male Centrism in K-12 Social Studies challenges and guides K-12 history teachers to incorporate comprehensive and diverse women's history into every region and era of their history curriculum.

Providing a wealth of practical examples, ideas, and lesson plans – all backed by scholarly research – for secondary and middle school classes, this book demonstrates how teachers can weave women's history into their curriculum today. It breaks down how history is taught currently, how teachers are prepared, and what expectations are set in state standards and textbooks and then shows how teachers can use pedagogical approaches to better incorporate women's voices into each of these realms. Each chapter explores a major barrier to teaching an inclusive history and how to overcome it, and every chapter ends with an inquiry-based lesson plan on women or using women's sources which stands counter to the way curriculum is traditionally taught, a case in point that tasks readers to realize how women have been integral to every period of history.

With expert guidance from an award-winning social studies teacher, this guidebook will be important reading for middle and high school history educators. It will also be beneficial to preservice teachers, particularly within Social Studies Education and Gender Studies.

Additional resources for educators are available to view at www.remedialherstory.com.

Kelsie Brook Eckert is an award-winning history teacher; the Coordinator of Social Studies Education at Plymouth State University, USA; and the Executive Director of the Remedial Herstory Project.

Teaching Women's History

Breaking Barriers and Undoing Male Centrism in K-12 Social Studies

Kelsie Brook Eckert

Routledge
Taylor & Francis Group
NEW YORK AND LONDON

Designed cover image: Drazen Zigic / Getty Images

First published 2025
by Routledge
605 Third Avenue, New York, NY 10158

and by Routledge
4 Park Square, Milton Park, Abingdon, Oxon, OX14 4RN

Routledge is an imprint of the Taylor & Francis Group, an informa business

Funding for publishing this chapter open access was provided by Lamson Library at Plymouth State University.

ISBN: 978-1-032-75196-2 (hbk)
ISBN: 978-1-032-69311-8 (pbk)
ISBN: 978-1-003-47288-9 (ebk)

DOI: 10.4324/9781003472889

Typeset in Palatino
by SPi Technologies India Pvt Ltd (Straive)

Dedication

For my grandmother—
    The historian and scholar.

Contents

About the Author

Kelsie Brook Eckert (she/her) is the Coordinator of Social Studies Education at Plymouth State University, the Executive Director of the Remedial Herstory Project (RHP), the New Hampshire State Coordinator for National History Day, and a Board Member for the New Hampshire Council for the Social Studies. She is the 2024 recipient of the Theo Kalikow award for her efforts toward the advancement of women in New Hampshire and the Transformative Teaching Award at Plymouth State. She taught high school social studies and was a two-time New Hampshire History Teacher of the Year, awarded by National History Day and the Gilder Lehrman Institute. She has developed dozens of inquiry-based lesson plans on diverse women's history, hosts a podcast on women's history, and is the Project Director for the RHP. She has a TEDx talk about the importance of diverse women's history, titled *It Has to Be Half*. Eckert is a world traveler and former college athlete, now a many-time ironman triathlete. She is also a wife and the mother of two amazing boys.

Preface

Our mental, cultural template for a powerful person remains resolutely male.[1]

—Mary Beard

I was sitting in the sun outside my favorite coffee shop on Main Street, the awning providing just enough shade from the summer heat. As I usually do, I had my books splayed out over the small circular table, which was dubiously balancing on the uneven sidewalk. Occasionally, a breeze would catch on the tall shops that lined the street and whip down, sending my pages, labels, and notes scribbled on scrap paper into momentary chaos.

Summer, for public school social studies teachers, is a time to rejuvenate through relaxation and outdoor activity as well as hone our craft. For me, this meant reading. I taught at a small school, so in my short time there I had taught every subject offered in the social studies. There is always more to learn, so I usually picked one book for each subject and then a few more for fun.

On this particular summer day, I was diving into two new books on world and US history: *America's Women* by Gail Collins and *A Women's History of the World* by Rosalind Miles. These books were my first (now of many) surveys in women's history, which was strange because I teach history and had already read substantially on both. My friends and family would not find it surprising at all that I'd chosen these books to read, given my passion for women's rights. I honestly didn't think I would glean much from these books. At best, I hoped I'd learn about a few women I didn't know about who had impacted history. I believed, as most people do, that few women had broken the glass ceiling and made a mark worthy of a historical footnote.

Sitting at the café, I found myself highlighting and tabbing frantically. It was almost overwhelming how much there was to know. I was around Chapter 3 or 4 when I looked up from the page. Whatever the particular page was about, I don't remember. I was struck by a sickening feeling: *Why have I never heard this?* I knew generally about some women, but nothing this comprehensive. No history book I'd read discussed things that impacted women's lives so intimately. Never had I come across such detailed accounts of extraordinary women. I knew about many women mentioned in the books, but for every woman I was familiar with, there were three or four more I'd never even heard of.

On this day, I was years into my career as a state-certified social studies teacher. I was highly skilled and a two-time New Hampshire history teacher of the year, among other honors. On paper, I looked pretty great. But despite the accolades and qualifications, I knew so little about what I was reading. It became obvious that despite my attempts, I, like many, had failed to teach a history that really included women. *Why?*

I taught secondary social studies in the public school system. My first years of teaching, I easily put in 60 hours a week. I spent most of that time doing research and growing my own understanding of my subjects. I dedicated my world to excelling in the classroom. I earned a variety of professional awards and recognitions. One of my lesson plans, on Mercy Otis Warren, was published by the HISTORY Channel. I studied D-Day in France as part of the Albert H. Small Normandy Scholar program. I was named the Outstanding Graduate Alumna from my graduate college. I succeeded in holding high expectations while scaffolding to allow every student the potential for success. My AP history students consistently got scores that earned college credit and were above the state and national averages, I regularly sent five or more students to the national history competition, and while I did a lot for the high achievers, I also worked to make sure students of all preconceived abilities succeeded.

I was, and remain, passionate about social, political, and economic equality for women of all races and sexual orientations, but despite the passion, I have failed to execute it well. If anyone should have been giving women fair representation in the history classroom, I should. And yet I looked back at my work and accomplishments and felt a bit like a fraud. My lessons were inadequate to address, and provide context for, the complex issues that women and people of color face and have faced every day. I began to ask, *Why were my lessons inadequate? Is it the culture? Is it the school? Is it me?*

One of the things I quickly acknowledged was that I worked in one of the best public schools in the nation, consistently ranked in the top ten by *USA Today* in a state consistently ranked in the top five. The school values the social studies and put trust in me to stay up-to-date with current literature on best practice in my subjects. When I'd spoken with my principal about how to give women a more accurate representation in the curriculum, I got full support. My school was well funded but economically below average in the state, with many students on free and reduced lunch. Class sizes were small, with an average of 12 or so students. The superintendent's office was down the hall, and I worked in one of the rare secondary schools with a female superintendent. The school was supportive of pretty much every initiative I tried and willing to invest money in it. My principal was a former social studies teacher who regularly had my back on curriculum development. The community in general was supportive of the school, and parents from all social and political backgrounds were relatively engaged. Though my situation was ideal, it was still the root cause of my constant anxiety: *I have absolutely no excuse to not "do it right."* I didn't have as many external forces to blame as other teachers did, and thus there was a constant guilt and this nagging question: *If I can't do it in my incredible circumstances, how can anyone else?*

This question has driven me to this point. A piece of my personal challenge is that my social studies education was inadequate. I began to ask, *What are my barriers to inclusive history education?*

My achievements launched me toward involvement with a variety of history and social studies education organizations in the state and around the country. At every stage, I was looking for guidance on how to do it better. I quickly realized that in every organization, very few people knew what they were doing. Many of the women who had been working on this for decades weren't trained as historians, and those who were struggled for legitimacy. I began to investigate the scholarship surrounding this problem. I stumbled upon article after article, mostly by women lamenting the lack of women's and gender history in the curricula dating back as far as the first women's history programs. Sick of hearing the same tune in the research, I decided to found the Remedial Herstory Project (RHP), a nonprofit working to get women's history into primary and secondary classrooms by producing ready-made classroom materials for educators to fight the issue from the grassroots. I spent years researching the barriers to inclusive women's history. With teams, we wrote multiple free, online textbooks for secondary classrooms. I identified problems and began to systematically hack at them. RHP grew in its following, scholarship, and support—with people, mostly women, regularly thanking us for *doing something* about the problem.

Note

1 Mary Beard, *Women & Power: A Manifesto* (London: Profile Books, 2017), 53.

Acknowledgments

If I have seen further it is by standing on the shoulders of Giants.[1]
—Sir Isaac Newton

Thank you to my husband, who listened and read different versions of this book over the last decade. It is rare to find a person who will endure your obsessions, engage intellectually with topics outside their sphere of interest, edit, advise, and support so enduringly. You are exceptional.

Thank you to Brooke Sullivan, who jumped at the chance to join me on this journey. Her constant support, cheerleading, and time have made our nonprofit, the Remedial Herstory Project, and this book possible. Thank you for really showing me what women supporting women looks like.

Thank you to my mom, who raised me and my sisters to be strong women. Because of her, I always knew I could achieve whatever I could dream of. And even better, I knew she would be my number one fan. Thank you to my grandmother, great-aunt Martha, and great-uncle Munn for inspiring a love of history and helping me see women in it.

Thank you to Dr. Heidi Snow, Chrissy Calkins Steele, Vanessa Gans, Dr. Julie Blase, and Dr. Marcia Blaine, my professors for whom I was encouraged to write history papers about women's lives before I knew this was a passion. Although only one was a professor of history, these women showed me that women had a place in history and teaching it. Thank you to my undergraduate advisor, Dr. Brian Roberts, who fostered my love for political science; despite being the only girl in freshman seminar, I was encouraged by Dr. Roberts to believe that I belonged.

Thank you to Sue Noyes and Dr. Rebecca Noel, two women who championed me and made my career possible. How amazingly lucky I was to apply for jobs in a mostly male field and have the honor of being hired by women at every stage. Thank you also to my first school principal, Andy Coppinger, who, beyond being a coach and mentor, supported my attempts to incorporate greater diversity into all my classes.

Thank you to the thousands of women's historians in the centuries before me who made it possible for me and my organization to do the work we do getting these resources into classes. If it wasn't for that archivist, that researcher, PhD candidate, and local historian diving into archives and making the stories of these women available, I would not have been able to begin this journey.

Thank you to the board of the Remedial Herstory Project and all the work each of you does to bring more awareness of women's lives and experiences in the past and present. A special thank-you to Dr. Barbara Tischler, Michelle Stonis, Elizabeth Dubrulle, Dr. Alicia Gutierrez-Romine, and Dr. Valerie Moyer, who read early versions of this book and provided insightful feedback and ideas. Your advice and reviews made me a better writer and feminist. Thank you to Dr. Alicia Gutierrez-Romine for responding to my pestering texts about the publishing process and helping me to write my pitch. Thank you for being in my corner.

Thank you to all the professors and authors who have joined me on our podcast to share their knowledge and insights on women's and gender history. Thank you for teaching me what I missed in history class.

Note

1 Sir Isaac Newton, Letter to Robert Hooke, 1675.

Introduction

History is no longer just a chronicle of kings and statesmen, of people who wielded power, but of ordinary women and men engaged in manifold tasks. Women's history is an assertion that women have a history, although that history has been distorted, even erased by the biases that pervade our culture and scholarship. We have to see women as a force in politics, as reformers, as revolutionaries, searching for an identity in their nation, their class, themselves. Women as producers, peasants, workers, artisans, domestic servants, in their roles in the family, as wives, daughters, and mothers have to become visible. The totality of women's lives is the concern of women's historians.[1]

—Aparna Basu

Women Are Half of Humanity

History is dominated by the stories of men. It has long been time for women's stories—her-story—to be told and, more importantly, taught. His-story is not the only story—it's just the one we are most acquainted with. But his-story will remain *the* story if the lives and accomplishments of half the population are all but excluded from the narrative. Women's stories are known and recorded. Scholars for the last century or more have been working to bring them into the public discourse, yet most teachers *still* don't know them, oversimplify them, or neglect their significance.

DOI: 10.4324/9781003472889-1

To begin to understand the problem, it's important to stare at the wall of barriers and puzzle through what reinforces them. What are the barriers to a collective understanding of women's history? Why do these barriers persist despite scholarship and research? Why is the history taught in schools consistently devoid of diverse women's narratives? As a history teacher who is passionate about women's rights and intrigued by the stories of women from the past, I asked these questions every time I stumbled upon *yet another* woman I had never heard of.

The barriers to an inclusive and comprehensive women's and gender history are many but are not insurmountable. Each barrier has a breaker—a linchpin that makes the towering wall of challenges fall apart. Too many people see the wall and are intimidated by it. They claim, "women's stories are just lost" or "records by women just weren't kept," but these are convenient ways to ignore the known stories and avoid digging for the unknown ones.

Many people have been so denied an education in women's and gender history that they claim, "Women just didn't do or accomplish much." This statement tells us much more about *their* understandings and values than it does about the accomplishments of women in the past, and it cleverly outlines a multitude of false beliefs about women, beliefs which we have come to accept. The statement is ignorant and offensive to half the population. For example, simply because women's names were not attached to accomplishments in the past does not mean they did not participate in those efforts. Students must learn to appreciate the cultural norms that blocked women's names from being included, even when they did *all* the work. Examples of real women help illuminate these falsehoods.

The incredible story of Albert Einstein's first wife—Mileva Einstein-Maric, who arguably was the brains behind this brilliant couple—exemplifies the butchering of women's history. Denied degrees from two universities, first because she was a woman and second because her husband already had a degree and somehow more than one degree in the family was wrong, Mileva spent her days as a homemaker and her evenings as a collaborator on the theory of relativity. Both roles were demanding and important. The letters she and her husband exchanged show that this work was a shared endeavor, with regular references to "us" and "our" work. Albert once said, "I need my wife. She solves for me all my mathematical problems."[2] But when the work was complete, Mileva's name was left off the essay. Why? Was Albert embarrassed? Would it have been poorly received by the academic community? Those would perhaps be feminist answers. Is it possible Mileva didn't want the fuss? Is it possible she was proud of the work they accomplished together and was happy for him to take credit for both of them? We may never know.

History is butchered when we ignore the role women played in it and how they were affected by it. Many of us know the name Einstein, but his wife? We don't mention her. Albert Einstein discovered relativity, but did he do it alone? Isaac Newton's humility about his discoveries said it best: "If I have seen further, it is by standing on the shoulders of Giants."[3] Every husband who accomplished things in his profession likely stood on the work of his wife, who kept the home and provided childcare, meals, support, and myriad other things. In Einstein's case, the giant was his wife, but not because of her wifely duties, although she did those as well.

Some women's stories were buried when the next victor came to power. If their stories are preserved, it's often a cautionary tale of women's rule. Student should learn to read between the lines. For example, most of Western Europe was controlled by two women for almost a century in the early Middle Ages—and few know the names or full history of Brunhild and Fredegund because their male successors attempted to erase or at least minimize their history.[4] As queen consorts, and queen regents under their sons, they held so much influence. To make things even more interesting, they hated each other since Fredegund likely had Brunhild's sister assassinated in order to secure the throne.[5] Fredegund, a known conspirator in at least 12 murders in her quest for power, died peacefully in her bed. Brunhild outlived her sons, leaving the then-elderly woman to fight battles with her young grandson against Fredegun's adult son—they lost. As a consequence, most of her bloodline was killed, and she was executed in the most brutal way possible, by dragging her behind a wild horse—yikes! This type of intrigue is a recipe for what should make history class—powerful leaders, military history, and diplomacy. Where were these women? They should have been a main narrative in the story of the early Middle Ages, not a buried one.

Similar stories occurred during and after the rise of Chinggis Khan. While he was an expert at conquering, his wives, daughters, and daughters-in-law were experts at organizing and governing. At its height, most of the great Mongol Empire was actually governed by women.[6] His daughters, like Alakhai Bekhi who ruled over a huge swath of land along the Silk Roads, was given the title "Princess Who Runs the State."[7] The story of the Mongol Empire is only half accurate when told without women (Figure I.1).

This phenomenon happens with more contemporary history too! When most people teach and learn about the Montgomery Bus Boycott, they learn about segregation, not sexual assault of Black women.[8] The power dynamic created by white supremacy also was a breeding ground for sexual assault of Black women. Bus drivers had the powers of police to enforce segregation laws, and sexualization, harassment, and assault were common on the busses.[9] Rosa Parks was not the first, nor was she the last Black woman to protest

Figure I.1 Robinson is erased from the narrative in this 1957 comic book by the Fellowship of Reconciliation. Parks is also minimized while King is centralized, which is factually inaccurate.

Source: Fellowship of Reconcilliation, "Martin Luther King and the Montgomery Story" Civil Rights Movement Archive, 1957. https://www.crmvet.org/docs/ms_for_comic.pdf.

this treatment. JoAnn Robinson was the head of the Black women's club and for months had been planning to boycott the busses without the support of the male clergy. When Parks was arrested, Robinson put the plan in motion, copying thousands of flyers.[10] The club women distributed the flyers to families, and overnight the busses lost most of their passengers. After the first week, the male clergy took over, and Robinson along with other women's names were buried behind that of then-26-year-old Martin Luther King Jr. In Figure I.1, a widely redistributed cartoon used to show other communities how to do what Montgomery did, Parks is reduced to a tired woman and Robinson and the women's club are entirely erased and replaced by King. King is literally shown making the copies Robinson is known to have made. There will be more on the Montgomery women in Chapter 5. The examples go on and on in region after region, era after era.

Often this falsity of what we know about history is hard for people to confront. Teachers and students must undo what they think they know to include women. Women are half of us and half our history. When history presents itself differently, it is a failure of the historians and teachers, not of actual events. Orville Wright, of the famous Wright Brothers who were pioneers in aviation, once said, "When the world speaks of the Wrights, it must include our sister. Much of our effort has been inspired by her."[11] The version of history that included Katherine I never learned, and I bet readers didn't either. If the Wright Brothers can tell the whole story, so can teachers.

Statement of Thesis

The problem is not just that a few crucial women are overlooked, it's that women's experiences, their diversity, and the complexities of their lives are lost in an entirely male-defined field. When history fails to include women's and gender history comprehensively, neglecting the layers of race and class, it leaves white, middle-class women as the norm, and women's history, like most men's history, is whitewashed. Women are half of humanity, not an interest group. Their history, their experiences, their challenges, and disagreements should be *half* the content of the history curriculum, and at present it's not even close.

Women, their interests, and challenges are not only unstudied but undervalued, which perpetuates the devaluing of women and their work today. Students need to see themselves in history, and half the population leaves high school with just a small handful of un-behaved and white historical models. When secondary teachers do teach women's history, it is often oversimplified, feminist, or even sexist, ideals. Both perspectives perpetuate the cycle of devaluing women's traditional contributions and acknowledging the ways women have sat outside of the ideals imposed on them. Our world is plagued with continuing gender discrimination, unequal treatment, and violence against women. In the primary and secondary classrooms, we can give all students the opportunity to study these problems and be part of the solution. History allows societies to see patterns in the past. History informs the present. If teachers take these problems seriously and teach women's and gender history, we can change lives. Without women's history, society is doomed to repeat the past.

A wall of social norms, customs, policies, and ignorance exists that barricades women's inclusion in the secondary history classroom. Teachers must stare at it long and hard to find the chinks and dismantle it. It's not as easy as saying, "Let's just put women in." We need to understand why they haven't been there and adjust accordingly.[12] Mistakes in inclusion are made when teachers don't know their subject matter well enough—I should know. I've made them. In secondary schools, if women are mentioned, it is often as a sidebar to the main narrative—yet women are central to the story. Pop-up, or sidebar, history leaves us with the impression that all women agree with one woman's perspective.

This book explores the barriers to women's and gender history and suggests important history that should be included as well as practical methods to include women in content already taught. This book argues that false and sexist ideas about women impact what is currently taught, that teachers must and can include women in the curriculum they already teach, and that they should shift to include themes that better incorporate women. Further, teachers must dismantle the illusion that women are a monolith and allow for women's diversity and disagreements. Teachers are responsible to both halves of the student body both in accessibility and in content selected for inclusion. Women should be half our content.

Conceptual Background
Women or Gender History
Women or gender history? Answer: both. Women's history is gender and sexuality history. It includes the exploration of masculinity and gender discussions. For a while, the move to include gender and sexuality in discussions of women's history was controversial among scholars. Many women feared that inclusion of gender and sexuality would decrease the much-needed attention to the sheer absence of women. However, scholars soon found that gender and sexuality research illuminated the stories of women in the past and that the fields complemented one another well. In their review of the status of women and gender history studies, Cornelia H. Dayton and Lisa Levenstein explained, "most practitioners in the field today would not consider studying women without also studying gender."[13] All of it is deeply needed, and more is more.

I will reference the histories of queer women throughout this text. The challenge of telling queer histories is that the figures didn't have the same words for their gender and sexual identities that we do today, so I use the term queer to highlight the non-cis, non-heterosexual nature of their personal life. In class, I take a brief pause to out these figures so that my LGBTQ+ students can see themselves in the past. Queer history is all over women's history. I think it's important that those connections be made so we can see how the patriarchal reliance on male providers and protectors was problematic for queer women. Most of the women who *are* taught in school were lesbian or queer and that crucial layer to their experience was left out. Many suffrage leaders fit into this category: Susan B. Anthony, Carrie Chapman Catt, and Alice Paul were all queer. Catt, the final president of the National Women's Suffrage Association, was buried next to her female partner, not her late husband, with an endearing epitaph on the headstone. Exploring sexuality and gender alongside women's history is crucial.

The Inquiry Model
I believe the teaching of women's history fails when we abandon academic principles for preaching ideas. Both the right and the left do this. So while I'm passionate about women's rights and women's history, *how* we teach that

is the same way we teach any social science or humanity subject: by getting the material and evidence into students' hands. To really teach critical thinking, social studies teachers around the world have adopted the old-turned-new-again approach to instruction called the inquiry model. The National Council for the Social Studies has grounded their pedagogy in inquiry in the recent College, Career, and Civic Life standards for the social studies. Inquiry is the essence of academia: asking questions and testing and retesting hypotheses.

I will expand on the inquiry model and its uses for teaching a diverse women's history in Chapter 2: "His-Story is not the Only Story." From my experience and for my purposes, many teachers want to teach women's history and simply don't have the evidence or materials to do it well, so I've ended each chapter with a sample "inquiry" that allows historic or present debates to be investigated in the classroom using primary material. Teachers can use these in class or use them as a model to build one more related to the content they want to teach. These inquiries are a handful of the over 100 inquiry-based lesson plans available for free on my nonprofit's website: www.remedial herstory.com. There, teachers can find articles, primary sources, and inquiries about women for government, economics, every period of history, and every region of the world. The development of most of those inquiries was funded by the Library of Congress, administered by Waynesburg University.

Phase Theory
There are many conceptual frameworks on how best to integrate women into the history curriculum, but the most referenced is Mary Kay Thompson Tetreault's "Phase Theory." Tetreault's theory is an expansion of Gerda Learner's 1975 essay on the systematic ways that historians were integrating women into the narrative.[14] Learner said that, first, historians were compensating by just throwing in notable women. Second, they were discussing the women's sphere and the rich themes of women's experience: contribution history. And she envisioned a third stage where history is holistic and intersectional.

Tetreault broke this three-part framework down further to give them more form. Her Phase Theory is a useful tool for teachers to reflect on where they are and see where they need to go. She expanded the three stages into five phases:

1. Male History
2. Compensatory History
3. Bi-Focal History
4. Feminist History
5. Integrated History

Her five phases are designed to cease the oversimplification of women's history and get into the nuances and complexities before finally integrating all of it into a human history.[15] It is also a helpful framework, because while Phase Five: Integrated History is the goal, it's hard to do that if you don't know key women, Compensatory History. Teachers certainly can't teach the history of all of us if they don't know how the layers of race, ethnicity, class, ability, sexuality, etc. impacted various groups. This book will use her framework to pull teachers through each phase, providing them with strategies, pedagogies, and packaged tools so they can finally access an integrated history.

Most secondary classrooms are in Phase 1: Male History.[16] So the first thing those teachers need to do is find notable women worth knowing. Inquiry will be deployed as a gateway strategy to integrate women's voices and biographies into the history curriculum and pull them from Phase 1 to Phase 2: Compensatory History. To move into Phase 3: Bi-Focal History, teachers should explore women's generalized experiences and contrast those with men's. At this Phase, I will also draw from the work of Jessica B. Shocker, specifically her paper "A Case for Using Images to Teach Women's History."[17] Her work makes plain that women's inclusion can be achieved today using some pedagogic strategies. Once key women and some general understandings of the female experience are known, educators will be primed to enter Phase 4: Feminist History, where the diversity of women's experience is explored. There I will build on Tetreault's ideas with the contributions of other scholars like Nel Noddings, Margaret Smith Crocco, Christopher Martell, and Kaylene Stevens, who have all explored strategies used by educators to teach histories that are more inclusive. Armed with this conceptual framework, knowledge, and many pedagogic tools, educators will be ready for Phase 5: Integrated History.

Chapter Summaries

To tackle the massive challenge of attaining an integrated history, each chapter presents a barrier, aligned with Tetreault's Phases, and then explores how to break them. Each chapter starts with a personal anecdote from my career or education. I call this "Background." This Background is used to orient and connect with readers through my firsthand experiences trying to teach inclusive history or train teachers. The goal of the Background is to show teachers that I've been there, too. There are many Barriers to teaching women's history. I've chosen to focus on the heavy hitters: male-defined themes, male domination in the history field, too little instructional time, pop-up history, teacher toolkits, the so-called glass ceiling, and the effective campaigns that make women's history controversial. These barriers are tackled in the order of Tetreault's phase theory.

For each Barrier, there are anecdotes, or strategies to Break through the Barrier, which I call "Breakers" and "Blueprints." The Breakers are historical examples or perspective shifts that are needed to clear the path for women's inclusion. Think of the Breaker as the pump-up speech, while the Blueprints to follow are the more practical framework, sets of questions, primary documents, revised standards, or revised periodization of history. At the end of each chapter, I have included an inquiry-based lesson plan that teachers can use in class. These inquiries correspond to each phase in Tetreault's phase theory, becoming more layered and complex as they go. I selected them intentionally to show a range of inquiry types, topics, and approaches.

Chapter 1—"History is Male-Defined and -Centered"—lays out the problems and inaccuracies of a male history and the way the whole structure of what we define as history is male. It argues that when we define history as political, diplomatic, and military history, we have chosen topics that women have historically been barred from. To begin to make space for women in substantive ways, teachers must understand that there are other themes to explore. I highlight three: economic, medical, and religious history.

Chapter 2—"His-Story is not the Only Story"—explores ways teachers can retrain themselves to find women's experiences to include. It starts by exploring why history is male-dominated. This chapter draws primarily on data from academic studies of the social studies education profession. To break these barriers, teachers need to find women's sources and experiences. With all the research, scholarship, and published primary sources, the excuses for teachers to ignore the stories and accounts by and about women are dwindling. Teachers need to look for the voices of women and include them in every history lesson they teach.

Chapter 3—"Finding Time to Teach Diverse Women's Stories"—addresses the constant challenge of teaching social studies: having enough time to teach everything. Yet teachers reprioritize all the time based on current events. We make room all the time, *so why don't we value making room for women—half the population?* Women's rights issues are in the media every single day. This chapter creatively shows how teachers can continue to teach their favorite subjects while including women. It pushes back against additive, pop-up history and heroification of the few women figures who often make history and encourages a more comprehensive approach to women's history. This chapter pulls us from bi-focal history into a more feminist history phase. Many historians and teachers, in an effort to incorporate more women into their narrative, reverted to a type of trivial history called "pop up history," which is damaging as it gives one woman a platform to represent all women and doesn't explore the diversity of the female perspective and how race, class, sexuality, religion, and many other factors changed the "women's view." To break this barrier, I introduce the Eckert Test. This test is a minimum requirement for women's diversity.

The next two chapters are also about the Feminist phase and how they could be applied to economics and government classes. Chapter 4—"Representation Matters"—highlights how seeing oneself in history can create opportunity for students. It also explores contemporary problems facing women and how a failure to discuss women's themes in the history and economics classroom may contribute. The breaker is to develop inclusive pedagogies that include women not only in the content but in the reinforced behaviors in the classroom. Inclusive, feminist classrooms make space for all girls to contribute and feel like they belong in the field of history.

Chapter 5—"Learning to Embrace Controversy"—tackles the Feminist phase in government and history classes. It examines the many controversial ways that women make history, such as rape, sexual assault, abortion, and other topics that are too controversial and thus shied away from in the secondary classroom. Yet social studies teachers teach other brutal and controversial topics, like war and lynching. Women's history should not be subjected to a double standard, and teachers must be prepared to defend against claims that teaching about women's very real lives is controversial. One in a handful of girls *in every classroom* will be sexually assaulted or raped in her lifetime. How dare teachers not discuss it and miss an opportunity to empower strong boys and girls to be part of the change.

Finally beginning to shift toward Integrated History, Chapter 6—"Strategies and Guidelines to Bypass the Sexists"—reviews the way that textbooks and standards are sexist and exclusionary. It draws on available data and studies on the inclusion of women's history in textbooks, standards, teacher preparation, and professional development. It examines how the social studies are politicized and underfunded and how this larger problem contributes to reform challenges. It ends with professional development woes and how teacher education programs fail to prepare educators to integrate women's history into the curriculum. This chapter draws from abundant research in these areas, including Mary K. Chick's "Gender Balance in K-12 American History Textbooks," *from Social Studies Research and Research*, as well as Tetreault's study. It also pulls on the recent "Where are the women?" study published by the National Women's History Museum in 2018. The Breakers are many, though, and thankfully scholars and I have done some of the grunt work. I provide possible new standards and women for every era as well as new ideas for periodization. The chapter is a launching pad, not a full solution to the problems.

The goal of this book is to improve curriculum and instruction. In order to do that, reference to historical examples is made throughout. These historical references are intended as cases in point. Often several are provided in a row. Because the goal is not to write a history here but rather to give short examples of history that could be included, someone may find that the examples provided lack context or nuance. Please consider these references a launching point to further inquiry—not the whole story.

This book takes an apparently radical stance, that women's history has to be half of the curriculum. Yet the approaches to such dramatic shifts in inclusion are mainstream, well researched, and grounded in theory. These Breakers and Blueprints combined will allow any teacher to improve their curriculum tomorrow and better include the voices of the other half of the population. If women and men are equal, they should be equally represented in our history. Women are half of humanity; they should be half of the content taught in classrooms. It's basic math.

Notes

1 Aparna Basu, "10. Women's History in India: A Historiographical Survey," in *Writing Women's History: International Perspectives* ed. by Karen M. Offen, Ruth Roach Pierson, Jane Rendall (London: MacMillan, 1992), 181–182.
2 Rebecca Banovic, "Does Albert Einstein's first wife Mileva Maric deserve credit for some of his work?" Independent, June 13, 2018, https://www.independent.co.uk/news/long_reads/mileva-maric-albert-einstein-physics-science-history-women-a8396411.html
3 Isaac Newton, Letter to Robert Hooke, February, 1675.
4 Shelley Puhack, *The Dark Queens: The Bloody Rivalry That Forged the Medieval World* (New York: Bloomsbury Publishing, 2022), xii.
5 Andrew Eubanks, "Brunhilda of Austrasia," *World History Encyclopedia*, June 23, 2022, https://www.worldhistory.org/Brunhilda_of_Austrasia/
6 Anne F. Broadbridge, *Women and the Making of the Mongol Empire* (Cambridge: Cambridge University Press, 2018), 72.
7 Jack Weatherford, *The Secret History of the Mongol Queens: How the Daughters of Genghis Khan Rescued His Empire*. New York: Crown Publishing Group, 2010, 72.
8 Danielle McGuire, *The Dark End of the Street: Black Women, Rape and Resistance—a New History of the Civil Rights Movement from Rosa Parks to the Rise of Black Power* (New York: Vintage Books, 2010), 63.
9 McGuire, *The Dark End of the Street*, 49.
10 Robinson, Jo Ann Gibson, Announcement- Another Negro Woman has been Arrested, December 2, 1955. https://kinginstitute.stanford.edu/king-papers/about-papers-project/research-and-editorial-process

11 Judith E. Rinard, Book of Flight (New York: Firefly Books, 2001), p. 71.

12 Nell Noddings, "The Care Tradition: Beyond 'Add Women and Stir'" 31.

13 Cornelia H. Dayton and Lisa Levenstein, "The Big Tent of U.S. Women's and Gender History: A State of the Field," The Journal of American History 99, no. 3 (2012): 796–798. http://www.jstor.org/stable/44308391

14 Gerda Lerner, "The Majority Finds Its Past," (Oxford: Oxford University Press, 1979), Smith-Rosenberg, C., "The New Woman and the New History," Feminist Studies, 1975, 3 (1 and 2), 185–198.

15 Tetreault, "Integrating Women's History," 213.

16 Tetreault, "Integrating Women's History," 215.

17 Shocker, J. B. (2014). A case for using images to teach women's history. The History Teacher, 47(3), 448.

1

History Is Male-Defined and -Centered

The assessment of ideas considered important for historical purposes has placed emphasis on published books, monographs, and political documents. Women have had little access to these forms of expression, and their other forms of expression have received little or no attention.

—Janis L. McDonald

What is history? On the surface, this is a straightforward question. Most respond, "The study of the past." But what is the past? The past we study is the story of the record, with an emphasis on the "reliable" *written* record. Without records, there is no history—there is theory and myth. There are other ways of knowing, like oral histories or anthropology, which also inform the record. The more reliable the records, the more reliable the history. Video surveillance of a battle is infinitely more valuable than a picture. A government report on a military intervention paints a much broader picture than a soldier's letter home, and presumably the government official is a more objective and better-informed source than the soldier. Of course, each of these sources presents its own biases, which is why a collection of sources from a variety of backgrounds and perspectives helps in corroborating the story, or the history that one is telling. History is like a puzzle, one that takes lots of pieces, or sources, to reveal the whole picture.

For most of human history, the vast majority of women were illiterate. This was not by their own choosing but rather because reading and writing

DOI: 10.4324/9781003472889-2

were denied to them. The sheer number of sources by men and about men makes writing a male-centered history very easy. Finding the rare sources about and by women is difficult, so writing women's history is difficult. Most historians now and in the past were men. Every source written by a man about women must be read understanding his bias and his probable inability to fully take a woman's perspective. Consequently, the historian is imposing his own perspectives on what the woman may or may not have been thinking. This is not to say male historians haven't loved and honored women in the past; quite the contrary, men have been writing and representing women in art as long as men have loved women. None of that exempts him from the high possibility that the historian's biases as well as norms from *his* time influence the history he writes.

Legal documents often record the lives and experiences of women. Historians can trace their lives through the crimes women were accused and convicted of. But again, the laws women violated were laws written by men. The police officers enforcing the laws were men, and while women could sometimes serve as witnesses or accusers in trials, the judge, jury, and executioner were all men. Women who wrote about these events often had to conform to patriarchal expectations to be accepted. Historians must consider this context and analyze the situation and events with this in mind. They must be careful not to impose their own biases and cultural norms on the women of the past. Modern historians must be cautious not to impose feminism where it doesn't belong.

In most places and times, elite women were allowed access to an education. As a result, the easiest perspectives to access are those of the wealthy: queens, empresses, nobility, and even nuns. But these women are the exception, not the rule. These women do not speak for all women. Their view of the world is a privileged one. The historian must wonder how the lives of poor working women may have been different. Anthropology can sometimes fill in the gaps using scientific evidence from digs to corroborate and support ideas. For example, the classicist Mary Beard used anthropological evidence from the trash pits of Rome to better understand the real lives of citizens, including the women in her book *SPQR*.

Modesty for women sometimes led to their erasure. In the nineteenth century, Harriet Beecher Stowe toured England to promote her book *Uncle Tom's Cabin*, which arguably started the American Civil War. On this "speaking tour," she sat in the audience while her husband read her speech from the stage.[1] Modesty was and remains preferable for women—all else is considered too masculine. Thankfully we know her name—but how many women wrote under pseudonyms or anonymously? Worse, how many were denied credit or had it stollen from them by a man with legal privileges? As Virginia

Woolf put it, "Indeed, I would venture to guess that Anon, who wrote so many poems without signing them, was often a woman."[2] Her words are often abbreviated to "Anonymous was a woman."

Given the challenges women faced in recording their stories, it is no wonder that men's history is everywhere, and women's history is hard to find and know. A lack of sources, however, does not equal a lack of existence. It does not mean a lack of impact, intrigue, or, frankly, significance. A lack of sources means just that. Women's history is just as interesting, and it has taken exceptional historians to uncover it.

For decades, social studies scholars have been calling for greater inclusiveness in social studies curriculum. Their efforts focused on multicultural, racial, and, yes, sexual and gender diversity. Scholars pointed out that the social studies have focused on the public sphere of citizenship rather than the private. In 2001, scholar Margaret Smith Crocco wrote:

> In a rapidly changing society of shifting gender roles and greater openness about issues of sexuality, the future of a healthy society may depend on a social studies curriculum that considers these issues in a more forthright manner.[3]

How do we do this? How do teachers shift focus and include women?

Noticing the Blanks

Background: I Fell in Love With Male History

My first year of college, I took a freshman-level class titled "Presidential Leadership." I showed up on the first day of class and discovered that I was the only woman in the room—out of about 20. It would be one thing if this story took place in the nineteenth or twentieth century, but I went to college in the twenty-first century. This was 2005. Where were all the women in political science?

Sometime in that first week, the male professor pulled me aside to check in on me and assure me that I *belonged* in political science. He made space for me and encouraged me. He became my advisor for the next four years.

In that class, I was asked to choose a president and one policy *he* championed. I wrote a 15-page thesis paper on Jimmy Carter's energy policy, and I was hooked. I declared a political science major and packed my course load with all things related to government, history, international relations, and religion. My college institution invested heavily in growing strong writers. I went on to write many more biographical papers. I wrote one on the moral courage, or lack thereof, of General Douglas MacArthur, an exegesis on the book of Genesis, a paper on the life of Muhammad, and shorter papers on political thinkers like Hobbes, Plato, and Rousseau. That was just my freshman year.

I loved what I was learning. I fell in love with the stories of men. *I fell in love with male history.* At the time, I didn't fully realize how male-centric my education was. I knew it was sexist. It's impossible to read Plato's ideas about women and not. But if you'd asked me, I wouldn't have minded it. I wanted to learn political science and history, and it seemed, because nobody was talking about it, that women didn't exist in *rigorous* academic subjects. Of course, I believed that women could carve out a space, and I hoped to be one of them.

I just didn't realize there already were *so many* women who already had. According to these classes, political science and history didn't include women. There had been no lessons on women. In my political science classes, there was no emphasis on gender analysis, women's firsts in politics, women in executive roles and cabinet positions, or on the first woman to run for the office—before she could vote. There was no acknowledgment of the emphasis women put on running for low-level offices in order to build the credibility of the sex in executive or political roles. There was no reference to the sexism Shirley Chisolm faced when she ran for president. I never heard the name Geraldine Ferraro, the first female vice-presidential candidate on a major party ticket, mentioned once.

I was also not really encouraged to think about how these issues debated by men impacted women. It's not that I should have written all my papers on women, but seriously, not one? The women in my life were smart, had ideas and opinions, and did bold things. Have women's roles so fundamentally changed in my lifetime that this is only now true? Or is the rendering of past women fundamentally flawed?

My junior year, a major presidential election occurred. Hillary Clinton was the front-runner in the Democratic primary against Barack Obama, but she eventually lost the nomination, perhaps because of the handicaps she faced as a female candidate with so much history in politics. Another woman would have a chance to make history. Alaskan Governor Sarah Palin became the second woman ever to be nominated on a major party ticket as vice president, next to American hero and veteran John McCain. Women were everywhere in politics, and my classmates and I were unprepared to help them get elected.

I may have fallen in love with male history and male politics, but the male experience is only half the human experience. My peers and I missed out because we were given no examples of women in history or politics, no gendered analysis, no foundation, no history, and no theory about women and their lives. Women may not have been president yet—but women had run for president and held other offices. Women were gunning for the top office, just as they had been since before they could vote. We just had no idea of the backstory.

Barrier: Emphasis on Male Themes

Changing history curriculum to be more accurate and inclusive very quickly becomes political. The expertise of reformers is questioned in favor of commentary from political pundits who essentially argue that this "new history" isn't what they learned in school and must therefore be inaccurate or antifactual. In their book *History on Trial: Culture Wars and the Teaching of the Past*, Gary B. Nash, Charlotte Crabtree, and Russ E. Dunn explain the intense reaction to the new history standards they introduced in the late 1990s, which were intended to more fairly present history and emphasize critical thinking skills. The reaction mainly came from the political right, which was bent on inspiring patriotism and nationalism. They said, "In all modern nations, educators and political leaders have regarded history as a vehicle for promoting *amor patriae*, for instilling in your people knowledge and attitudes that promote national cohesion and civic pride."[4] Their reforms limited the deification of figures like George Washington and Paul Revere and included lesser-known leaders who were also instrumental in the forming of our nation. The reaction was harsh.

Rush Limbaugh and other conservative pundits went wild. These new standards diminished the founding fathers and incorporated more voices of typical Americans, minorities, and poor people. Nash and his colleagues said Limbaugh "catechized" his listeners with misguided definitions of what history was. He said, "History is real simple. You know what history is? It's what happened."[5] What Limbaugh and many others didn't understand is *how* historians determine what happened.

Memorization of facts does not help students determine how those "facts" became facts! They miss out on the whole point and challenge of history: sifting through piles of information to determine a greater truth. Historical facts are different from mathematical or scientific facts. Historical facts rely on individual documents and records. Not all records and not all sources are reliable. Unlike other subjects, history doesn't happen in a vacuum in which we can replay time to try and catch events again. History happens in real time, sources miss details, and we pull together truths based on a collection of those details. We weigh the evidence and find truth based on the skills of a historian: reason, logic, and hypotheses from imperfect records. We are plagued by a history where the piles of women's documents were excluded from the first drafts of history. It's not that those documents aren't there, but that the predominantly male historians didn't study them.

To demand facts is to be dishonest about what the field of history is at its essence. It may appear to be a neutral and objective request, but history is interpreted. Nash and his colleagues believe that historical inquiry is far from unpatriotic; they suggest that it is the core of the philosophy on which the United States was founded:

> [O]ne of the most important of all American traditions is education and citizenship that requires open inquiry and healthy skepticism about any account of the past, and open-mindedness to the possibility of new historical perspectives. This kind of tolerance and receptivity is itself a cardinal tenet of Enlightenment thought.[6]

The attack on historians who reexamine historical evidence and draw different conclusions from their predecessors is unheard of in other fields. In no other discipline do people protest that revisionism based on new evidence or a different method of analysis is corruptive. The experiences of these reformers in the 1990s is similar to the reactive and hostile environment seen in schools today over the C3 Framework, AP curriculum, and state laws over Critical Race Theory.

These debates are not new—they have been reinvigorated in every decade since the rise of public secondary education in the late 1880s. It seems that what sparks this reinvigoration is a random, perhaps trivial, survey of college students about American history and governmental structure. Questions include subjects such as *Freedom of speech is guaranteed by what document?* And students fail almost every time, which as a social studies teacher saddens me, but as someone who specializes in education and thus brain science, I'm not at all surprised. We all know that if we don't use it, we lose it, and knowing which document secured freedom of speech is far less important than knowing one *has* freedom of speech and in what contexts, how to best *use* one's free speech, and the skill of being able to find the correct answer. There is a time and a place for rote memorization—I certainly would be embarrassed if that answer hadn't flown off my tongue—but for the typical American in the digital age, this kind of rote knowledge is a thing of the past. Thus, it saddens me when laypeople use trivia questions as a substitute for valid assessments of the quality of history education our students receive.

James Loewen best articulates the issue:

> College teachers in most disciplines are happy when their students have had significant exposure to the subject before college. Not teachers in history. History professors in college routinely put down high school history courses. A colleague of mine calls his survey of American history "Iconoclasm I and II," because he sees his job as disabusing

his charges of what they learned in high school. In no other field does this happen. Mathematics professors, for instance, know that non-Euclidean geometry is rarely taught in high school, but they don't assume that Euclidean geometry was mis taught. Professors of English literature don't presume that *Romeo and Juliet* was misunderstood in high school.[7]

Loewen explains how textbooks are primarily responsible for the failures in secondary history education because they are nationalistic, provide simple moral narratives, fail to dig into the moral gray areas, and do not present history the way it happened: with an incredible amount of conflict and debate. He says, "The titles themselves tell the story," citing several examples with glowing patriotic cover titles "graced… with American flags, bald eagles, and the Statue of Liberty."[8] University history professors feel that high schools have done it wrong. We need students to *do* history, not memorize it. They need to learn facts, yes, but they must know *how* we know those facts. These are the skills of historians.

Everyone should be alarmed by any "fact-based" curriculum that disproportionately represents men, who are only half the population. Now, more than ever, focus on women in history curriculum is needed. With increasingly more women filling jobs in every field, holding leadership positions, participating in our democracy, and engaging in public discourse, women deserve to be mentioned in school curriculums to provide real models of women who tried, failed, succeeded, struggled, and overcame. Students of all genders need to see women with strengths and weaknesses in the history that they learn, so they can see women venturing into a world that has been traditionally male-dominated. Teachers need to acknowledge the sexism in the texts, the standards, and the system to find ways to bypass it.

When it comes to women's history, what *did* happen? Seriously. Women were there and yet are absent from the pages. The answer for women, as for men, is: it's in the sources. Nash explained, "The number of 'facts' is limitless, restricted… only by the number of documents that have survived floods, fires, and the trash barrel."[9] H. Stewart Hughes, a Harvard historian, explained the stark difference between history and every other field of scholarship:

[H]istorians—in contrast to investigators in almost any other field of knowledge—very seldom confront their data directly. The literary or artistic scholar has the poem or painting before him; the astronomer scans the heavens through a telescope; the geologist tramps the soil he studies… The historian alone is wedded to empirical reality and condemned to view his subject matter at second remove. He must accept the word of others before he even begins to devise his account.[10]

For women, their stories were often told by men, and thus there is an even more complicated removal and confrontation of the sources on their lives.

History being his-story has a long… history. To illustrate how history was male-defined, historian Janis L. McDonald showed the failure of historians to include the work of women. She used Mercy Otis Warren, one of America's first historians, as a case in point. She dissected Warren's life, her writings, her overall legacy, and the general devaluing of her historical works and found that the descriptive biographical approach to writing history used up to the 1950s would, by definition, fail to include women because the benchmarks for inclusion were defined by men. McDonald cited the earlier work of historian William Raymond Smith, who agreed that the "categories and periodization have been masculine by definition, for they have defined significance primarily by power, influence, and visible activity in the world of political and economic affairs."[11] McDonald explained that the standards for historical inclusion, while good for reliability and validity, and while providing a clear measure of how widespread the readership was, almost completely exclude women. She explained that the field of history has defined evidence as published works and political documents. Given that most women could not secure publishing opportunities and all were barred from politics in all early democracies, this fundamentally excludes women. The first novel penned by an African American woman was not published until 1859, leaving the Black female perspective on early America out entirely. The various forms of expression recorded and available, said McDonald, "have received little or no attention."[12] Women who did gain attention often provided information about important men, not women.[13] So it's not that women's writing or significant contributions to our story are absent—it's that the process of canonizing their story is rigged to exclude them.

Mercy Otis Warren's works should be a staple in any course on the American Revolution, right there with Thomas Paine's *Common Sense*. She wrote play after play, poem after poem that riled up New England in the years leading to the war.[14] She was willing to say "independence" long before the male representatives of her time and was brazen in her published literary attacks on the king.[15] She, like Paine, wrote so the layperson could read and understand, but was more colorful. Her plays were widely read. John Adams and Washington admired and encouraged her writing. The difference between her and Paine is that to maintain her ladylike humility, she wrote under an anonymous pen name, "the Columbian Patriot." Her name would become obscured in history despite the fact that she wrote the first history of the American Revolution, titled *History of the Rise, Progress and Termination of the American Revolution* and published in 1805.[16]

Warren knew and corresponded with many of the founding fathers and their wives. Both from Massachusetts, the Adamses and Warrens were close acquaintances. John Adams had once written that he "had a feeling of inferiority… whenever [he] approached or addressed her" and that her "attainments dwarf those of most men."[17] Warren was a revolutionary to the core and a staunch opponent of anything that appeared monarchical. She was critical of Adams's federalist leanings and wrote about them in both her history and her critique of the Constitution. Thomas Jefferson, Patrick Henry, and Sam Adams all supported her work, and even Jefferson ordered copies for his cabinet.[18] John Adams, however, did not take to some of her critiques of him. Perhaps it was their shared revolutionary experience that made his positions on federalism more infuriating. She wrote, "His passions and prejudices were sometimes too strong for his sagacity and judgment."[19] She joined the many who suggested he was a monarchist. Adams sent her a letter on April 11, 1807, that resulted in a contentious exchange and an ultimate falling out. Warren said his letters were "so marked with passion, absurdity, and inconsistency as to appear more like the ravings of a maniac than the cool critique of genius and science."[20] After failing in logic, Adams issued the final blow, remarking to a friend, "History is not the Province of the Ladies."[21]

Subjects like music history, art history, and many others taught by elective teachers are "soft histories." Women's history, too, is treated as "soft history," left for someone else to teach. This is one of the ways that the history classroom systemically excludes and marginalizes women and people of color. Women have contributed to society in both their grueling daily work and fruitful careers. Few are aware of these contributions because they are not part of what we define as history—they are intentionally or unintentionally excluded. If we define the social studies through the public political and economic themes, we are denying academic attention and competence to private domains.

Many historians have tried to write a more accurate his-story, better referred to as our-story—to tell "people's histories"—and they have succeeded in including the voices of marginalized men. However, the particular challenges of writing a women's history in conjunction with men's history is difficult at best, and those who try often include far more middle-class white women than they do women of other races and classes.

James Loewen and Howard Zinn are the most prominent in their attempts to dismantle the top-down approach to history. Though ranting at times, they are wonderful historians who have shed light on the importance of real, people's history, but their wonderfully inclusive works fall short of achieving a history that is half female. Neither is even close! Loewen only includes

Helen Keller in order to point out how oversimplified and whitewashed she has become in our cultural memory. Loewen left it up to another generation to take his lessons and make it better. Before Loewen died in 2021, he wrote to me in an email, "You sound like the kind of hist. teacher every kid needs. Carry on!" It meant a great deal.

In the afterword of Zinn's book *A People's History of the United States*, which is probably the best example of an inclusive history, he reflects on his success in including the underdogs, minorities, and previously voiceless. He writes,

> It did not occur to me, when I first began to immerse myself in history, how badly twisted was the teaching and writing of history by its sub-mersion of nonwhite people. Yes Indians were there, and then gone. Black people were visible when slaves, then free and invisible. It was a white man's history.[22]

He explains, as I have done, how distorted his history education was and yet, like his predecessors, leaves out the ladies. Even in this brief excerpt, he uses Native and Black people to make his argument and, while he claims it's a "man's history," skips an example of women. Zinn knew he had failed. He wrote,

> I wanted in writing this book, to awaken a greater consciousness of class conflict, racial injustice, sexual inequality, and national arro-gance. But even as I tried to make up for what I saw as serious omis-sions, I nevertheless neglected groups in American society that had always been missing from orthodox histories. I became aware of this, and embarrassed by it, when people wrote to me..."[23]

His book has one chapter completely dedicated to women: Chapter 6, titled "The Intimately Oppressed." He gives one paragraph to Black women in his chapter on the end of slavery. Women's suffrage is allotted two pages and gives honorable mentions to women activists in the Progressive Era. He doesn't really mention women until Chapter 19, "Surprises," in which he dives into a variety of women's issues hotly advocated for in the femi-nist movement of the 1960s and 1970s. Even Zinn tells history in a way that involves women only when they manage to squeeze into men's politics. *What was half the nation doing during the rest of the chapters? Where are the women?*

If Loewen and Zinn, the "people's historian," didn't do it, few others are likely to. Since Zinn, comprehensive women's histories spanning US and world history have been written by women to close these gaps. The time has come for full integration of history. We need to validate women's work and contributions in the past to give women a place in the present. Men need to share the definition of power. Women who engage in traditionally feminine activities as well as fight for women and women's causes are important and significant. Women who have excelled as men have for millennia and been ignored by history must find a place in our cultural understanding of the past. Women must be recognized.

Take George Washington. There is no doubt he accomplished amazing things and is a character worthy of conversation in class. But it's accurate history to make plain that he could have done *none* of it if Martha Washington wasn't home managing the plantation, children, and enslaved people and *quite literally* fundraising for the revolution. Their plantation would not have been as profitable if it weren't for the forced labors of his slaves. If it wasn't for them, Washington would have been broke and the revolution would have stalled due to limited finances. Validating is acknowledging accurate history.

In a workshop with secondary students near London, researchers Bridget Lockyer and Abigail Tazzymant gave students three different sets of sources to explore the everyday lives of medieval women. These sources were unique types of records often overlooked in historical study: portraits of elite medieval women, women's wills, and a court case involving a woman's marriage. Students were encouraged to consider who recorded the documents and what implication that had for distorting the truth. Students discussed the women's class, potential for agency, and their significance.[24] Students left this experience with a much deeper understanding of women's lives but also with frustration that all of their history classes didn't provide this exposure.[25] This is an experience that occurs all over the world as marginalized groups learn the untaught history of people like them, but unlike some marginalized groups who make up a minority of people, women are half of the population.

Dr. Marie Cartier, who teaches women's and queer studies at California State University, Northridge, explained to me that she routinely asks her classes, "Who benefits from you not knowing your history?"[26] This is an important question. There isn't necessarily an intentional conspiracy to deny women an education, but there are beneficiaries. Denying women their place in the curriculum does have impacts. Governments benefit, as they aren't forced to resolve the patterns that have kept women as second-class citizens. Men benefit, as they aren't responsible for considering the ways in which the patriarchal system has benefitted them. There are many other beneficiaries.

Laurel Thatcher Ulrich once wrote for *Harvard Magazine* that

> Most people assume that history is "what happened" in the long ago. Historians know that history is an account of what happened based on surviving evidence, and that it is shaped by the interests, inclinations, and skills of those who write it. Historians constantly rewrite

history not only because we discover new sources of information, but because changing circumstances invite us to bring new questions to old documents. History is limited not only by what we can know about the past, but by what we care to know.[27]

Many secondary teachers, me included, have not taught about women, instead recycling the themes we were taught. It's time we break that pattern.

Breaker: Compensate by Asking Women-Centric Questions

Women are in every story, they just aren't often at the center of it, because that's how the patriarchal society we live in functions. Sociologist Allan Johnson wrote, "A male center of focus is everywhere. Research makes clear, for example, what most women probably already know: that men dominate conversations by talking more, interrupting more, and controlling content."[28] To focus on women requires looking with a different lens, and old models of exploring history may not entirely apply.

Finding the history of women is only a research question away. Once you start to notice the blanks, you can begin to ask, "Where are they?" Mary Kay Thompson Tetreault's phase theory established in "Integrating Women's History" in 1986 encourages teachers to become aware of the blanks. At this phase, teachers have the "ah ha" moment where they realize their history is skewed. She first recommends that teachers "compensate" by adding in women in topics they already teach, whose stories and experiences contributed something to the same history.[29] I often hear from teachers in this phase because they are shocked by the names and lives of prominent women they had never heard of. This phase is called Compensatory history, which I joke is the "Have you heard of Susan B. Anthony?" phase.

Teachers trying to drag themselves out of a male-centered curriculum should ask:

◆ Who are the notable women missing from history, and what did they contribute in areas or movements traditionally dominated by men?
◆ What did they contribute in areas that are an extension of women's traditional roles?
◆ How have major economic and political changes affected women in the public sphere?[30]

Investigating these questions in lessons and units already taught can begin to bring women in. Once I was teaching with a lesson on the Chinese Exclusion Act from the Stanford History Education Group. Integral to this history is that the Chinese men immigrating to the US were largely unmarried. I taught this lesson many times in my class, but one year it hit me like a brick: *where are the women?* Why weren't Chinese women immigrating? What economic or political changes were impacting their choices prior to the Chinese Exclusion Act? So, I Googled, and sure enough I found an article about the Page Act, a law that severely curbed Chinese women's immigration and that preceded the better-known Chinese Exclusion Act. As my students worked through the primary material in class, I sat in the back building an inquiry-based lesson plan for the next day that centered the lives of Chinese women.[31]

The biggest reason women's history is not yet integrated is that women's history is not required to graduate with a history or social studies education degree! Teachers, like me, who took typical routes to teacher certification never studied women's history. Women's history is often offered as an elective or independent course: Women's Studies or Gender Studies. What message does that send? That there is HISTORY and then *women's history*?

The task of educators today is to blend these two spheres of scholarship by simply adding women to their questions. In leading professional development with educators, there's enough scholarship to easily do compensatory history, so I tell educators to take their topic and search "women in the _____." In other words, just Google it. In one teacher training, an experienced educator exclaimed, "I was surprised how much was there just by adding 'women' to my search results." But isn't that how it is with our students? If they aren't finding the right information, check the search terms. The algorithm will give you the default his-story until you tell it to include the other half: women.

Looking for fascinating, diverse, and complicated women's history is as simple as a Google search. Seriously. The field of women's history has come so far in the last several decades, and teachers simply need to capitalize on the labors of those who dug in the archives to find the lost stories of women. But despite the robust evidence, women's history has not made it to the mainstream.

Simply asking the right questions—ones that intentionally focus on women's experiences—will transform the sources that students seek and tell a whole story of human sacrifice, discrimination, and patriotism. It is not that the sources are not there—it's that secondary teachers are not asking the right questions.

Blueprint: Know Women in the Themes Already Taught

History is a white male-centric subject because it is taught from a top-down perspective that emphasizes the fields of politics, diplomacy, military, and business. Dr. Bettany Hughes suggested that only 0.5 percent of history is written about women.[32] Historian Aparna Basu proclaimed, "The only women who found a place in traditional history textbooks were either women who successfully performed male roles or whom great men loved."[33] It is no won-der that teachers teach his-story—it's the one out there!

Yet women *have* made history in these fields. Topics like suffrage, tem-perance, and progressive reforms are routinely taught in schools. I am still shocked at how few people know who Susan B. Anthony is—really know her the way they do Washington or Lincoln. They *should* know her with the same depth. Her involvement in American politics across reform movements like abolition, temperance, and, of course, suffrage spanned decades—greater than Washington and Lincoln. The 19th Amendment, which gave women the right to vote, is named after her. In US history, it's not just Anthony: each of the first ladies and people like Pocahontas, Weetamoo, Phillis Wheatley, Elizabeth Freeman, Nancy Ward, Sacajawea, Lucretia Mott, Sojourner Truth, Harriet Jacobs, Sarah and Angelina Grimke, Harriet Tubman, Carrie Chapman Catt, Alice Paul, Lucy Burns, Frances Perkins, Mary McLeod Bethune, the list goes on and on, are all deserving of deep examination in the same way men who make political history are. A standardized list of agreed upon women to include is provided in Chapter 7.

If your history education was so sexist as to exclude *even* the women above, then you have some work to do in compensating for history erased. It is guaran-teed that these women are mentioned in a high school textbook with an edition published in this century. If you do know and mention them, how deep is that examination? A dive into the nuances of these women's lives may be in order.

To start, the process of compensating means looking at the themes already taught and noticing when women are not present. In every topic, there is a woman worth mentioning. Manhattan Project? Lilli Hornig. Westward Expansion? Ah Toy. Mongol Empire? Borte. Viking Exploration? Gudrid. Find the women. (In Chapter 6, I provide an organized list for every era and period of US and World history.)

If teachers don't have mastery of suffrage, temperance, progressive women, and the feminist movement, then that is where they should start. These four units of study are the easiest way to compensate with what is already taught. They are rich in source material, interesting, and debatable. They involve politics and diplomacy, overlap with and are exacerbated by wars, and impact the economy.

Squeezing women into the spaces already dominated by men is only half of it. No matter how hard you look for women in the political, military, diplo-matic, and economic fields, men will outnumber women because of the long history of women's exclusion from those spaces. Eventually, to really com-pensate, teachers must ask what other fields or themes would include more women? They must ask, if a housewife wrote the first draft of history, what topics would have been important and prioritized in her daily life? More on this in Chapter 2.

The assumption that women did not record their history, as a justification of not digging for it, allows the mistakes of our past to repeat: our ancestors neglected the stories of women, and we fulfill the cycle by not examining their lives and records. Rosalind Miles suggested, "For even the most cursory survey of women's work reveals that its range, quantity and significance has been massively underestimated, not least by women themselves."[34] Women have been writing their stories since the beginning of writing, but few of their stories have made the canon of historical reading and contemporary knowing.

We can find primary sources by women with proximity to writing men. Many men recorded the stories of the women around them, and those stories can be told through their eyes. Unfortunately, tracing women through history can sometimes be hard because of the patriarchal way names are assigned, with women dropping surnames at marriage, and if they marry several times, their name will change several times. Further, those norms often insist on female humility, so women would often go not by their personal identifying names at all but instead by "Mrs. So-and-So." These layers of complexity are a challenge but are not insurmountable barriers. Historians must uncover *how* a woman may have identified to find her in the historical record.

All historians struggle with the preservation of their primary material, but women's historians have mountains of struggles. In addition to encountering the typical delete buttons of the past, like floods and fires, women's historians have the added challenges of the devaluing of women's writing and contributions as their contemporaries saw it. Too much of their writing ended up in the trash pile. In so many cases, their ideas, perspectives, and opinions are lost to history. One interesting approach is the book *Sexuality and Slavery: Reclaiming Intimate Histories in the Americas*, in which the contributing authors traced the lives and experiences of African women as far back as the written record would go. They traced the experiences of these women along the slave trade and into their lives in the Americas through the Antebellum Period. Almost all the sources describing the lives and experiences of African women were European and then American men. At the end of the book, the authors added a chapter by Jim Downs imagining what these women would have said and thought if they had been recorded.[35] It was a tremendous intellectual undertaking and one that could be replicated in classrooms whenever an absence of sources is noted but other primary material has been exhausted.

All of that said, primary and secondary teachers today have little excuse not to find and incorporate primary material from women into their classrooms because women's historians have painstakingly worked to make it available. There exist collections that contain primary material on women specifically, or that include the voices of women, from every topic produced by scholars in that field. Teachers need only do a simple Google search and *use* what they find.

Male hegemony over history must be challenged. Teachers and historians must shift the sources deemed legitimate and reliable to allow our history to include marginalized people who were historically denied access to the spaces that legitimized them. Sources from the educated, Western, white, cis-gender, heterosexual, and, yes, male population have been falsely idealized in our society as the epitome of the neutral, logical, and sophisticated intellectual.[36] Yet all of those characteristics also privilege, separate, and bias the intellectual or source from the ability to understand disadvantage or the unique experiences of the marginalized. This is where diverse women primary sources and historians are vital.

Assume Women Are There

The best teachers start assuming women were in this history, they just haven't known enough to include them. At the Compensatory Phase, teachers don't need to structurally change their classes to add in lessons or partial lessons on the lives and experiences of women. Women are already all over the history they teach; they just may not know it yet. For a world history class, the following are women easily includable because they rose to the rank of figures who typically make history: figures who intersect diplomatic and military history. The Julias dominated Roman politics; highlight them. Empress Lu, Empress Wu Zhao, and Empress Cixi each held immense power over China in their times; highlight them. Buddica, Zenobia, and Cleopatra against Rome and the Track sisters against the Han, all led armies against expanding empires. Brunhild and Fredegund controlled most of Western Europe, while Theodora influenced Byzantium in the Middle Ages. Catherine Medici ruled France as regent through the Protestant Reformation and conflicts with the Huguenots. Queen Elizabeth and Queen Victoria of England often top lists of important figures in history because entire eras were named after them. Catherine the Great of Russia and Maria Theresa were two of the few Enlightened monarchs of the Enlightenment Period. In African history, you will find a long list of powerful queens, as many societies were matrilineal. Nzinga, an important example of a woman whose history is well known, used her brilliance and power to help her people resist Portuguese encroachment into their territory in the 1600s. Or the Dahomey, who used women warriors to defend against Europeans in the 1800s. Likewise, the Japanese and Koreans have long histories of female leadership.

Many women were involved in the wars we typically teach in history classes, and while many of them served as nurses and camp followers, roles so often devalued and overlooked, others had roles that rivaled male contributions in traditionally male fields—which we all know make history. Many women served as spies in war, a fact which led to their erasure due to the nature of clandestine work. The most well known of these was Harriet Tubman, often credited for helping the enslaved escape the south in the American Civil War, but Tubman also led the Union army in a raid that liberated hundreds of enslaved, making her the first woman to hold a command position. Intelligence work is often classified as the first drafts of history are being written. When the documents are finally declassified, insufficient effort is made to integrate this work into the narrative.

The story of Empress Lü Zhi is fascinating and illustrative of the way that teachers should critically analyze what sources say about major women historical figures. Any teacher of world history will discuss the consolidation of the Han Empire, and they probably will name her husband, Emperor Gaozu. Teaching the Han without teaching about Lü Zhi is folly. She was the first and most notable female empress consort of the Han Dynasty.[37] By surviving accounts, she was a vicious woman. She and Emperor Gaozu were a formidable pair: he had a good eye for talent and recruited experts to guide him, and she was a ruthless defender of his rule.[38] After the empire was secured and enemies of the Han defeated, she assassinated two of the generals who had elevated her husband to his position. While this may have been politically savvy, it was also harsh, to say the least.

Lü Zhi's position was still tenuous because she had a whole harem of her husband's concubines and their sons to contend with.[39] Her husband was particularly fond of his concubine Lady Qi and their son Liu Ruyi, giving him lands and wealth. But the emperor was convinced that he should maintain the line of succession. When Emperor Gaozu died, Lü Zhi controlled the empire with cruelty and executed rivals of her son, including sons within her husband's former harem, to consolidate her power. Lady Qi's son was poisoned, and she was imprisoned in a pigsty, where soldiers pulled out her tongue, blinded her, and then chopped off all her limbs. She ruled the Han Empire as regent for about 15 years. Were the sources for this information slandering her? Were they accurate? Did she really torture Lady Qi? How horrible was she really? It's hard to say. Powerful women in history are often treated well by their contemporaries and then slandered by their successors. Teachers should examine the sources with students, emphasize the importance of context, and stress an understanding of the biases of sources.[40]

World War II is a big topic in most secondary social studies classes—hello women's history! I've seen a lot of teachers emphasize women's roles on the home front, holding down the home, rationing, donating, volunteering with the Red Cross, and so on. All of that is accurate and incredibly important; however, there is so much more to women's involvement. Also, the emphasis on those aspects of women's contributions promotes gendered stereotypes: women in their domestic roles as homemakers. How we have been teaching *the war* without women is beyond me. Women remobilized (for they had been mobilized for the First World War); every branch opened women's service options that *enabled* men to serve on front lines. Women were pilots, nurses, secretaries—you name it.

Women were vitally important; in fact, they carried out the majority of intelligence efforts during the war.[41] Thousands of women were mobilized on all sides of the war; they were recruited on college campuses and even via newspapers ads asking if they enjoyed crossword puzzles. Girls left their homes for Washington, DC; Bletchley; and other centers of intelligence operations. Women also led these operations. Elizabeth Freedman and her husband were the founders of American cryptology. Freedman and her team broke almost every Nazi and Japanese code within a year of US entry into the war. They also uncovered the location of Admiral Isoroku Yamamoto, the architect of the attack on Pearl Harbor, and had him shot down. These women not just had the back of the male personnel at war, they actively defended them through their efforts.

Similar refocusing could happen with the Cold War. Juanita Moody was one of the few American women who had risen through the ranks in cryptology and was in charge of an intelligence unit during the Cuban Missile Crisis. It was her team that discovered that something sketchy was going on in Cuba. She could see ships from the Union of Soviet Socialist Republics (USSR) bringing in supplies under the cover of night. Plus, microwave towers were being installed. Moody's report was taken to the White House. President John F. Kennedy read it, but she worried that not enough was being done. So, she pressed the National Security Agency to make an unprecedented move: publishing the information to the larger intelligence community. She said, "It has reached the point that I am more worried about the trouble we're going to get in having not published it, because someday we're going to have to answer for this. And if we do…"[42] The report pushed the government to investigate. The government flew U2 planes over Cuba and saw nuclear launch sites.

As the crisis continued, Moody spent sleepless nights on a cot in her office. The Soviets sailed for Cuba with nuclear weapons. The United States installed a naval blockade. Moody used a new technology known as teletype to pass the most current, relevant, top-secret information from her team to the powers that be. With ships facing off and active war as close as it could be, Kennedy struck a deal with Nikita Khrushchev, the Soviet leader. The United States would remove weapons from Türkiye as long as the Soviets would not bring their weapons to Cuba.

Moody received the Federal Woman's Award, which was established to honor "leadership, judgment, integrity, and dedication" among female government employees—despite being the brains behind the most dangerous moment in human history. When she was asked about her past by those outside the intelligence community, Moody would say, "Oh, I've done lots of interesting things for a country girl from North Carolina."[43]

Women's Historians

Men have had millennia to craft the field of history, and the field of women's history is only in its infancy, so attempts to redefine it are necessary to right historical inaccuracies. In its newness, mistakes will be made, perhaps overemphasis made on some topics, and ill-fitting definitions developed, but we need more women and men to weigh in for us to find the proper points of emphasis and ways to include women.

Women's absence from the history classroom has left us with the false impression that their thoughts and feelings on major issues were not recorded. And yet, in every period and in every culture, when women were barred from academia, discouraged, and even forced from literacy, women wrote, drew, and told their stories. The problem faced by historians is that the volume of women writers is fewer, the authority of women writers is usually questioned, and the sexism or other issues of their time led to many women writers being hidden.

The first professional historians were Greek and Roman; it is from them that the Western precedent of defining history as his-story, and not her-story, comes. Beard explained that, in the ancient tradition, subordination of females was an important part of being a man and was deeply ingrained in the culture and the accounts of the time. Beard did a gendered analysis of Homer's *Odyssey* using Penelope as an example. In the story, she said, "As Homer has it, an integral part of growing up, as a man, is learning to control the public utterance and to silence the female of the species."[44] She explained that entire works were dedicated to the absurdity and inferiority of female power. Examining the stories about the mythical Amazon women, Beard concluded that "the underlying point was that it was the duty of man to save civilisation from the rule of women."[45] She elegantly showed that oratory and power in the West have always seemed to be a male sphere of influence. Therefore, putting women into the history curriculum is an act of resistance against a society bent on excluding them—even when they are the center of the story.

But the nineteenth and twentieth centuries were not the beginning of women's historical writing. Unprofessional and usually elite women historians from around the world wrote centuries before the professional women of the later centuries. At best, their gender, focus on women's issues, and lack of education kept their works hidden; at worst, blatant sexism, violence, and repression banished their works forever. It has been the work of women's historians in the last centuries to bring the work of their sisters from the past into the light.

Modern history brought increasingly greater numbers of women writers. The Golden Age in the Muslim world saw women recorders of the Hadith, chronicling the words and deeds of the prophet, most notably through his favorite wife, Aisha.[46] In Japan, the world got its first novel, *The Tale of Genji*, a timeless classic written by a woman centering the lives and experiences of court women.[47] The Protestant Reformation disrupted educational opportunities for women.[48] On the one hand, it criticized the Catholic structure that had long given educational opportunities to women within the convents. There women were scholars, chroniclers, poets, and writers. Outside the convent, the emerging universities were barred to women. On the other hand, the reformations that took place around Europe encouraged the widespread education of people, including women, so that they could read and understand the Bible. This was a game changer for women across class, their key to intellectualism. Wherever education went, so went women authors and historians.

The relatively new desire to write social history from the perspectives of typical people's experiences rather than that of the elite created space for women's history.[49] Women began writing professionally in the late nineteenth and early twentieth centuries, and their focus was, not surprisingly, to close the gaps on what we know about women's past. They sometimes co-wrote with their historian husbands. The first drafts of professional women's history paralleled the rise of women's colleges. These women tended to write about women but certainly would not have considered that they were creating a new field of history.[50] The contributions that those women made to this field, digging for their sisters' voices in the past, are underacknowledged.

There is a false idea, however, that women weren't historians in the past. The irony, of course, is that the world's first named chronicler was a woman! Enheduanna, the daughter of Sargon of Akkad, lived between 2285 and 2250 BCE and was the high priestess in the ziggurat in Ur, a city in Ancient Sumer. She is best known for her powerful recorded prayers to the goddess Inanna during a time of conflict and upheaval in Sumer. The fact that the first named chronicler chose to write about a powerful goddess is also significant as it shows how, when you solicit women's sources, you can learn more about other women—in this case, a mythical one. But this pattern is true for other early women historians.

In China, the first known woman historian was Ban Zhao, who lived during the later Han Empire. She was from a prominent and accomplished Chinese family that was well integrated into the imperial court. Her father, Ban Biao, was a historian eager to write a better history than his predecessors had.[51] He began writing a multivolume text too ambitious to complete in his lifetime, so Ban Zhao took on the task of finishing it.[52] As a tutor at the Dongguan Imperial Library, she was permitted access to the texts and archives.[53]

Given that she was surrounded by powerful and bright women, it is not surprising that, after finishing her father's history, Ban Zhao wrote about women. She wrote a manual for women's education that largely emphasized their submission and was the first Chinese philosophy about women, which endured far beyond her lifetime. Ban Zhao was not immune to her time; her ideas were heavily influenced by the dominant Confucian thought. Confucianism valued filial piety, or respect for and obedience to one's ancestors. It encouraged strict hierarchies within families, where one's authority was garnered by age and gender, with women being subordinate.[54] Ban Zhao wrote:

> A woman (ought to) have four qualifications: (1) womanly virtue; (2) womanly words; (3) womanly bearing; and (4) womanly work. Now what is called womanly virtue need not be brilliant ability, exceptionally different from others. Womanly words need be neither clever in debate nor keen in conversation. Womanly appearance requires neither a pretty nor a perfect face and form. Womanly work need not be work done more skillfully than that of others.[55]

Ban Zhao encouraged women to go about their work wholeheartedly and to submit to their husband and his family in all things. Who knows what pressure she felt to uphold these ideals of male domination and superiority. She did little to discuss the plight of poor women in China and did not address the issue of female infanticide, which was rampant. Perhaps she feared that her work would be discarded if it was not in line with contemporary thinkers. Or perhaps Ban Zhao saw her instructions as women's path to relative liberation. Modern intellectuals often critique her work as diminishing women's role and potential, and perhaps they are correct, but without Ban Zhao, attention to women's education may not have come at all.[56] Seeking out a woman author, like Zhao, allows us to know about women in her time, a history that male authors neglected to record thoroughly.

As a final example, in the West, the first known female professional historian was Byzantine Princess Anna Comnena, who, similar to Ban Zhao, was a noblewoman whose incredible privileges allowed her to record her ideas on philosophy and history.[57] Her life was wildly fascinating. She was a primary witness to both her father's and brother's reigns. She also plotted to overthrow her brother and place her husband on the throne, a plot that failed, leading to her forced seclusion in a convent for the remainder of her life.[58]

Comnena wrote her history in the twelfth century with the aid of the monks while imprisoned.[59] Her 15-volume historical account was based on records available at the convent and her own experience, which included witnessing the first Crusade. Her history was more accurate than those of some of her male contemporaries, who tended to exaggerate. She wrote of her repugnance at her husband's timidity and failure to secure the throne. She speculated that "perhaps their genders should have been reversed."[60] Of course, Comnena, like other historians, wrote about politics and the military, but, similar to Enheduanna and Ban Zhao, she saw an opportunity to write about women and took it. She honored her grandmother, Anna Dalassena. She spends many passages on the power, skill, and empathy with which her grandmother led and credits her with control of the government during her father's reign.[61]

Women and the pitifully small fraction of male historians who write women's histories are needed if a true human history is ever to be written. Most women's histories include a caveat about the peculiar challenge of writing a women's history. Mary Ritter Beard, one of America's first women's historians, wrote, "Naturally, as a novel undertaking, the book may appear weird and unsymmetrical to the masters of system with a pro-founder knowledge of history... There is sure to be an over-emphasis in places but my apology is that, when contentions have long been weighted too much on one side, it is necessary to bear down heavily on the other."[62] Rosalind Miles said she was filling in the blanks. The classicist Mary Beard threatened that if she sounded as though she was asking men to step aside, she'd be willing to look them in the eye. Any student of women's history must accept that women's history is *our* history. It is not an alternative to the narrative of men.

The task of teachers and historians is to look for places where women have been silenced in the topics they already teach and add those women's voices in. Teachers need to learn the history they missed or skipped over in their own educations. This is compensatory history, the first step toward teaching women's history.

Resources for Compensatory History
Recommended Reading: Surveys of Women's History
This first chapter provided a crash course on themes of women's history often left out. It's important to compensate and correct the history we know by reading surveys about women. The Remedial Herstory Project has a free online textbook for young and old learners. Topics I've summarized in this book in a sentence or paragraph have an entire chapter dedicated to them there. The bibliography for each chapter can also be a fruitful place to find scholarly texts for an even richer study.

For US History, teachers should consider surveys like *A Black Women's History of the United States* by Diana Ramey Berry and Kali Gross or *America's*

Women: Four Hundred Years of Dolls Drudges Helpmates and Heroines by Gail Collins. Both texts influenced me a great deal. For World History, Bonnie Smith's *Women in World History: 1450 to the Present* is a strong place to start, alongside the collections of essays in Sarah and Brady Hughes's two-volume *Women in World History*. Works like those by Rosalind Miles, author of *The Women's History of the World, Who Cooked the Last Supper?*, and her most recent on modern history, are easy to read.

Teachers can also begin to look for more narrowly focused books by experts rather than generalists. *SPQR* by Mary Beard gives a strong foundation for Ancient Rome. *Women and the Making of the Mongol Empire* by Anne Broadbridge challenges the centrism of Chinggis Khan in Mongol history. *Patriots, Prostitutes, and Spies: Women and the Mexican-American War* by John M. Belohlavek pulls women from the margins of the conflict. These books are out there. It's time that teachers are familiar with them.

Sample Inquiry: What Were the Human Sacrifices on D-Day?
The best example of finding women where they are assumed not to be is D-Day. On D-Day, not a single woman was allowed to be part of the Allied invasion of Normandy—this was no place for a lady! Boys were led by men to beaches where they would become men by fighting other men, to be honored by older men. Or at least that's how it would seem. Few people mention that women also landed that day or that the majority of the civilians living on the Normandy coast were women. If you make it past the beach scene of *Saving Private Ryan*, you might have an inkling that women worked for the War Department as secretaries drafting letters home to the mothers of fallen soldiers. And the next scene shows the true story of a mother getting notified that three of her sons had died. But these show women in their traditional roles and give little context to the full extent of the sacrifice that women made in the war, despite the fact that this war was the decisive turning point in modern feminism and the civil rights movement of the twentieth century. *If women weren't allowed on the beaches, what direct roles did women play in the invasion?*

Virginia Hall was an American woman who lost her leg to gangrene before the war and wanted to serve. She had studied abroad in Paris and was fluent in French. She was turned away by American intelligence, so she turned to the British and was eventually recruited by Vera May Atkins, who worked in the France Section of the Special Operations Executive. Atkins correctly observed that men in French villages were sparse, as most were serving out the war in Nazi POW camps. Any male intelligence officers, especially young ones, would be immediately suspected as spies; women, she insisted, were necessary for the invasion to succeed. She sent Hall and women like her into France, where they lived among the Nazis, radioing intelligence back to Britain, gathering internal resisters, and facilitating the drops for weapons and supplies to the French Resistance. These efforts ensured that when the invasion came, a willing and armed France was waiting.

Women were also on the ships crossing the English Channel the morning of the invasion—even if they weren't supposed to be. Martha Gelhorn, who is sadly noted most frequently for her short marriage to Ernest Hemingway, was also a well-established journalist and writer. The morning of D-Day, she hoped to join the many male journalists covering the story but was not permitted to be there. She wrote letters to military leaders, demanding that she be permitted to witness the invasion on behalf of her magazine. She said, "It is necessary that I report on this war. I do not feel there is any need to beg as a favour for the right to serve as the eyes for millions of people in America who are desperately in need of seeing but cannot see for themselves."[63] She was denied again. Hemingway, her estranged husband, applied for her spot even though he didn't even work for a magazine. He got it.[64]

The morning of the invasion, she got on a ship on the pretense of interviewing nurses and stowed away in a bathroom on board so she, like the male journalists, could write a firsthand account of the day. After the initial assault on the beach, she emerged with some doctors and helped them tend the wounded. At this point, 9,000 Allied soldiers were dead. It is important to note that she got there before Hemingway.[65] Her account was later published in *Collier's* magazine, and many people found it a better read than the more widely published work of her ex because it was more human. She said, "All of us knew that our own wounded were good men and that with their amazing help, their selflessness and self-control, we would get through all right."[66] Gelhorn was stripped of her accreditation and sent to a nurse's camp simply for wanting, like other journalists, to do her job; her only offense was that she was a woman. She subsequently escaped and flew to Italy to continue covering the war.

Many perhaps forget to consider the French women who witnessed the occupation and invasion firsthand. One of the best eyewitnesses was Marie Louise Osmont, who kept a diary throughout the war, including the morning of the invasion. Her gorgeous home, which I have been to, sat moments from the beaches. It had been occupied by the Nazis since the fall of France. On June 4—two days before D-Day—she wrote, "Quiet, warm day; night by contrast, filled with the noise of six drunks staggering and bawling."[67] On June 6, she wrote a much longer entry: "Landing! During the night… I am awakened by a considerable rumbling of airplanes and by cannon fire, prolonged but really far away. Then noises in the garden and in the house: talking, loading ammunition boxes, nailing."[68] After a long account of the raising alarm, she wrote, "We're deafened by the airplanes, which make never-ending round." She went on to explain how she had to feed her farm animals during the invasion, that parts of her home were hit by shells, and how her Nazi occupiers were "nuts," but how she had to keep cooking during the onslaught. At some point, one of the Nazis said, "The Tommies are here" and left.[69] She didn't see English soldiers for several hours. The next day, she witnessed what she called a "horrifying" airplane battle. Her windows were broken. She said, "You have the feeling that a runaway train is passing over your body."[70] That day, a French flag was rehung over the school by the Allied soldiers, and soldiers passed out chocolate, cigarettes, and other goods that the French had not seen in years. Her diary went on to describe many more weeks of fighting, the numerous times she almost died, the deaths of her farm animals during the battle, and her impressions of the much-younger American men who took over her home after the Germans vacated.

Back in Britain, Canada, and the United States, families were anxiously waiting news of the invasion. A thorough book called *The Bedford Boys* is a social history of Bedford, Virginia, the city that lost more sons than any other city in the world on D-Day.[71] The chapters flip back and forth between the families back home and the soldiers preparing for war. The women back home spent their days rolling bandages and worrying. Each of them slept with the radio on for news of the invasion they knew was coming. In the middle of the night, the women heard the radio man make the announcement that the landing was on. They were up. They glued themselves to the radio and called family. No one could sleep. It would be weeks, maybe months, before they learned whether their loved ones lived or died. One mother who lost a son never forgave then-Gen. Dwight D. Eisenhower, who oversaw the planning of the invasion, for what she considered needlessly wasting her son's life.

During the war, Eleanor Roosevelt wrote a column titled "My Day" to inspire and relate to the American people. Six days a week, she wrote to uplift and inspire the women of the United States as First Lady. On June 7, she wrote:

> So at last we have come to D-Day, or rather, the news of it reached us over the radio in the early hours of the morning on June the 6th… I have no sense of excitement whatsoever. It seems as though we have been waiting for this day for weeks, and dreading it, and now all emotion is drained away… The best way in which we can help is by doing our jobs here better than ever before, no matter what these jobs may be.[72]

She signed it "E. R."

Even when women are intentionally excluded, they were there, and we deny students a greater understanding of the layers of various events if we exclude women's stories. Historians and educators *can* find examples like these for wars long before World War II—from every era and region of the world—just by adding "women" to their search terms. The inquiry activity for students that follows is one of my favorites because the subject is mostly about men, but the sources are all from women. It is downloadable on the Remedial Herstory Project's website.

What were the human sacrifices on D-Day?

Before reading, consider the source of the following documents. Then examine and analyze the document by responding to the analysis questions provided.

Background

The invasion at Normandy, France, known as D-Day, occurred on June 6, 1944 and was the largest sea-to-land invasion in world history. This amphibious assault required the cooperation of multiple nations armies, navies, and air forces to succeed.

Data

D-Day Data	
Sailors	195,700
Ships	6,939
Infantry	156,115
American	73,000
British and Canadian	83,115
Aircraft	3,262
Tons of Bombs Dropped	3,200
Nazi Germans on shore	50,000
German Mines	4,000,000
German Aircraft	est. 108
Casualties	
Allied	4,413
German	est. 4,000–9,000

Battle of Normandy Data	
Allied Troops Landed in 5 Days	326,547
Allied Vehicles Landed	54,186
Allied Supplies (in tons)	104,428
Casualties	
Allied	53,714
German	est. 200,000
French Civilian	19,890 + est. 15,000 prior to invasion

Data from: "D-Day the Numbers." D Day Center. 2020. http://www.dday.center/d--day-facts-and-figures.html.

Document A: Martha Gelhorn

Martha Gelhorn was the only American female eyewitness to the D-Day invasions, in violation of military orders. She was also one of the first journalists to witness the event. Gelhorn was denied a press card because she was a woman. She appealed her case claiming, "It is necessary that I report on this war. I do not feel there is any need to beg as a favour for the right to serve as the eyes for millions of people in America who are desperately in need of seeing, but cannot see for themselves." She was still denied. On the morning of D-Day, she stowed away on a ship so she could write a firsthand account of the day. She was among the first wave and the earliest correspondents to reach the beaches. Her account appeared Collier's *magazine and was widely read. As a consequence for violating orders, Gelhorn was stripped of her accreditation and sent to a camp. She escaped by plane to continue covering the war.*

Then we saw the coast of France and suddenly we were in the midst of the Armada of the invasion. People will be writing about this site for one hundred years and whoever saw it will never forget it. First it seemed incredible; then there could not be so many ships in the world. Then it seemed incredible as a feat of planning; if there were so many ships, what genius is required to get them there, what amazing and unimaginable genius. After the first shock of wonder and admiration, one began to look around and see separate details. They were destroyers and battleships and transports, a floating city of huge vessels anchored before the green cliffs of Normandy. Occasionally you could see a gun flash or perhaps only hear a distant roar, as a naval guns fired far over those hills. Small-craft Beatles around in a curiously jolly way. It looks like a lot of fun to race from shore to ship in snubnose boats beating up the spray. It was no fun at all, considering the mines and obstacles that remained in the water, the sunken tanks with only the radio antenna showing above the water, the drowned bodies that still floated past. On an LCT [landing craft, tank] near us washing was hung up on a line, in between the loud explosions of mines being that needed on the beach dance music could be heard coming from its radio. Barrage balloons, always looking like comic toy elephants bounced in the Highwind above the mast ships, and invisible planes drone behind the gray ceiling of cloud. Troops were unloading from big ships too heavy cement barges or to light craft, and on the shore moving up for brown roads that scarred the hillside, our tanks clanked slowly and steadily forward.

Then we stopped noticing the invasion, the ships, the ominous beach, because the first wounded had arrived. And LCT Drew alongside our ship, pitching in the waves; a soldier in a steel helmet shouted up to the crew at the aft rail, and a wooden box looking like a lidless coffin was lowered on a pulley, and with the greatest difficulty, bracing themselves against the movement of their boats, the men on the LCT latest structure inside the box. The box was raised to our deck and out of it was lifted a man who is closer to being a boy than a man, dead white and seemingly dying. The first spoon did Mandy brought to that ship for safety and care was a German prisoner.

Everything happened at once. We had six water ambulances, light motor launches, which swung down from the ship's side and could be raised the same way when full of wounded. They carried six litter cases apiece or as many walking wounded as could be crowded into them...

The captain came down from the Bridge to watch this. He was feeling cheerful and he now remarked, "I got us in all right but God knows how we will ever get out." He gestured toward the ship that were stick around us as cars in a parking lot. "Worry about that some other time."

Wounded were pouring in now, hauled up in the lidless coffin or swung aboard in the motor ambulances... An American soldier on that same deck had a head wound so horrible that he was not moved. Nothing could be done for him and anything, any touch, would have made him worse. The next morning he was drinking coffee. His eyes looked very dark and strange, as if he had been a long way away, so far away that he almost could not get back. His face was set in lines of weariness and pain, but when asked how he felt, he said he was okay. He was never known to say anything more...

We waded ashore in water to our waists... It was almost dark by now and there was a terrible feeling of working against time.

Everyone was violently busy on that crowded and dangerous shore. The pebbles were the size of melons and we stumbled up a road that a huge road shovel was scooping out... The dust that rose in the gray night light seemed like the fog of war itself... all of us knew that our own wounded were good men and that with their amazing help, their selflessness and self-control, we would get through it all right.

Gelhorn, Martha. The Face of War. *New York: Simon and Schuster, 1959.*

Sourcing
1 Is this a primary or secondary source?
2 Do you find Gelhorn to be a reliable source for the invasion? Why or why not?

Document
3 Describe the scene in your own words.
4 Describe the human sacrifices witnessed by Gelhorn.

Analysis
5 How might this description be helpful to families of soldiers back home?

Document B: Marie Louise Osmont

Americans often forget that wars happen in people's backyards. The Atlantic and Pacific oceans prevent Americans from facing the full realities of war that other nations feel so deeply. So, of course, many perhaps forget to consider the French women who witnessed the invasion firsthand. One of the best eyewitnesses to D-Day was Marie Louise Osmont. She kept a diary throughout the war and the morning of the invasion. Her gorgeous home sat moments from the beaches. It had been occupied by the Nazi's since the fall of France. In the diary, she refers to the "Tommies," a nickname for the English.

June 6, 1944

Landing!! During the night of the fifth to the sixth, I am awakened by a considerable rumbling of airplanes and by cannon fire, prolong but fairly far away. Then noises in the garden and in the house: talking, loading ammunition boxes, nailing. I get up, go to the window. I see the big fifteen-ton truck arriving, coming from the drive and pulling up in front of the stoop... They're dragging sacks, boxes; they come up and go down... They don't look happy. I stay by the window. The airplanes fly over in tight formations, round and round continuously...

Coming from the sea, a dense artificial cloud; it's ominous and begins to be alarming... I go to get Bernice to get into the trench, a quick bowl of milk and we run – just in time! The shells his explode continually in the trench in the farmyard.... with short moments of calm; we take advantage of these to run and deal with the animals, and we return with hearts pounding to burrow into the trench... The fact is that we're all afraid...

The afternoon is endless.

Osmont, Marie-Louise. The Normandy Diary of Marie-Louise Osmont. *New York: Random House, 1994.*

Sourcing
1 Who is the source? What bias do they likely have?

Document
2 Describe the scene in your own words.
3 Describe the human sacrifices witnessed by Osmont.

Analysis
4 Why do you think Osmont is "horribly sad"?

Document C: Eleanor Roosevelt

During the war, First Lady Eleanor Roosevelt wrote a column entitled "My Day" to comfort the American people. Six days a week, she wrote to uplift and inspire the women of America. On June 7th, she wrote the following passage.

So at last we have come to D-Day, or rather, the news of it reached us over the radio in the early hours of the morning on June the 6th… I have no sense of excitement whatsoever. It seems as though we have been waiting for this day for weeks, and dreading it, and now all emotion is drained away…

The time is here, and in this country, we live in safety and comfort and wait for victory. It is difficult to make life seem real. It is hard to believe that the beaches of France, which we once knew, are now places from which, in days to come, boys in hospitals over here will tell us that they have returned. They may never go beyond the water or the beach, but all their lives, perhaps, they will bear the marks of this day. At that, they will be fortunate, for many others won't return….

This is the beginning of a long, hard fight, a fight for ports where heavy materials of war must be landed, a fight for airfields in the countries in which we must operate. Day by day, miles of country may be taken, lost and retaken. That is what we have to face, what the boys who are over there have been preparing for and what must be done before the day of victory. That day is coming surely. It will be a happy and glorious day. How can we hasten it?

The best way in which we can help is by doing our jobs here better than ever before, no matter what these jobs may be.

E.R.

Roosevelt, Eleanor. "Eleanor Roosevelt's 'My Day,' 6/7/1944: sacrifice on D-Day." White House Historical Association. Electronically Published 2020, https://www. whitehousehistory.org/eleanor-roosevelts-my-day-6-7-1944.

Sourcing
1   What would likely motivate the First Lady's words the morning of D-Day? How might her motivations be different than other Americans?

Document
2   Does Roosevelt seem optimistic?
3   Describe the human sacrifices mentioned by Roosevelt.

Analysis
4   Why is this source important to understanding the impact of D-Day on American and world families?

Based on these accounts, what were the human sacrifices on D-Day?

Notes

1   Gail Collins, *America's Women: Four Hundred Years of Dolls Drudges Helpmates and Heroines* (New York: William Morrow, 2003), 98.
2   Virginia Woolf, *A Room of One's Own* (New York: Harcourt Brace and Company, 1929), 49.
3   Margaret Smith Crocco, "The missing discourse about gender and sexuality in the social studies," *Theory into Practice*, 40(1), 66.
4   Gary B. Nash, Charlotte Crabtree, and Russ E. Dunn, *History on Trial: Culture Wars and the Teaching of the Past*, 15.
5   Nash, Crabtree, and Dunn, *History on Trial*, 6.
6   Nash, Crabtree, and Dunn, *History on Trial*, 11.
7   James Loewen, *Lies My Teacher Told Me* (New York: New Press, 2018), 1–2.
8   Loewen, *Lies My Teacher Told Me*, 3.
9   Nash, Crabtree, and Dunn *History on Trial*, 9.
10 H. Stewart Hughes, *History as Art and as Science*, (Harper & Rowe, 1964), 4–5.
11 William Raymond Smith, *History As Argument: Three Patriot Historians Of The American Revolution* (The Hague: Mouton & Co., 1966), 207.
12 McDonald, "The Need for Contextual Revision," 186–187.
13 McDonald, "The Need for Contextual Revision," 186–187.
14 Debra Michaels, "Mercy Otis Warren," *National Women's History Museum*, 2015, https://www.womenshistory.org/education-resources/biographies/mercy-otis-warren
15 Erick Trickey, "The Woman Whose Words Inflamed the American Revolution," June 20, 2017, *Smithsonian Magazine*, https://www.smithsonianmag.com/history/woman-whose-words-inflamed-american-revolution-180963765/
16 McDonald, "The Need for Contextual ReVision," 186–187.

17 McDonald, "The Need for Contextual ReVision," 186–187.

18 Jone Johnson Lewis, "Mercy Otis Warren," Thought Co., February 4, 2019, https://www.thoughtco.com/mercy-otis-warren-biography-3530669

19 Lewis, "Mercy Otis Warren."

20 Lewis, "Mercy Otis Warren."

21 Lewis, "Mercy Otis Warren."

22 Howard Zinn, *A People's History of the United States* (New York: Harper & Row), 685.

23 Howard Zinn, *A People's History of the United States* (New York: Harper & Row), 685.

24 Bridget Lockyer and Abigail Tazzymant, "'Victims of History,'" 13.

25 Bridget Lockyer and Abigail Tazzymant, "'Victims of History,'" 14.

26 Marie Cartier interview with Kelsie Eckert, *The Remedial Herstory Podcast*, podcast audio, June 2022, https://open.spotify.com/episode/1leKzesTU x5kJHjHVYqhLb.

27 Laurel Thatcher Ulrich, "Womanless," Harvard Magazine, 1997, https://harvardmagazine.com/1999/11/womanless.html.

28 Johnson, *The Gender Knot*, 12.

29 Tetreault, "Integrating Women's History," 213.

30 Tetreault, "Integrating Women's History," 215.

31 This lesson plan, and many others are available for free at www.remedial herstory.com. It was part of my original collection of inquiries published there and is now surrounded by dozens of others authored by many other contributors.

32 Bettany Hughes, "Why Were Women Written Out Of History? An Interview With Bettany Hughes," English Hertiage, February 29, 2016, http://blog.english-heritage.org.uk/women-written-history-interview-bettany-hughes/.

33 Aparna Basu, "Women's History in India: An Historiographical Survey," in: Offen K., Pierson R.R., Rendall J. (eds), Writing Women's History (Palgrave Macmillan, London, 1991) https://doi.org/10.1007/978-1-349-21512-6_10.

34 Miles, *The Women's History of the World*, 149.

35 Daina Ramey Berry and Leslie M Harris. *Sexuality and Slavery: Reclaiming Intimate Histories in the Americas* (Athens Georgia: University of Georgia Press, 2018), 189.

36 Stopford, "Teaching feminism," 1208.

37 Encyclopedia Britannica Editors, "Gaohou," *Encyclopedia Britannica*, October 19, 2015, https://www.britannica.com/biography/Gaohou

38 "Empress Lu," Traditional East Asia, n.d., http://projects.leadr.msu.edu/traditionaleastasia/exhibits/show/badass-female-rulers/empress-lu

39 Hans Van Ess, "Praise and Slander: The Evocation of Empress Lü in the Shiji and the Hanshu," NAN NU -- Men, Women & Gender in Early & Imperial China 8, no. 2 (September 2006): 221–54. doi:10.1163/156852606779969824.

40 The Remedial Herstory Project has an inquiry-based lesson plan on their website about Lü Zhi.

41 Liza Mundy, *Code Girls: The Untold Story of the American Women Code Breakers of World War II*, First ed. (New York: Hachette Books, 2017).

42 David Wolman, "The Once-Classified Tale of Juanita Moody," Smithsonian Magazine, March 2021, https://www.smithsonianmag.com/history/juanita-moody-woman-helped-avert-nuclear-war-180976993/

43 David Wolman, "The Once-Classified Tale of Juanita Moody."

44 Beard, *Women & Power*, 4.

45 Beard, *Women & Power*, 4.

46 Shahla Haeri, *The Unforgettable Queens of Islam* (New York: Cambridge University Press, 2020) 61.

47 Motoko Rich, "'The Tale of Genji' Is More Than 1,000 Years Old. What Explains Its Lasting Appeal?: The book is often described as the world's first novel and a touchstone of Japanese literature. But some of its themes, including its take on gender and power, have echoed over centuries," *The New York Times*, April 20, 2023, https://www.nytimes.com/2023/04/15/books/tale-of-genji-japan-women.html

48 Kirsi Stjerna, *Women And The Reformation* (Oxford: Blackwell Publishing, 2009) 26.

49 Richard T. Vann, "Historiography: Women's History," *Encyclopedia Britannica*, January 17, 2020, https://www.britannica.com/topic/historiography

50 Vann, "Historiography."

51 Yuen Ting Lee, "Ban Zhao: Scholar of Han Dynasty China," World History Connected, last modified 2012, https://worldhistoryconnected.press.uillinois.edu/9.1/lee.html

52 Lee, "Ban Zhao: Scholar of Han Dynasty China."

53 Lee, "Ban Zhao: Scholar of Han Dynasty China."

54 The Editors of Encyclopaedia Britannica, "Ban Zhao". *Encyclopedia Britannica*, January 1, 2022, https://www.britannica.com/biography/Ban-Zhao

55 Ban Zhao, Nancy Swan, trans., *Lessons for Women*, c. IV.

56 Lee, "Ban Zhao: Scholar of Han Dynasty China."

57 Meghan Kelley, "The Good Life of Anna Comnena: First Female Historian and Byzantine Princess," The Histories: Vol. 7: Issue 2, Article 3. https://digitalcommons.lasalle.edu/the_histories/vol7/iss2/3

58 Jone Johnson Lewis, "Biography of Anna Comnena, the First Female Historian," Thought Co, last modified May 15, 2019, https://www.thoughtco.com/anna-comnena-facts-3529667

59 Lewis, "Biography of Anna Comnena."

60 Lewis, "Biography of Anna Comnena."

61 Anna Comnena, Marcelle Thuebaux, trans., ed., *The Writings of Medieval Women*, vol. 14, New York: Garland Library of Medieval Literature, 1987, retrieved from http://www.womeninworldhistory.com/dalassena.html

62 Mary Ritter Beard, *On Understanding Women* (New York: Greenwood Press, 1968), v.

63 Martha Gelhorn, cited by Lyse Doucet, "The women reporters determined to cover World War Two," BBC, June 5, 2014, https://www.bbc.com/news/magazine-27677889

64 Martha Burk, "D-Day: 150,000 Men — and One Woman," Huffington Post, December 6, 2017, https://www.huffpost.com/entry/d-day-150000-men---and-on_b_5452941

65 Burk, "D-Day."

66 Gelhorn, "Committed to Reporting the Truth."

67 Marie-Louise Osmont, *The Normandy Diary of Marie-Louise Osmont* (New York: Random House, 1994), 39.

68 Osmont, The Normandy Diary of Marie-Louise Osmont, 40.

69 Osmont, The Normandy Diary of Marie-Louise Osmont, 43.

70 Osmont, The Normandy Diary of Marie-Louise Osmont, 47.

71 Alex Kershaw, *The Bedford Boys: One American Town's Ultimate D-Day Sacrifice* (Waterville, ME: Thorndike Press, 2003).

72 Eleanor Roosevelt, "Eleanor Roosevelt's 'My Day,' 6/7/1944: sacrifice on D-Day," *White House Historical Association*, Electronically Published 2020, https://www.whitehousehistory.org/eleanor-roosevelts-my-day-6-7-1944

2

His-Story Is Not the Only Story

To know nothing of what happened before you were born is to forever remain a child.

—Cicero

The absence of women's history in the mainstream curriculum leads us to believe that women's history doesn't exist, women didn't do much, and there isn't much to find. There are certainly blanks, but in large part this is false. In fact, the authors of the AP World History textbook *Ways of the World* argue, "No division of human society has held greater significance for the lives of individuals as those of sex and gender...The inequalities of gender, like those of class, decisively shaped the character of the First Civilizations and those that followed."[1] To assume that women did not record their history, as a justification for not digging for it, allows the mistakes of our past to repeat. Rosalind Miles suggested, "For even the most cursory survey of women's work reveals that its range, quantity and significance has been massively underestimated, not least by women themselves."[2] The further back people go in history, the more they tend to oversimplify and ignore women, but women were there, documented, and diverse in thought and action.

In some cases, we know only a small fraction of the story. Miles asserted that any women's history "must listen to the silences and make them cry out."[3] Pioneering American historian Mary Ritter Beard argued that the absence of women in history does not mean that women haven't been doing things—it's that their actions, though recorded, did not bypass the gatekeepers to history.[4]

DOI: 10.4324/9781003472889-3

When an event happens, do all people agree on how it played out? History was once current events. How many different perspectives are there of current events? The same is true of history. Is it possible to know what truly happened or what it felt like to be there? There could be as many histories as there are human witnesses. History has been written by victors and has suppressed the story of the losers; therefore, it has been not a truthful account of what happened but rather the dominating account. Good history is a consensus about what happened derived on the basis of evidence. As more evidence comes forward, the historical record changes. The record is a moving target. It is alive. It is ever-changing.

But this is not how some students learn history. In some classrooms, they are told what happened. In some classrooms, they read from a textbook that tells them what they need to know: a standard version of history—but there is no standard. There are an infinite number of sources and perspectives to consider. No such document exists for current events. Every newspaper has a different take. In history, we find our truths, just like in current events, by the strength of the source, by the evidence that is presented, and sometimes even by an average of everything that is being said.

A neat psychological phenomenon helps illustrate the importance of our-story: the wisdom of the crowd. Aristotle first referenced it, modern juries are based on it, and Galton found evidence to support it.[5] When a crowd at a 1906 fair speculated for fun on the weight of an ox, Galton found that the median of all their guesses was within 1 percent of the actual weight of the ox. This was significantly closer than the likelihood of any one person's guess being accurate. What does this mean for historical study? It suggests that the average of the stories told is perhaps the closest to the truth.

When women and other marginalized groups are excluded, we are not getting the truth of the past. We are getting less than half the story. Our history is better told, more truthful, and more accurate when everyone's voices are included. His-story serves the few. Our-story, which includes her-story, includes the voices, stories, and experiences of all of us.

Noticing the Biases

Background: But Can You Name the Women?

When I started speaking about women's history at professional conferences, I attracted people who were already open-minded and interested in women's history. Sometimes I got attendees who wanted to prove to me that they knew women's history. And, worse, despite all the obvious data, some wanted to maliciously prove that my work was unnecessary. So, I put my research methods to work and decided to turn it into a game. *You think you know women's history equally? Prove it.*

To start the talk, I had attendees make a list of ten important men from history. These dutiful historians and teachers quickly jotted down their list. What they didn't know was that I was timing them. Then I asked them to make a list of ten important women from history. *If* they could complete the list, not one person was able to beat the time they got on the men's list. What does this tell us? Men's names are easier to recall. Stories of men are more frequently taught, rehashed, and referenced in our culture to improve our memory of them. I win the men's list by recalling the US presidents I have so often been required to memorize. We are primed for men's history, not women's.

In her essays and public appearances, Gloria Steinem said that the rise in college courses and programs in women's studies was an attempt to make up for women's invisibility in history. She added that these courses were more like "remedial studies."[6,7] As I converse with college-educated professionals, I can't help but feel that Steinem was right. These adults know so little about these women, and, self-consciously, I know that's true of me too. When I tell my friends and students about the women I uncover, they are wowed as if I am an expert—but I know she should be better known and I actually know very little about her. The problem is that for all this work and research, the accomplishments of this field have not been made mainstream. Women's history is history, but if you have to take a separate, elective class to learn about it, the masses will never know it—heck, historians will never know it! If we can't name women, we don't know women's history.

Barrier: Male Domination in History

A total of 76.6 percent of all teachers in the US are women, and 59.8 percent of all secondary educators are women.[8] From the beginning, it's important to state generally that we need more men in education. More on this in Chapter 3. But it sometimes surprises people to learn that secondary and college *history* education is not only dominated by the stories and accomplishments of men but also primarily taught and researched by them. Women's lives are so infrequently discussed in history, and it's rare to see them teaching it. *Coincidence?* The predominance of male topics and male instructors leaves girls thinking this is not a subject for them.

The Brookings Institute found, consistent with other studies, that social studies courses were predominantly taught by men in the secondary classroom. They wrote, "Social studies teachers are disproportionately male… Among demographic variables, gender stands out the most."[9] *The most.* Their data showed that this differed from other subjects in which women were the majority (see Figure 2.1). In a field where most teachers are female, this glaring area of male majority stands out (Figures 2.1, 2.2).

PERCENTAGE OF MALE TEACHERS

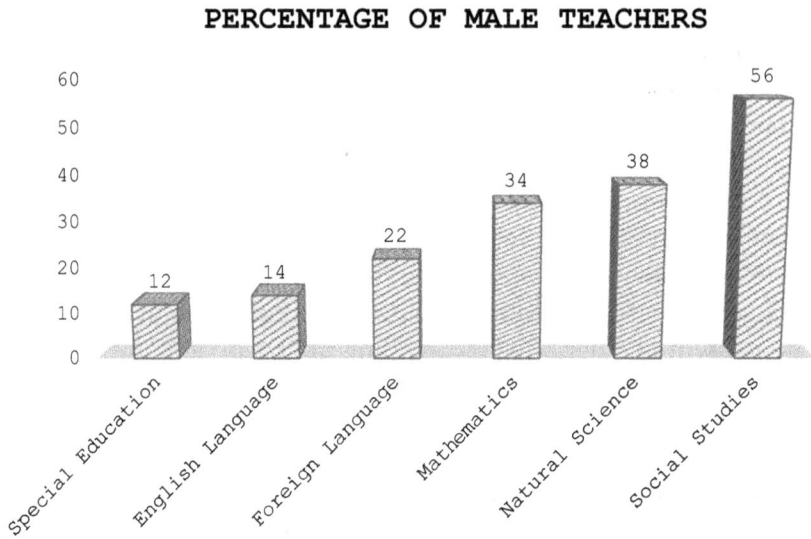

Figure 2.1 The Brookings Institute found that men predominantly teach social studies compared with all other subjects, demonstrating the potential for inherent bias in curriculum selection.

Source: Data from Michael Hansen, Elizabeth Mann Levesque, Jon Valant, and Diana Quintero, "2018 Brown Center Report on American Education: Understanding the social studies teacher workforce," June 27, 2018, retrieved from https://www.brookings.edu/research/2018-brown-center-report-on-american-education-understanding-the-social-studies-teacher-workforce/.

Male Historians' Biographic Subject

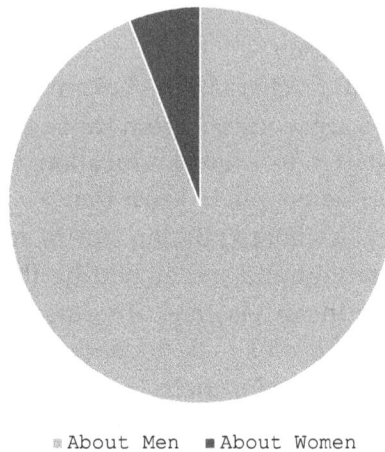

▨About Men ▪About Women

Figure 2.2 In a study, Slate found that only 6 percent of recent male biographers wrote about women. Female authors were far more likely to write about women.

Source: Data from Andrew Khan and Rebecca Onion, "Is History Written About Men, by Men?" Slate, January 6, 2016, http://www.slate.com/articles/news_and_politics/history/2016/01/popular_history_why_are_so_many_history_books_about_men_by_men.html.

Fewer Female History Faculty than Other Fields

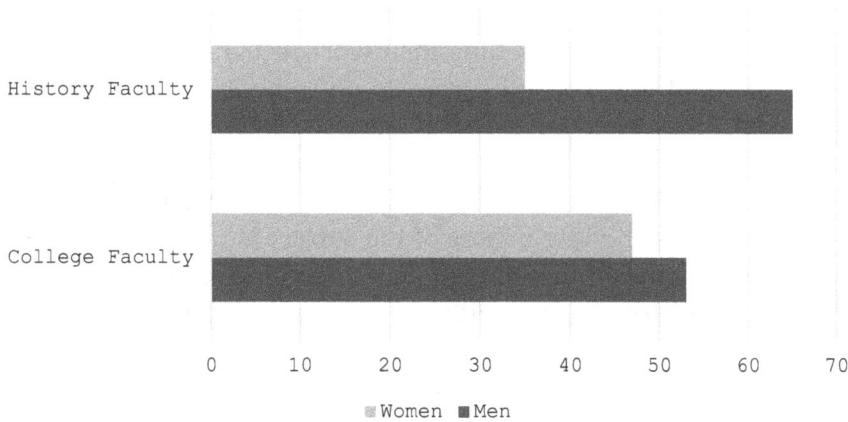

Figure 2.3 Women who hold full-time faculty positions in history are behind other fields.

Source: Eckert's table with data from Catalyst, "Quick Take: Women in Academia," January 23, 2020, https://www.catalyst.org/research/women-in-academia/.

Men teaching history at the secondary or collegiate level is not inherently problematic, except that only 6 percent of male historians write about women.[10] If scholars are not writing about women, it won't trickle down to the teachers. And if scholars have this selection bias for topics, it's likely that teachers do as well. Women tend to write about women more, but the number of available female historians remains low (Figure 2.3).

In 2008, women represented only 35 percent of history faculty, far below the average across subjects, where women make up almost half of tenure-track professors.[11] In the UK, the problem was worse: women made up only 21 percent of history faculty in 2012.[12] When Lynne Hunt wrote her 2018 book *History: Why It Matters*, she did a quick survey of a few California universities as case studies of inclusion and found that the ratios of men and women faculty members had not improved. One school had nine female history faculty out of 26. In colleges across the United States, Europe, and Australia, women are generally less likely to be promoted and earn less than their male peers—in the UK, over 15 percent less! In academia, women actually make up the majority of lower-level lecturer positions, but as you examine the upper ranking Assistant Professors and full Professors, women are more rare. In the US, women make up only 39.3 percent of tenure-track positions; 12 percent of those women were of color.[13,14]

Women historians are grossly underrepresented in various measurements of professional achievement, such as being cited and being conference panelists. Just as children are overwhelmingly taught history by men, the media utilize male historical experts far more than they utilize women, so when teachers show documentaries in class, it is highly likely that the historians featured reinforce the idea that history is for men and about men. Women historians have a harder time getting their work recognized, so teachers who want to read about women find it hard to do so because the information is harder to find. Scholars at the *Journal of Women's History* explained:

> Women's expertise is routinely disregarded, even when they are the primary authors and researchers of the subject in question. This dismissal not only means that the public is not seeing or hearing enough from diverse historians, but neither are students or our colleagues.[15]

The classicist Mary Beard zoomed out to the larger issue, stating, "Women in power are seen as breaking down barriers, or alternatively as taking something to which they are not quite entitled."[16] She asserted that society suggests that women belong "outside power,"[17] which is why women historians, even when they are the most qualified person on that subject, are often excluded from the dialogue.

Having women faculty at the college level allows the younger women in their classes to see themselves in the field. Subsequently, those women are more likely to choose topics in women's history for their research. More female professors and more research create a path for these ideas to trickle down to secondary educators.

One might hope that the overall growth of women in various graduate programs would help improve these data, but in history, women's growth in the field has remained stagnant. In the last two decades, only 42 percent of history PhDs were women.[18] Robert Townsend, assistant director for research and publications for the American Historical Association, wrote,

> The problems start with the students attracted to history. Over the past 20 years history has graduated some of the smallest proportions of female undergraduates of any field in higher education—well below all of the other humanities and social science disciplines outside of religious studies.

He continued,

> The most troubling aspect of the trends in female student enrollment and graduation is the way history has plateaued at both the undergraduate and graduate level. If women continue to earn barely 40 percent of the degrees in history, that seems to set a rather hard ceiling for the representation of women among those employed in the discipline.[19]

Include Women's History

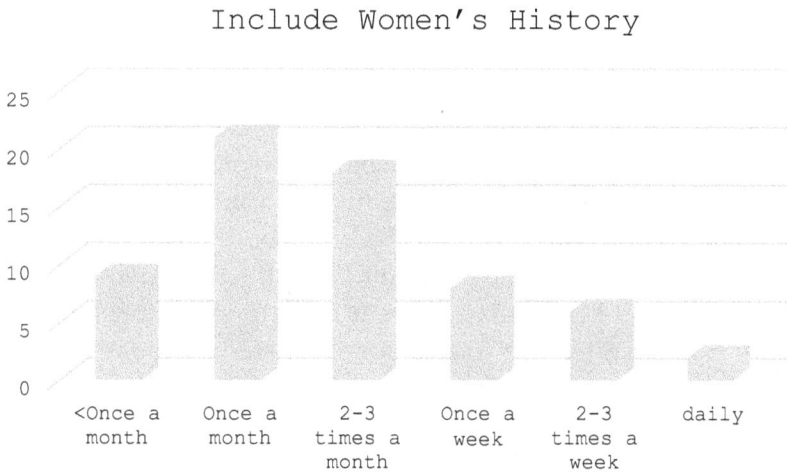

Figure 2.4 Cicely Scheiner-Fisher's study of Orange County Schools, in Florida, shows that educators barely teach women's history.

Source: Data from Cicely Scheiner-Fisher, "The Inclusion of Women's History In The Secondary Social Studies Classroom," Electronic Theses and Dissertations, University of Central Florida, 2013, https://stars.library.ucf.edu/etd/2848, 41.

If women are not studying history, they certainly wouldn't be qualified to teach it (Figure 2.4).

Those who study history often do not know women's history and therefore struggle to teach it. In her 2013 dissertation, Cicely Scheiner-Fisher found that while 91 percent of teachers in Orange County Schools, in Florida, incorporate women's voices in the curriculum, only 25 percent do it once a week or more, and 46 percent do it once a *month* or less![20,21] The plurality are teaching women's history 5 percent of the time, and a majority teach it less than 20 percent of the time. Although it clearly varies by the teacher, in a ten-month school year, the median student was learning about women's history once a month: a ratio of 1:10 women's history to men's history. In essence, most teachers barely teach women's history.

In a 2021 study in Massachusetts schools by Christopher Martell and Kaylene Stevens, different results were found, yet the same problems were there. The researchers acknowledged that their geographic context likely produced these results. In Massachusetts, they said, we would expect teachers to have different perspectives on teaching race and gender than other states. Massachusetts is politically liberal, and its population, including teachers, may be more likely to support views of race and racism aligned with liberal political beliefs.[22] Still, 62.5 percent of teachers reported that they covered women weekly, compared to 60.2 percent who said they covered men *daily!* So while this is certainly better than the study from Florida a decade earlier, it is appallingly sparse when comparing the treatment of male and female figures. In both studies, while the majority of teachers taught about men in 100 percent of their classes, women's history remained somewhere between 5 percent and 20 percent of the curriculum.

This became evident when Lockyer and Tazzymant worked with students in a UK study. Teachers had "crowbarred" women in by adding a separate unit on women. Students observed this and found the gesture politically motivated and performative. It sent the message that the *real* history was male-dominated. Students said, "I don't think it's deliberately more about men though, without being sexist, there is more to learn about men, they've done more."[23] Later, after five workshops facilitated by the researchers, student perceptions about women's history changed. One student said, "I found it quite interesting the fact that I thought before this that the reason why women weren't really talked about is because nothing was really recorded about them, because it was mainly men doing the recording. But having seen this and seen how much actually has been recorded about women I found that surprising why we don't really learn more about women."[24] If five workshops can change student perspectives, imagine what 180 school days can do.

Narrowly covering women creates fallacies about women's history. In Martell and Steven's study in Massachusetts, 72.8 percent said they taught about the gender pay gap and 30.1 percent said they taught about incidences of rape on college campuses. Both of these were framed in the contemporary context, which again creates a false belief that only modern women have been dealing with these things and fighting against them. Women's ideas and perspectives need to be incorporated from pre-history, through early civilizations and ancient, medieval, and modern history to reinforce over and over that women were active and engaged agents.

These problems are pervasive not only in the history curriculum but across all subjects. Word problems in math reinforce gender stereotypes, science teachers fail to credit women who have now been proven to be the real brains and discoverers of new scientific ideas, and so on. In a study of teacher education texts, Karen Zittleman and David Sadker found:

> Given the decades of research documenting the impact of gender bias in schools, the authors anticipated stronger, fairer texts than those analyzed 20 years ago. Clearly, there has been progress, but it is minimal. Introductory/foundation texts provide slightly more than 7% of content to gender issues; methods texts average little more than 1%. Although a commitment to gender fairness is verbalized in several of the texts, specific resources and strategies to achieve that goal are often absent.[25]

Does the gender of teachers matter? It shouldn't, but there remains the pervasive problem of women being excluded from the curriculum and men being the ones to primarily research and teach it. This should give us pause. The cycle will continue until a shift occurs in our cultural expectation that history is about men and its teachers are male or that male teachers can't, for some reason, teach about women and gender. I'm white but have spent my career deepening my understanding of Black history. It can be done. The cycle that keeps women out of the curriculum will continue until the social studies teachers on the front lines know her-story and know how to fit it in. Society needs more women both in history and teaching it.

When women are teaching history, their lived experiences impact what they select for inclusion. Therefore, diversity in the profession can lead to diversity of theme and topics within the content—and that is where the women are. It is important that the social studies curriculum acknowledge histories outside military, political, and diplomatic themes as legitimate and worthy of study. That said, studies have shown that men in particular may have greater social freedom to talk about women—and thus how wonderful is it that the majority of social studies teachers are men. More on this in Chapter 3.

Breaker: Bi-Focal and Diverse Themes

Once teachers begin to examine the writings by and about women, they can move to a "bi-focal" approach where they can look at history in the binaries: male and female. In this second phase, teachers can begin to ask broader, comparative questions about the human experience.[26] In these investigations, students can be invited to explore gendered norms and expectations. They can compare the experiences of women to men to more deeply understand how society shapes their experiences, work, and relationships. They can explore the different ways that oppression manifests for different groups and begin to ask the following questions:

- How does the division between the public and private spheres explain women's lives?
- Who has oppressed women, and how are women oppressed?
- How did notable and ordinary women respond to their oppression?
- What did women contribute to areas or movements traditionally dominated by men?[27]

Centering women's experiences means not shying away from hard questions above because they are about things that impact women's everyday lives both in the past and at present. Sometimes teachers shy away from questions because the answer themselves are hard, but those hard answers will help young students understand and navigate the society around them.

Women's history is harder to find in the historical record, especially using common methodology for research. Women writers were rarer, and published women's works were hard to come by. Because of the sexism of their time, few women's diaries or other personal writings were preserved—but nonetheless the sources exist.

Imagine a history that, in addition to politics, military, diplomacy, and business, included medical history, more robust religious histories, and other themes. These themes would necessitate including women, among others. Records on all these topics exist from as far back as records have been kept. Emphasis on these themes would mean that more women would be part of history.

Of the themes that so often make history, economics is one that should be reexamined to include the labors of women, which are all but erased from the traditional curriculum. In her piece titled, "The Care Tradition: Beyond 'Add Women and Stir,'" Nel Noddings argued for "Homemaking," to stand alongside economic themes.[28] Topics that cross so many fields connected to the social studies certainly belong in a secondary classroom, but perhaps the most appealing aspect of these topics for contemporary study is their immediate application to the lives of young people. After all, why do we study the social studies? To learn about our world, our society, human lives.

My honest gut reaction to the topic of homemaking, as a woman who has done my best to avoid it, was that it wasn't as important as major industry-changing topics like how the Bessemer process influenced the shift from iron to steel. That gut reaction *is the problem*. That gut reaction is how I have internalized the beliefs that women's work is less important and less deserving of historical study.

In all of these areas, thorough exploration leads to juicy discussion of women's exploitation and oppression, but it also leads to conversations about our contemporary world. Today, young people of all genders expect the opportunity to be breadwinners, but caregiving is so "denigrated" in Western society that few want or are prepared for it.[29] A piece of this is due to the low pay for caregivers (more on this in Chapter 4), but again, whom does this lack of preparation serve? Noddings phrases it as a possible inquiry:

> Were homemaking and child rearing ever well taught in homes? How many youngsters—even girls—failed to get adequate education for these important tasks? Did their ignorance serve pernicious (if unintended) societal goals? Is such ignorance widespread today? Who gains and who loses from such ignorance?[30]

Who benefits from women not knowing their economic history? It's not women. Not a single country in the entire world has achieved gender equity.[31] Our entire economy is run on the backs of women's free labor.

What follows is a brief, very brief, survey of three themes of history often left out of curriculum: women's economics, medical, and religious history. I've included this history, despite not being an expert on these themes, because it's hard to explain what teachers are missing out on if I don't pause to teach the content. I've written these less as histories and more as a conveyance of key understandings that teachers should be teaching. Obviously, there is nuance to each of these themes, and any attempt to summarize women's experiences across time and place will fail. Therefore, consider the following a launching pad for further study.

Economic History

Economies run on the backs of women's free labor as homemakers, childcare providers, chefs, housekeepers, laundresses, pick-up and drop-off drivers, administrative assistants to plan and execute scheduling of doctors' appointments, event planners—the list goes on. Despite incredible social change in the last half century, women remain the default caregivers in most families, and our social, cultural template puts immense pressure on them to serve—for free. It's long overdue that we legitimized this labor with greater academic study in K-12 curriculum so that we can build a more fair and equitable economy.

Most teachers of economics acknowledge that measures of an economy fail to consider the full experience of the human laborers within that economy. Happiness levels, for example, aren't usually in the nation's economic report. Economists study exchanges that are financial through gross domestic product; they measure financial investments, inflation of prices, and unemployment. They measure the hours that people work every day and conclude that women work less than men, because, well, they work less in paid wages. But women work *more* hours than men when unpaid labor is factored in.

In the United States, men average about 17.5 hours a week performing unpaid domestic labor. Women, on the other hand, spend 28.4—an 11-hour difference *per week*![32] Men who work 5 hours more a week at their salaried job are not working more. This is a semantic, yet fundamental, piece of the equal pay conversation. If you add women's unpaid and paid labor together, women work longer hours—women are just unpaid for huge chunks of their labor.[33] So much of the work that women do is unseen. To help make that labor visible, Eve Rodsky compiled a list of many of the domestic tasks that need to be done daily, weekly, monthly, and annually. She wrote a book titled *Fair Play*, which breaks down the importance of sharing this domestic labor. Often spouses, mostly men, were unaware of just *how much* of this invisible, undervalued domestic labor women do.[34]

Why have we erased women's labor from measures and collective memories? Because women make up only 26 percent of economists. This erasure also happens in our schools in the way we teach about the economy, businesses, and labor history. Most of us who teach about the Industrial Revolution will emphasize the rise in coal, oil, and railroads but not the labors of women. How many times have I shown pictures of the horrifying working conditions of the period and shown images of mostly men. We teachers highlight the big men: Andrew Carnegie, John D. Rockefeller, Cornelius Vanderbilt, and JP Morgan. But we fail to ask who cooked their supper? Who cleaned their house? Who cared for their children? If we did, we would learn a very different lesson of exploitation, racial and class differences, and dangerous conditions. Even if we chose to highlight only the big women alongside the men, we would learn a great deal about how women invested their monies differently, on social causes and reforms.

So, what was that history we skipped? In the ancient world, this can manifest in exploring the nuances of "women's work"—where and when it was different from men's and where and when it was the same. It is vitally important to teach about the seismic shift the Agricultural Revolution had on women's work: increasing birth rates and thus the amount of time women spent in domestic labor. The effect can be seen in the way the fertility goddesses went from being housed in religious centers to hearthside. Teaching about the Silk Roads inclusively should *start and end* with women, as poor women in China were the primary producers of silk and elite women's betrothals to men abroad kept peace on the routes.[35]

In the medieval world, women's labors are more deeply understood and can provide interesting nuances to history when the layers of class and race are examined. Generalizing women's work, like generalizing men's work, is dangerous because, when over-simplified, middle-class women's work dominates the narrative. Elite women were better educated than their common sisters and thus their work involved tasks that were more intellectual. Poor women often worked alongside men and rarely had the opportunity to live the secluded lives of homemakers. They unsexed themselves in male worlds. In the Ottoman Empire, for example, it was elite women who veiled and stayed in cloistered spaces, not poor women who labored in marketplaces surrounded by men.[36]

In world history courses, transnational comparisons of the work that women did would highlight similarities and differences. Noddings explained how homemaking strategies and philosophies vary regionally and have changed over time and yet, in some ways, remain the same. The way women's labor was respected or not is also interesting.

Across time and place, women served as midwives. This is a constant and necessary role for women. This vital role was one of the few paid and acceptable professions left open to women. It's also interesting because it contributed to both the productive and reproductive labor of women. Successes in midwifery were vital to the larger economy because improvements decreased infant and maternal mortality and increased the number of available laborers, central to all economic concepts like employment rates and gross production.

In feudal societies, women were active in doing work such as milling grain, laundering, spinning, and working in retail and prostitution. It is difficult to estimate, but approximately one third to one half of all merchants in feudal Europe were women.[37] These women were often unattached or widowed, continuing their husband's business after he passed.

Too often teachers oversimplify so as to dismiss women's labors as drudgery when that "drudgery" is desperately vital to the economy. During the Age of Exploration in world history and in western expansion in US history, women were scarce among the populace, so the skills they had been trained in as homemakers were also scarce. Women who monetized these skills in the market made fortunes running boarding houses, cooking, and serving as seamstresses and prostitutes.

Slavery, as with the labors of most people on the bottom of the social caste, did little to distinguish women from men in their labors. Enslaved women did backbreaking labor alongside men and died at similar rates. Enslavers gradually shifted toward valuing enslaved women's reproductive labor, which would decrease the need to import new slaves and instead regenerate the enslaved population year to year.[38] Women who proved fertile were monetarily valued higher at auction and less likely to be sold. In US history, Black women's labors often are usually discussed only in relation to their role as slaves, and this too needs to cease. Free Black women living in the antebellum South were part of the merchant class, owned businesses and land, and were vital contributors to the economy.[39]

As the centuries-long process of industrialization and professionalization began, women's work saw dramatic shifts. Women's guilds began to disappear, laws barred women from lucrative businesses, and industrialization pulled women's work from the cottage to factories. Married women were driven from the paid workforce as a result.[40] Their male managers and employers found these women to be agreeable and hardworking and were pleased that they were willing to work for a small fraction of the male wage.[41] Weaving, long a staple of women's labor, was now produced on looms in mills owned by men. Male doctors, with degrees from medical colleges that women were denied entry to, began to replace midwives—despite the fact that they had no lived, cultural, or practicum experience with birth.[42] Unions headed by men worked to protect male wages, often at the expense of women.[43] Women's work, once vital, became universally seen as "pin money"—extra.

One of the few women to win the Nobel Prize for economics was Dr. Claudia Goldin—a history-making woman herself as the first woman to earn tenure in Harvard's Economics Department. Her research, which won her the prize, highlighted how only in the 20th century, with the expansion of service-sector jobs and the development of high school education, did a more familiar labor pattern emerge for women. One of her characteristic findings was that women and their economic participation formed U-shapes, like the one she found between the size of Western economies and women's labor force participation. The pay gap declined in the early 1900s as industrialization entered other industries, but discrimination began to play a more significant role in the gap.[44] In the factory setting, employees could be paid based on the unbiased measure of output, but the turn-of-the-century employers began using ambiguous factors like job tenure which penalized women who were expected to leave their careers when they had children.

Most women, however, remained in domestic labor, where the advances in factory technology offered little benefit to their daily lives. Skyscrapers were being built, but only one quarter of American homes had indoor plumbing as of 1890.[45] "It took an hour a day to take care of even the most modern stove... All in all, sweeping, dusting, cleaning lighting fixtures, washing windows, and maintaining the furnace and fireplaces took an estimated twenty-seven hours a week."[46] There is no shortage of primary documents that explore effective, ethical, and efficient homemaking strategies. Women like Catherine Beecher, a prolific writer, shared their ideas in home journals and magazines.[47] These writings and magazines have long been dismissed as soft history, by a historical elite made up mostly of males, who don't do or need this type of training.

The efficiency that developed in men's work would not be brought home until women demanded or made it themselves. It is no surprise that many of those reforms paralleled women's access to higher education and growing numbers of professional women. *How much more quickly could these achievements have been made with more women in business, science, and politics?* Women took it upon themselves to invent what they needed to innovate. Vacuums, laundry machines, dishwashers, and other home appliances popped up throughout the late 19th and early 20th centuries, shifting the nature of and time commitment to domestic work. Josephine Cochran's dishwashing machine, patented in 1886, is a neat example.[48] As the decades continued, improvements on these technologies increased their effectiveness and further decreased women's time spent on homemaking. This paralleled higher rates of college degrees among women and decreasing birth rates.

In the study of suffrage, we can see the role that the male government played in creating a second-class status for women. When we gender economic history, it becomes incredibly obvious why women have struggled to find pay equity with men—everything from the types of jobs that women could do to the pay they got and how the government would protect them when they were treated unjustly. These governmental failings are deeply evident in the case law in the 20th century in the US and around the world. In the US, male-centrism and thus sexism were embedded in New Deal policies; the Economy Act of 1932; laws that barred women from opening bank accounts and having credit cards and other means of financial freedom from men; codes that prevented women from certain jobs; union contracts that allowed for differential pay; tax codes that benefited salaried work over domestic work; a lack of healthcare, pension, social security, etc. for homemakers; and the way laws made it easier to harass, discriminate, and pay women unfairly and easy to get away with that behavior.[49] The 20th century is packed with example after example of women taking their newfound political freedom and demanding that it apply to their financial futures.

Central to all conversations about women and the economy is what Claudia Goldin simplified to "Career and Family." To put women and gender explicitly in economics class, teachers must analyze how organizations and economies incorporate women who menstruate, get pregnant, give birth, go through menopause, have children, and caretake for loved ones into the paid labor force. In many ways, these parts of being female have been treated as an obstacle to paid work, perpetuating the huge wealth gap between men and women. Students should analyze the return on investment of various policies like family leave and learn to do what economists do. Goldin's research explored how different the options available to women in the last five generations were. For some generations of women, the economy was inflexible and they chose career *or* family. For other generations, science, legislation, and culture allowed women to get closer to having both. I will address each of these in much more depth in Chapter 4. For now, let's understand that it is difficult to talk about women and the economy without other themes that affect women at work: the history of medicine and religion. The medical field established the "science" that justified women's place, while religions shaped the cultural context and environment in which women lived and worked. Most history curriculums leave out these two themes of history, which is why most fail to teach about women.

Medical History

For men, their value in society and history has been measured by their productive accomplishments, which we study. For women, it was their reproductive value which has most defined their lives and worth in history.

Why should we not study it? Medical history tells us so much about the lives of women because women, now and in the past, rely on physicians more than men do. Across time, physicians kept records of their patients which now can be studied to understand the lives of women. Therefore, medical history is women's history.

Reproduction impacts women's bodies, health, careers, and, sadly, societal value. Reproduction requires medical care following puberty, and for women this is their reality. All students deserve the chance to learn about women's health as far back as we can go in time, showing the ways it was treated differently across cultures and the advances that dramatically improved and saved the lives of women and children. This includes access to various methods of anesthesia, abortion, birth control, and menstruation treatments, among other measures.

Reproduction crosses social studies subjects. Anthropology, for example, tells us a great deal about the female experience. As the human species developed larger brains, which allowed us to move from hominid to *Homo sapiens*, women's bodies literally morphed to birth these larger-skulled beings.[50] As brains continued to enlarge, evolution favored women who gave birth earlier, before the skull was so large that it could not pass through the birth canal. Still death during childbirth around the world was incredibly high, so much so that the Mayans called birth the "woman's war."[51] Communities and families were regularly devastated by the death of yet another woman in childbirth.

In history, we know a great deal about the practices surrounding birth because Greek physicians wrote about them. Because so much of a woman's life revolved around her uterus, it's no wonder medical writing of this time focused primarily on that. Hippocrates is known today for the Hippocratic oath, which doctors take to do no harm. He was an ancient Greek physician whose ideas were written down by other male physicians years later. This work, the Hippocratic Corpus, included treatises like *Diseases of Women*, *Nature of Women*, and *Diseases of Young Girls*, from which almost all Western medical thinking is derived—even today. You can examine women's experience through the meticulous records kept by physicians.

But women were not just the patients. In economics, we can explore this topic through the careers that birth offered, and continue to offer, women and the ways in which government oversight, certification requirements, and other economic pressures have both helped and endangered women patients and the careers of women physicians. Being a midwife was one of the few accepted ways that women have run businesses beyond their home around the world. But in the 1500s, the first obstetric text was published, starting a push toward "professionalizing" the industry—tell the women who built

their careers around serving pregnant people that they weren't professionals! This professionalization damaged women patients.[52] Their physicians
had never been through what they were going though, and Victorian gendered expectations respected women's modesty. As a result, doctors sometimes thought it immodest to look under a woman's gown while assisting in
a delivery! Also, male medical students weren't allowed to observe births, so
instead they learned from textbooks![53]

By the 1800s, despite the professional-male takeover of midwifery, women
continued to suffer from the failure of the profession to cure some horrible
conditions caused by birth, including tearing and a dropped uterus lodged
deeper in a woman's pelvis, making any movement severely painful. A terrible ailment was a vaginal fistula, in which the wall between the vagina and
the bladder or rectum would rip, leading to urine or feces leaking through
the vagina, causing infection.[54] Some historians think these issues increased
because of instrumental practices invented by doctors. J. Marion Sims, like so
many male doctors before him, wanted to help women with these maladies
but needed to experiment with surgery. So, without anesthesia, he went looking for women to experiment on. He was an enslaver from Alabama who sub-
scribed to the racist belief that Black women didn't feel as much pain as white
women.[55] He felt that white women could not have endured the pain of these
unproven surgeries; therefore, he tested his ideas on enslaved women, whom
he essentially tortured for the "greater good." Lucy was one of these women.
He wrote in his notebook, "That was before the days of anesthetics, and the
poor girl, on her knees, bore the operation with great heroism and bravery."[56]
Anarcha was the first woman to have her fistula surgically repaired by Sims,
but it took 13 operations.[57] Consent to these operations has been up for historical debate. In a 1941 paper titled "The Negro's Contribution to Surgery"
published in the *Journal of the National Medical Association*, Dr. John A. Kenney
of the Tuskegee Institute, considered the dean of Black dermatology, wrote,
"I suggest that a monument be raised and dedicated to the nameless Negroes
who have contributed so much to surgery by the 'guinea pig' route."[58]

One would be remiss not to include the story of Dr. James Barry in any
course. In 1826, Barry was responsible for one of the world's first recorded
successful Caesarian sections in which both the mother and child survived. He
was also a contemporary of Florence Nightingale. Barry was assigned female
at birth and raised as a girl by the name of Margaret Ann Bulkley.[59] When
his uncle died, he assumed the name James and used the new identity as
an opportunity for self-betterment, enrolling in medical school in Edinburgh,
Scotland. Barry had been raped as a child, and the resulting child was raised
by his mother, but the stretch marks from pregnancy remained his entire life.
Barry had a highly successful and controversial medical career, serving as a

physician all over the world, including during the Crimean War.[60] While in South Africa, he performed the Caesarian section. The grateful mother named her new baby James in his honor. When Barry died years later, it was discovered that he had female genitalia. How he would have liked to be remembered is unknown except that he had requested to be buried in the clothes he died in. It was evident that those close to him had known his secret (Figure 2.5).

In hospitals, before germs were understood and sterilization common, doctors would go from surgery to surgery, carrying infections to women in labor. By the 1800s, the maternal death rate reached between 2 and 8 per 100 deliveries—around ten times the rate outside of hospitals.[61] In New York in 1840, 80 percent of women who gave birth in a hospital died.[62]

This quick survey of women's medical history is merely an introduction to the ways that the medical field has documented the lives of women. Abundant scholarship in this field is available for educators and scholars to relearn and add dynamics and perspectives to the history they know. To recount history without including medical history and the story of reproduction is to fail to tell the complete history and to leave out the records of women's lives and experiences. Rosalind Miles explained, "The renewal of the

Figure 2.5 A portrait of Dr. James Barry.

Source: Portrait of Dr. James Barry, 1820s. Wikimedia Commons, https://commons.wikimedia.org/wiki/File:James_Barry.jpg.

species has always been the sole, whole, unavoidable and largely unacknowl-edged gift to the future of the female sex worldwide."[63] To equally represent them, teachers must proudly acknowledge women's work in child-rearing throughout history.

Religious History

Religious history is women's history. Faith needs to be understood as both a culture and a belief system. While followers can believe what they want about spirituality, the rights and privileges afforded in those cultures are worth examining and comparing. All around the world, religions have played an interesting role in creating the cultural and belief-centered structures that both oppressed and inspired women. Women's religious history reveals the constant struggle experienced by these women. Religion and cultural move-ments for women are often a two-steps-forward-one-step-back kind of deal.

What we know about women and culture in the prehistoric past comes from religious stories, poems, and idols. These polytheistic goddesses were connected to the earth and daily human experience. Fertility goddesses were everywhere and sometimes the most powerful and awful of the gods, like Inanna or Ishtar.[64] As polytheism was replaced by monotheism, the centrality of women's reproductive importance dissipated. Sex became shameful, and women's bodies became more controlled by the increasing patriarchal norms.[65]

For faiths established or lasting into the period of written record, it's dan-gerous to generalize since they are so distinct from one another. If forced to syn-thesize, women were deeply involved in the founding of *every* major religion, and *every* religion—although some, like Islam, are revolutionary for women—eventually adopts norms or laws that severely limit the speech or involvement of women. In the following, we will examine these in chronological order.

Hinduism predates the historical record, so the lives of real women who may have been involved are unknown, but Hindus believe in a number of gods and goddesses who blurred gender lines. Some of the most powerful Hindu deities are female and display a mix of characteristics that our current Western gendered perceptions would consider both male and female.

Judaism's founder, Abraham, was joined in his exploration of monothe-ism by his wife, Sarah. Sarah was unable to have children and give him an heir, and, realizing her precarious social position, she offered him her slave woman, Hagar, to produce heirs with.[66] Eventually, Sarah had the first heal-ing recorded in the Torah and gave birth to a son and heir. Characters in the Hebrew texts all have flaws, evidenced when Abraham betrayed Sarah by saying she was his sister, instead of his wife, to save his own skin. Abraham's story without her just doesn't make sense, and it gives us a window into the strict patriarchy within which Judaism emerged.

Buddhism was founded by the Buddha, whose mother died in childbirth and who was raised by his stepmother, Yaśodharā. When he began his discovery, he abandoned not only the palace but also his wife, Pajapati, who remained loyal to him despite his abandonment.[67] When he finally founded his faith, his stepmother requested that women be allowed into monastic life, and he eventually relented after making some incredibly misogynistic comments that have been recorded for posterity.[68]

Jesus, who brought Christianity to the world, was joined in religious texts by a bunch of Marys. Jesus's story literally began with his miraculous birth—it's a birth story. There is so much to analyze with students about the portrayal of the Virgin Mother, Mary, and how the later church put her on a pedestal, while other women intellectuals and spiritual followers were portrayed as destitute or whores.[69] In the years after Jesus's crucifixion, women were among the many early converts and even martyrs in the Roman empire (Perpetua and Felicitas in particular).[70]

Islam was founded by Muhammad, who was bankrolled by his older business-owning wife, Khadija.[71] She became the first Muslim convert and supported him as he founded a faith that dramatically improved women's lives and curbed female infanticide. Although he favored Khadija, Muhammad took other wives. Islam allowed polygamy, presumably to protect women from the harsh realities of Arab life. Muhammad married the young Aisha, the daughter of his closest ally, Abu Bakr, the first rightly guided Calif.[72] Aisha not only attempted to defend the empire from Ali following the death of Muhammad in the Battle of the Camel—titled thus because she rode a camel into battle—she also joined the many female followers who contributed significantly to the recorded teachings of Muhammad that informed the practice of the faith for centuries.[73]

To discuss the role that religion has played in women's lives might be difficult in a school setting, but it is possible. World history courses have been tasked with teaching about the world religions. To teach about only some of the beliefs while ignoring how those beliefs impact half the population is a systemic failure. Students are frequently asked to explain the core beliefs of these faiths and how they are structured in practice. These are not questions of opinion, nor do they preach. *Could teachers not ask students to research and explain how women are treated in these religions?* Students learn about the Spanish Inquisition and how church leaders treated the nonbelievers. Students would need no guidance to find that none of the major world religions allows substantive female leadership, few honor female prophets, and few have valued women's scholarly contributions, Aisha being a powerful exception. To ignore the role of women in religion leaves students with an incomplete view of world history and a false perception that religion is somehow innocent of sex discrimination.

Despite women's centrality to the founding and spreading of these faiths as well as the fact that most of them ensure equal spiritual potential, every religion in the world eventually moved to condemn women as sinful, lustful, and beings to be restrained by men. Monotheism was probably preferable to the heavily patriarchal pagan faiths that surrounded it, and it's important to put those faiths and their treatment of women in that context. In other words, it may have been restrictive, but it was freer than the alternative.

Religion is the backbone of our cultural and systemic beliefs, and throughout the commentary on women in religious literature, one can find commentary that promoted male supremacy. Every culture values the silence and obedience of women.[74] Women around the world have been barred from the places where men discussed government, politics, and religion, and women's public commentary was policed.[75] Early Christian leaders definitely seemed to hold contempt for women. Saint Paul, who spread the faith in the first century, wrote the most quoted line to silence and subordinate women, in 1 Corinthians 14:34:

> Women should keep silent in the churches, for they are not allowed to speak, but should be subordinate, as even the law says. But if they want to learn anything, they should ask their husbands at home. For it is improper for a woman to speak in the church.

In this quote, Paul was writing to Christians in Rome and Corinth with advice on how to avoid being slaughtered by the Roman pagan majority. The quote is more political than theological. Romans were more patriarchal, if that's possible, compared with the early Christians. So, in other words, Paul is saying that women should keep quiet in church to help the Christian minority stay "under the radar" and keep them safe.[76] But regardless, the effect was a lot of people interpreting it to mean that Paul wanted women to shut up. Taking their cue from Paul, theologians encouraged husbands to monitor their wives and limit their public communications.[77]

Buddhists, Christians, and Muslims all allowed the education of women who dedicated their life to God in convents. Unlike in portrayals in films, women joined enthusiastically for a variety of reasons. A European woman from the aristocracy had two life paths available to her: marry into financial security or become a nun.[78] About half of Europe's monasteries were for women, and they were never short on recruits. Convents also improved women's quality of life and longevity. Medieval women in nunneries lived two to four times longer than their married sisters because of the role that high-risk childbirth played in women's lives.[79] Many women joined nunneries for piety, but there were also more practical reasons—like self-preservation. Historian Joshua J. Mark stated, "The nunnery was a refuge of female intellectuals."[80]

Figure 2.6 A line engraving portrait of Hildegard de Bingen.

Source: Hildegard de Bingen. Line engraving by W. Marshall, 1642. Wikimedia Commons, https://commons.wikimedia.org/wiki/File:Hildegard_von_Bingen._Line_engraving_by_W._Marshall._Wellcome_V0002761.jpg, licensed under CC BY 4.0.

But even in all-female convents, all the opportunities for status and advancement available to male scholars were denied to them and given to male monks (Figure 2.6).

Some women of the Middle Ages were able to bypass misogyny and forge meaningful careers through the church. One of the more notable was Hildegard de Bingen, a nun turned abbess, turned scholar and Christian mystic.[81] The research and works of this brilliant woman touched many fields, from philosophy to musical composition, herbology to medieval literature, cosmology to medicine. She regularly defied the patriarchal hierarchy of her profession and pushed boundaries for women. She was unanimously selected as abbess when the previous woman died, and after enhancing the reputation and wealth of the convent for many years, she requested permission to build her own further away from patriarchal influences.[82] Although she was denied, she persisted, even falling sick and claiming God was working to ensure she got her nunnery, and eventually she founded the convent at Rupertsberg in 1150 CE.[83] There, Hildegard de Bingen was freer to explore her spiritual and intellectual ideas. She reintroduced the old idea of the divine feminine and wrote that God had just as many female characteristics as he did male. Hildegard de Bingen was also likely gay. She fell in love with a fellow nun, and their letters were passionately loving. Shortly into their relationship, her lover was pulled from the nunnery by her brother, who was a Bishop, and she died from sickness. She was devastated. Nonetheless, she was widely popular and went on four speaking tours in defiance Christian prescriptions that women should stay silent.[84]

In Christendom, it wasn't until the Protestant Reformation that restraints on women's intellectualism improved to some extent.[85] Although Martin Luther was no friend to female intellect, he did believe that all Christians should be trained to read the Bible, so in spite of some of the horrible things he said and believed about women, his preaching is a notable turning point for women's education in the West, but not necessarily a step toward liberation.

Some religions extended privileges to women and allowed them to find their voice in the church. The Quakers, notably, gave equal footing to their women "friends" and even allowed women to be preachers. Many later women's suffragists would come from the Quaker faith, having grown up being treated equally at church and finding the social and political contradictions in society unreconcilable.[86] In the United States, Lucretia Mott, the organizer of the Seneca Falls Conference, was a Quaker preacher. Elizabeth Cady Stanton scandalized the suffrage movement by claiming that religion was the root of women's subordination and writing her own Bible, called *The Women's Bible*.[87]

To tell history without religion is folly and yet is often the case in schools. But to teach religion without women is not only sexist but false history. The role that women played in their founding and the way religions treated women are crucial to understand the faith. It is not enough to summarize and say all religions limit women, because that leaves out the interactions that these religions have with one another. Women are central to interfaith conversations and used to promote and condemn ideologies. Women in the West today struggle to understand how women in the Muslim world can feel empowered by a veil, while those Muslim women look at the unchaste Western culture with critique.

Economic, medical, and religious history are essential for students to get a broader understanding of human life—not just the narrow experiences of men in the public world. By shifting focus and acknowledging that there is primary material we have ignored or under-referenced, we can begin to see women in our past. Teachers with their new, wider lens may notice that the history they have been teaching is entirely male-defined and -centered.

Rethinking Objectives

This chapter started with the idea that teachers should reimagine themes and consider the possibility that different themes would lead to different outcomes, ones that included women. I'd like to end with a reimagining of what we deem important for historical study. With ever-looming climate disasters, I wonder what my classes have taught students about how to effect public policy change to protect our health and our earth? I spent so much time discussing the process of industrialization and not enough on the processes of cleaning rivers, reforestation, removing toxic waste, and the heroes who made effected communities livable. Sure, I mentioned John Muir, Teddy Roosevelt, and Rachel Carson, but they were outweighed by the sheer number of tycoons of industry I taught about. Efforts to protect the environment are centuries old, and many have been successful. Aren't there historical lessons to learn that are more valuable than the net worth of JP Morgan, which was long a staple in my US history course?

The more I investigated protectors of nature, the more I found women. Indigenous women were everywhere. Valuable lessons on respect, consensus building, and appreciation for natures gifts were embedded in this history. Nineteenth-century women were amateur botanists and ornithologists, who collected vital information that impacted climate science. I learned about a whole field known as ecofeminism. Women also worked professionally in the field of science to address climate issues. Nonscientist women became some of the leading activists to protect their communities from toxic waste. If my classes celebrated the preservers of nature instead of the perpetrators of climate abuses, how different would my outcomes be?

My state recently mandated that high school history courses have some sort of genocide prevention unit. I realized that in my classes I taught a lot about genocide but not about the ways that one could recognize and prevent it. *Shouldn't that be the main objective of talking about genocide?* Not to rehash all the horrible things that happened but to talk about the choices that people made along the way that would have prevented the horrors of a genocide from happening?

When I began writing the Remedial Herstory Project's online textbook, it was a lot easier than people might imagine. The decades of women's history scholars who preceded me have made available so much rich information. All we had to do was synthesize it down for a secondary audience. But when I got to the world wars, I found the framework that I had for teaching about it was difficult to bring women into without a bit of a stretch. Of course, women were there, women marines were established, they were nurses and administrators and played many other roles in the war, and they also started the White Feather movement, which bullied men into enlisting by emasculating them—but that all felt a bit disconnected from the geopolitical issues I wanted students to understand about the war.

With World War I, I always teach about the "MAIN" causes of World War I: militarism, alliances, imperialism, and nationalism. I talked about figures like Franz Ferdinand, and, of course, I could mention his wife Sophia, but it's also a bit like there was a whole theme I was missing. Afterall, where were women? Then I remembered the movie *Iron Jawed Angels*, one of the first feature-length films about women's history in existence. One of the main characters and a real American lawyer, Inez Milholland, abandons the suffrage cause to go abroad on a peacekeeping mission. So, I started researching that, and I found mountains of scholarly research about these women activists who organized and worked to try to prevent what felt like inevitable war.

For the first time in my life, I was introduced to the transnational feminist movement, which really began during the world wars for the purposes of peacemaking. One of the fruits of their decades-long labor was the UN Declaration of Human Rights. My research led me to some interesting findings that showed that treaties with more women who were participants were more likely to last. Scholars found that "[w]omen's participation increases the probability of a peace agreement lasting at least two years by 20 percent, and by 35 percent the probability of a peace agreement lasting 15 years."[88] I wondered how many women signed the treaty of Versailles? How many women were involved in the Nuremberg trials? Focusing on women led me to peace.

I've often thought that by teaching about war, I was helping to prevent it. People could see how horrible war is and learn to take steps to stop patterns. I still think that is valid. However, I'm wondering if focusing on "war" leads to normalizing it and desensitizing people to its inhumanity. I wonder if by teaching about the causes of war, we're outlining a template on how to create war.

I want my students to learn how to create peace, build consensus, talk across difference, and respect one another. These are things that have been fostered in women for millennia. What if instead of learning the causes of war, my students learned about the pathways to peace? What if the heroes of my new classroom were not generals but organizational leaders who dedicated their lives to peace.

Blueprint: Don't Add, Modify

Talking about gender does not have to, initially, reshape entire curriculums. It can simply be a modification of content already taught. Taking male-centered content and asking about women, gender, and sexuality can make inclusive something that is exclusive, as discussed in Chapter 1. Another strategy is to modify the analysis of sources to include a gendered lens.

In 2001, scholar Margaret Smith Crocco recommended that educators use their platform to critique gendered social scripts that make men initiators and women receivers and that reinforce sexism, homophobia, or heteronormative ideas in schools.[89] These changes, still unaccomplished, would allow schools to better reflect the private experiences of many families and be a catalyst for a new wave of social integration. How should educators begin to add this analysis? My answer: with things they already teach.

Analyze Images

One of the oldest tricks in the book for teaching not only women's history but also the history of any marginalized group is to teach what you always teach but adding gendered or racial analysis to the sources of information. This is best highlighted with images but could be replicated for textbooks or other text-based source material. For young people, images are part of their daily consumption of media. They are valuable tools to guide students toward a deeper historical understanding. Jessica B. Shocker, in her paper "A Case for Using Images to Teach Women's History," wrote, "One of my goals as a history educator is to inspire my students to think like historians; therefore, it is essential that I teach tools such as image analysis to facilitate this type of scholarship."[90] After all, an image is worth a thousand words.

Teaching with images is a powerful way to examine gender dynamics and include women. Men have always loved women and represented their form in art. Regardless of the period of history, teachers could bypass the text and analyze these rich gender-driven dynamics through visuals (Figure 2.7).

Many visuals depicting women are ones that educators already use. Take Columbia, for instance. Columbia was used to represent the United States up until the 1920s, when she fell out of favor.[91] Perhaps it was the changing female dress that made her less fashionable, perhaps it was the rise in Uncle Sam as a symbol of the country during World War I, or maybe it was women's enfranchisement that led to the decline of using women as personified versions of their nation. *American Progress*, one of the most common images shown in US history courses, depicts Columbia in all her glory. It would not be too complicated to add a gendered analysis to an analysis of the implications of westward expansion. Students could consider these questions:

Figure 2.7 *American Progress* by John Gast (1872) shows Columbia leading the US westward across the plains, bringing light, industry, and technology in tow, while Indigenous people flee further westward into darkness.

Source: John Gast, artist, 1872, Crofutt, George A. American Progress., ca. 1873. Photograph. https://www.loc.gov/item/97507547/.

Why is the United States represented by a woman? Why is she dressed in those robes? Are there other women in this image? If so, how are they portrayed? How are real women portrayed differently from this female symbol? Where are Black women? Why are they erased? (Figure 2.8)

Using women as symbols is frequent throughout US and world history. Most often, women were used in wartime propaganda to influence public opinion and rile people up about the war. These images can tell us a great deal about the perceptions that people had about their enemy as well as women. This image, titled *This Is the Enemy*,[92] shows an ape-like Japanese soldier attacking a defenseless white woman. The inherent appeal to white racism is crucial for analyzing this image with students and understanding the war in greater depth (Figure 2.9).

Women were also artists and photographers themselves. Renaissance painters were women. The most famous photograph from the Great Depression—*Migrant Mother*—was captured by a female photographer, Dorothea Lange. Looking for works by women and analyzing them with students are also important. Women captured images of their experiences and

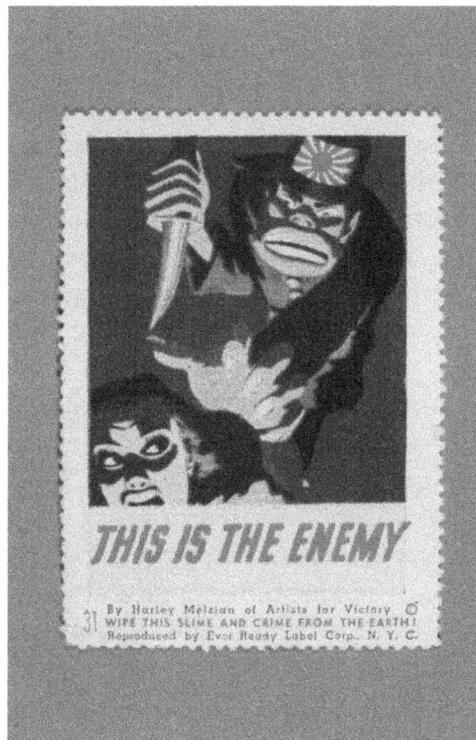

Figure 2.8 *This Is the Enemy* shows a racist depiction of an ape-like World War II-era Japanese soldier attacking a defenseless white woman from behind with a knife drawn.

Source: This Is the Enemy, 1942. United States Holocaust Memorial Museum Collection, Gift of Forrest James Robinson, Jr. https://collections.ushmm.org/search/catalog/irn612193.

Figure 2.9 *Migrant Mother* shows a destitute mother looking out of her makeshift shelter with her young children alongside her.

Source: Lange, Dorothea, photographer. Destitute pea pickers in California. Mother of seven children. Age thirty-two. Nipomo, California. United States Nipomo San Luis Obispo County California, 1936. March. Photograph. https://www.loc.gov/item/2017762891/.

world. These images are a window into understanding half of humanity in their own depictions rather than those that men have imposed on them.

In her paper, Shocker included a table of tools for teachers to improve their techniques for teaching with images. She wrote, "Images must be read critically rather than passively," and these methods guide teachers in how to do that.[93] Below is a smaller sample of the strategies she included (Table 2.1). [94]

Each of these methods was used in the class without explicitly teaching the method at first.[95] Teaching with images allows women to be easily and meaningfully included in the classroom.

These are also powerful strategies for including people of color. Shocker joined Christine Woyshner to do a content analysis of three major history textbooks, finding that Black women were significantly underrepresented compared with their white peers.[96] In the textbook, *America: Pathways to the Present*, women were in 207 images while men were in 682. Their study included one text from an African American history with even worse figures: 156 images of women and 926 images of men. Shocker and Woyshner recommended the intentional use of images in class to circumvent Black women's exclusion in other sources. We can help students see women in the past by showing students these visuals. After all, a picture is worth a thousand words.

Table 2.1 A sample of Shocker's Selected Strategies for Analyzing Images in the Classroom

Strategy	Author	Description
Close Looking	Woyshner	Students make observations of items they see without drawing conclusions. In the second phase, students make inferences and hypotheses.
Juxtaposition	Woyshner	Students examine two images and look for similarities and differences.
Sourcing	Wineburg/ Mattson	Students think about the creator of the image and how the life and context of their life impacted the image. Students consider motivations, biases, audiences, and so forth.
Inside-the-frame/ Outside-the-frame	Mattson	Students analyze what is happening in the image and then think about what they cannot see in the image, like what is behind the camera, etc.
Figuring	Shifrin	Students analyze cartoons and archetypes portrayed in images to consider how those images would be received by others.

Source: Jessica B. Schocker, & Christine Woyshner, "Representing African American women in U.S. history textbooks." *The Social Studies*, 2013, 104(1), 23–31.

Resources for Bi-Focal History

Recommended Reading: Primers for Teachers

This second chapter introduced themes often left out of history curriculum. Teachers will need to examine these with more depth. At this phase of teaching women's history, teachers may benefit from primers that help them reoutline their historical framework. *Clio in the Classroom* edited by Carol Berkin, Margaret S. Crocco, and Barbara Winslow is a great resource for US History. For World History, I recommend *A Primer for Teaching Women, Gender, and Sexuality in World History* by Merry E. Wiesner-Hanks and Urmi Engineer Willoughby.

Sample Inquiry: Why Is Mary Baker Eddy Controversial?

The Remedial Herstory Project has built inquiry-based lesson plans on every major world religion and philosophy and how women are viewed in scripture. We have one that explores passages from the Bible, another that compares the Quran to Hadith, another on Confucius sayings, and several on Hindu traditions and goddesses. In selecting a lesson to include here, it was important to me that the focus be on a woman who alone made history—not the support to a great, male prophet.

Mary Baker Eddy is a strong example of the overlapping nature of the themes of economics, health, and religion and how they bring women into the story of humanity. I was raised as a Christian Scientist, in the state where

Mary Baker Eddy was born: New Hampshire. I was surrounded by Eddy's historical sites my entire life. I found it weird that none of my peers had heard of her and she was never talked about in my classes—not because of some hero worship, but because in addition to being the first woman to found a sustaining religion in world history, she was the first woman from New Hampshire inducted into the Women's Hall of Fame in Seneca Falls, NY.[97] Why weren't New Hampshire teachers talking about her? In New Hampshire, we have few historical figures of note. The most prominent author at the New Hampshire Historical Society wrote two books: one on the first president from the state (Franklin Pierce) and Eddy. The capitol of New Hampshire, Concord, isn't a large city. The tallest building is the Christian Science church. In downtown Boston, the massive Christian Science center is a notable location that secular people recognize. Eddy lived much of her life in Massachusetts. Why isn't it a staple of Massachusetts history? But her influence goes far beyond New England. Christian Science churches can be found all around the world. This inquiry is a good example of bi-focal history, as it aims to add to secondary classrooms a character who has been all but erased and to focus on what was happening for women or a woman. (Figure 2.10).

Figure 2.10 Photo of Mary Baker Eddy by H. G. Smith, 1886.

Source: Photo of Mary Baker Eddy by H. G. Smith, 1886. Wikimedia Commons, https://commons.wikimedia.org/wiki/File:Public_Domain_Mary_Baker_Eddy.jpg.

Eddy was born into a strictly Christian family. She experienced severe health problems for most of her life and was often bedridden. Eddy sought cures from both God and contemporary medicine. After losing two husbands (one to death and another to abandonment) as well as having her only child taken from her because of her poor health and lack of financial means, Eddy fell on the ice and was told she would die.[98] That evening, she prayed and believed that she tapped into Jesus's methodology for healing. She rose the next morning and began her life's work, eventually living to the age of 89. Eddy wrote a book called *Science and Health*, in which she described what she called Christ's healing. She turned that work into a metaphysical college and eventually a church. Her church had no pastor and was gender-egalitarian. Women and men shared the podium, reading her book alongside the Bible. Her church grew rapidly and globally, maintaining its epicenter in Boston at what was called the "Mother Church." Eddy concurred with Elizabeth Cady Stanton in seeing religion's shortcomings and how it could be redesigned to be more inclusive of women.

Eddy's ideas, like those of so many women before her, were often attacked not for their religious merit but because she was female.[99] Eddy's critics were many and well known. Mark Twain called her conceited and unladylike.[100] She was ridiculed in the yellow journalistic press and found herself caught in the feud between William Randolph Hearst and Joseph Pulitzer, the former writing in her defense and the latter assaulting almost every aspect of her being.[101] She had the last word, founding her own newspaper and disrupting the market with reliable news. Her paper, the *Christian Science Monitor*, would go on to win many Pulitzer Prizes. She is a woman worth compensating for in history class. This inquiry looks at Eddy's writings and lets her contemporaries weigh in. The inquiry is downloadable on the Remedial Herstory Project's website.

Why is Mary Baker Eddy controversial?

In this inquiry, students will examine contrasting primary source accounts and form their own conclusions about Mary Baker Eddy and her significance in history.

Document A: Science and Health

Mary Baker Eddy reimagined the loving God from Christianity as representing good qualities that were ever-present rather than as a divine being one prayed to. Eddy represents these divine ideas in her writing by capitalizing the first letter of the word.

Leaning on the sustaining Infinite with loving trust, the trials of to-day are brief, and to-morrow is big with blessings. The wakeful shepherd tending his flocks, beholds from the mountain's top the first faint morning beam ere cometh the risen day. So from Soul's loftier summits shines the pale star to the prophet shepherd, and it traverses night, over to where the young child lies in cradled obscurity that shall waken a world. Over the night of error dawn the morning beams and guiding star of Truth, and the wise men are led by it to Science, to that which repeats the eternal harmony reproduced in proof of immortality and God. The time for thinkers has come; and the time for revolutions, ecclesiastic and social, must come. Truth, independent of doctrines or time-honored systems, stands at the threshold of history. Contentment with the past, or the cold conventionality of custom, may no longer shut the door on science; though empires fall, "He whose right it is shall reign." Ignorance of God should no longer be the stepping-stone to faith; understanding Him "whom to know aright is Life" is the only guaranty of obedience.

Since the hoary centuries but faintly shadow forth the tireless Intelligence at work for man, this volume may not open at once a new thought, and make it familiar it has the task of a pioneer to hack away at the tall oak and cut the rough granite, leaving future ages to declare what has been done. We made our first discovery that science mentally applied would heal the sick, in 1864, and since then have tested it on ourselves and hundreds of others, and never found it fail to prove the statement herein made of it. The science of man alone can make him harmonious, unfold his utmost possibilities, and establish the perfection of man. To admit God the Principle of all being, and live in accordance with this Principle, is the Science of Life, but to reproduce the harmony of being, errors of personal sense must be destroyed, even as the science of music, must correct tones caught from the ear, to give the sweet concord of sound. There are many theories of physic, and theology; and many calls in each of their directions for the right way; but we propose to settle the question of "What is Truth?" on the ground of proof. Let that method of healing the sick and establishing Christianity, be adopted, that is found to give the most health, and make the best Christians, and you will then give science a fair field; in which case we are assured of its triumph over all opinions and beliefs. Sickness and sin have ever had their doctors, but the question is, have they become less because of them? The longevity of our antediluvians, would say, no! and the criminal records of to-day utter their voices little in favor of such a conclusion. Not that we would deny to Caesar the things that are his, but that we ask for the things that are Truth's, and safely affirm, from the demonstrations we have been able to make, that science would have eradicated sin, sickness, and death, in a less period than six thousand years. We find great difficulties in starting this work right: some shockingly false claims are already made to its practice; mesmerism (its very antipode), is one. Hitherto we have never in a single instance of our discovery or practice found the slightest resemblance between mesmerism and the science of Life. No especial idiosyncrasy is requisite for a learner; although spiritual sense is more adapted to it than even the intellect; and those who would learn this science without a high moral standard will fail to understand it until they go up higher. Owing to our explanations constantly vibrating between the same points an irksome repetition of words must occur; also, the use of capital letters, genders and technicalities peculiar to the science, variety of language, or beauty of diction, must give place to close analysis, and unembellished thought. "Hoping all things, enduring all things:" to do good to the upright in heart, and to bless them that curse us, and bear to the sorrowing and the sick consolation and healing, we commit these pages to posterity.

Glover, Mary Baker. Science and Health, 1st ed. Boston: Christian Scientist Publishing Company, 1875.

Source
1. Who wrote this document?
2. When was this document written?

Document
3. Does it surprise you that she was the sole pastor of this new church?
4. What are some principles of her new church, recorded in the first chapter of her book?

Why do you think Mary Baker Eddy might be controversial?

Document B: Mark Twain

The immense popularity of Mary Baker Eddy and Christian Science drew praise and criticism from some of the greatest thinkers of the time. Mark Twain dedicated an entire book to critiquing Christian Science and specifically Eddy. The book began as a collection of essays, the first one published in Cosmopolitan in 1899.

MONOPOLY OF SPIRITUAL BREAD

Very properly, the first qualification for membership in the Mother-Church is belief in the doctrines of Christian Science.

But these doctrines must not be gathered from secondary sources. There is but one recognized source. The candidate must be a believer in the doctrines of Christian Science "according to the platform and teaching contained in the Christian Science text-book, *Science and Health, with Key to the Scriptures*, by Rev. Mary Baker G. Eddy."

That is definite, and is final. There are to be no commentaries, no labored volumes of exposition and explanation by anybody except Mrs. Eddy. Because such things could sow error, create warring opinions, split the religion into sects, and disastrously cripple its power. Mrs. Eddy will do the whole of the explaining, Herself—has done it, in fact. She has written several books. They are to be had (for cash in advance), they are all sacred; additions to them can never be needed and will never be permitted. They tell the candidate how to instruct himself, how to teach others, how to do all things comprised in the business—and they close the door against all would-be competitors, and monopolize the trade:

"The Bible and the above—named book [Science and Health], with other works by the same author," must be his only text-books for the commerce—he cannot forage outside. Mrs. Eddy's words are to be the sole elucidators of the Bible and Science and Health—forever…

THE LORD'S PRAYER-AMENDED

This is not in the By-laws, it is in the first chapter of Science and Health, edition of 1902. I do not find it in the edition of 1884. It is probable that it had not at that time been handed down. Science and Health's (latest) rendering of its "spiritual sense" is as follows:

"Our Father-Mother God all-harmonious, adorable One. Thy kingdom is within us, Thou art ever-present. Enable us to know—as in heaven, so on earth—God is supreme. Give us grace for to-day; feed the famished affections. And infinite Love is reflected in love. And Love leadeth us not into temptation, but delivereth from sin, disease, and death. For God is now and forever all Life, Truth, and Love."…

CHAPTER VII

"We consciously declare that Science and Health, with Key to the Scriptures, was foretold, as well as its author, Mary Baker Eddy, in Revelation x. She is the 'mighty angel,' or God's highest thought to this age (verse 1), giving us the spiritual interpretation of the Bible in the 'little book open' (verse 2). Thus we prove that Christian Science is the second coming of Christ-Truth-Spirit."—Lecture by Dr. George Tomkins, D.D. C.S.

There you have it in plain speech. She is the mighty angel; she is the divinely and officially sent bearer of God's highest thought. For the present, she brings the Second Advent. We must expect that before she has been in her grave fifty years she will be regarded by her following as having been herself the Second Advent. She is already worshiped, and we must expect this feeling to spread, territorially, and also to deepen in intensity.

Particularly after her death; for then, as any one can foresee, Eddy-Worship will be taught in the Sunday-schools and pulpits of the cult…

Twain, Mark. Christian Science. First published 1907. Retrieved from Gutenberg Press. https://www.gutenberg.org/files/3187/3187-h/3187-h.htm#link2H_PREF.

Source
1. Who wrote this document?
2. When was this document written? (See the annotation at the top in addition to the citation).

Document
3. What are some claims made about Mary Baker Eddy?
4. According to this document, why was Mary Baker Eddy controversial?

Document C: Mary Baker Eddy

Eddy responded in a published letter to Twain's critiques. Her self-defense follows.

It is a fact, well understood, that I begged the students who first gave me the endearing appellative 'mother' not to name me thus. But, without my consent, that word spread like wildfire. I still must think the name is not applicable to me. I stand in relation to this century as a Christian discoverer, founder, and leader. I regard self-deification as blasphemous; I may be more loved, but I am less lauded, pampered, provided for, and cheered than others before me. And wherefore? Because Christian Science is not yet popular, and I refuse adulation.

My visit to the Mother Church after it was built and dedicated pleased me, and the situation was satisfactory. The dear members wanted to greet me with escort and the ringing of bells, but I declined, and went alone in my carriage to the church, entered it, and knelt in thanks upon the steps of its altar. There the foresplendor of the beginnings of truth fell mysteriously upon my spirit. I believe in one Christ, teach one Christ, know of but one Christ. I believe in but one incarnation, one Mother Mary, and know I am not that one, and never claimed to be. It suffices me to learn the Science of the Scriptures relative to this subject. Christian Scientists have no quarrel with Protestants, Catholics, or any other sect. They need to be understood as following the divine Principle. God, Love and not imagined to be unscientific worshippers of a human being.

In the aforesaid article, of which I have seen only extracts, Mark Twain's wit was not wasted in certain directions. Christian Science eschews divine rights in human beings. If the individual governed human consciousness, my statement of Christian Science would be disproved, but to understand the spiritual idea is essential to demonstrate Science and its pure monotheism? One God, one Christ, no idolatry, no human propaganda. Jesus taught and proved that what feeds a few feeds all. His life-work subordinated the material to the spiritual, and he left this legacy of truth to mankind.

His metaphysics is not the sport of philosophy, religion, or Science; rather it is the pith and finale of them all.

I have not the inspiration or aspiration to be a first or second Virgin-Mother. Her duplicate, antecedent or subsequent. What I am remains to be proved by the good I do. We need much humility, wisdom, and love to perform the functions of foreshadowing and foretasting heaven within us.

Eddy, Mary Baker G. "Mrs. Eddy Replies to Mark Twain." Originally published in the New York Herald. Retrieved from Christian Science Sentinel. January 22, 1903. https://sentinel.christianscience.com/issues/1903/1/5-21/mrs.-eddy-replies-to-mark-twain.

1. Do you find Eddy's self-defense convincing?

Document D: Susan B. Anthony

As a leading women's figure, Anthony was questioned about her thoughts on Eddy and her new religion. Eddy was not a suffragist and never aligned her religion with any social causes.

"What of Mrs. Eddy? No man ever obtained so large a following in so short a time. Her churches are among the largest and most elegant in Boston, Chicago, and other cities. But it is only during the last half century that woman has been permitted by man even to offer a prayer aloud in public. The great Apostle Paul enjoined her to keep silence in the churches. For nineteen hundred years since the dawn of Christianity, man has been much occupied establishing faiths and formulating creeds for woman to follow. Since she found her voice and her tongue, fifty years ago, she has been too busy rising to her own level and adjusting her life to new conditions to do more than recognize the great need of humanity — fewer creeds and more of the divine Spirit. When woman does write her creed, it will be one of right actions, not of theological theories."

Anthony, Susan B. "The Work of Mrs. Eddy," Christian Science Sentinel, December 14, 1899, http://sentinel.christianscience.com/shared/view/a7xxv5h7cu?s=t.

Source
1. Who wrote this document?
2. Twain's original essay?

Document
3. Why do you suppose she doesn't talk about Eddy directly?
4. According to this document, why was Mary Baker Eddy controversial?

Document E: Peter Wallner, Historian

Twain wasn't the only man of the period to come after Eddy. A few years later, Joseph Pulitzer, the publisher of the New York World, *published a scandalous and defamatory article about Eddy where he claimed she was ill, dying of cancer, and being manipulated by her secretary-footman, Calvin Frye. It was sensational going so far as to claim another woman was impersonating her about town. It claimed that despite her annual income of a million or more, her money was not accounted for. The people of Concord, NH, where she lived were alarmed. Here, a New Hampshire historian explains the significant local defense of Eddy.*

The fact that none of the charges made by the World were remotely true was of little concern to Joseph Pulitzer, [a] yellow journalis[t], [his] one goal was to sell newspapers…

Church leaders and the citizens of Concord came immediately to Eddy's defense… Concord mayor… Charles H. Corning recorded the day's events in his diary as "a remarkable & red marked day" in his life… Bombarded all day with questions about Eddy from reporters investigating the "big scoop," Corning received a… "request to go out to Pleasant View & see with his own eyes the lady herself…"

After spending a half hour with Eddy, Corning recorded his final impressions.

> She is 85 years old & she shows her years, face sharp, form slight, hands veined but warm in shaking hands, her wrinkles & age lines are prominent, she is naturally tremulous & I noticed a shaking of the head… But considering her years & her life's work & the work to be done daily I saw a woman who surprised me. … That she rides out daily I have no doubt…

Corning then went to the Christian Science Church… where he addressed a packed house…

The next day, October 29, 1906, newspapers all over the country carried the statements of Corning. The [Concord] Monitor's editorial lambasted "a certain section of the American press" for publishing "grossly fantastic and entirely false statements."

Excerpt from Peter A. Wallner's book Faith on Trial: Mary Baker Eddy, Christian Science and the First Amendment. *Plaidswede Publishing: Concord, NH, 2014. Retrieved from https://www.concordmonitor.com/Archive/2014/11/faithontrial-cmforum-113014.*

Source
1. Who wrote this document?
2. When was this document written?

Document
3. Why would claims about Eddy's deteriorating health be a scandal for Christian Science?

Overall, why was Mary Baker Eddy controversial?

Notes

1 Robert Strayer and E. Nelson, *Ways of The World*, 3rd ed. (Boston: Bedford/St. Martin's, 2016), 73.
2 Miles, *The Women's History of the World*, 149.
3 Miles, *The Women's History of the World*, 13.
4 Mary Ritter Beard, *Woman's Work in Municipalities* (New York, Appleton, 1915). https://lccn.loc.gov/15007484
5 F. Galton, "Vox populi," *Nature*, 75 (1949): 450–451.
6 Gloria Steinem, Meenakshi Mukherjee, and Ira Pande, "A Conversation with Gloria Steinem," *India International Centre Quarterly* 34, no. 2 (2007): 90–105, http://www.jstor.org/stable/23006309
7 This line from her essay was the inspiration for the nonprofit, the Remedial Herstory Project.
8 Soheyla Taie and Laurie Lewis, "Characteristics of 2020–21 Public and Private K–12 School Teachers in the United States: Results From the National Teacher and Principal Survey," The National Center for Education Statistics at IES, First Look, Dec. 2022-113, 17. https://nces.ed.gov/pubs2022/2022113.pdf.
9 Michael Hansen, Elizabeth Mann Levesque, Jon Valant, and Diana Quintero, "2018 Brown Center Report on American Education: Understanding the social studies teacher workforce," June 27, 2018, retrieved from https://www.brookings.edu/research/2018-brown-center-report-on-american-education-understanding-the-social-studies-teacher-orkforce/
10 Andrew Khan and Rebecca Onion, "Is History Written About Men, by Men?" Slate, January 6, 2016, http://www.slate.com/articles/news_and_politics/history/2016/01/popular_history_why_are_so_many_history_books_about_men_by_men.html
11 Lynn Hunt, *History: Why it Matters*. Cambridge: Polity Press, 2018, 70.
12 Lynn Hunt, *History: Why it Matters*. Cambridge: Polity Press, 2018, 70.
13 Catalyst, "Quick Take: Women in Academia," January 23, 2020, https://www.catalyst.org/research/women-in-academia/
14 Catalyst, "Quick Take."
15 Emily Prifogle and Karin Wulf, "Why Women Also Know History," *Journal of Women's History* 32, no. 2 (2020): 113–117. doi:10.1353/jowh.2020.0014, 113.
16 Mary Beard, *Women and Power*, 57.

17 Mary Beard, *Women and Power*, 56.

18 Prifogle and Wulf. "Why Women Also Know History," 113.

19 Robert B. Townsend, "WHAT THE DATA REVEALS ABOUT WOMEN HISTORIANS," *Perspectives on History*, May 1, 2010, https://www. historians.org/publications-and-directories/perspectives-on-history/ may-2010/what-the-data-reveals-about-women-historians

20 Cicely Scheiner-Fisher, "The Inclusion of Women's History In The Secondary Social Studies Classroom," *Electronic Theses and Dissertations*, University of Central Florida, 2013, https://stars.library.ucf.edu/etd/ 2848, 41.

21 Her sample size was 69 social studies teachers from the same school district in Orange County, FL.

22 Christopher C. Martell and Kaylene M. Stevens, "Perceptions of Teaching Race and Gender: Results of a Survey of Social Studies Teachers," *The High School Journal* 101, no. 4 (2018): 274–99. https://www.jstor.org/stable/ 26785824

23 Bridget Lockyer and Abigail Tazzymant, "'Victims of History,'" 11.

24 Bridget Lockyer and Abigail Tazzymant, "'Victims of History,'" 14.

25 Karen Zittleman and David Sadker, "Gender Bias in Teacher Education Texts: New (and Old) Lessons," Journal of Teacher Education 53, no. 2 (March 2002): 168–80. https://doi.org/10.1177/0022487102053002008, 168.

26 Tetreault, "Integrating Women's History," 215.

27 Tetreault, "Integrating Women's History," 215.

28 Noddings, "The Care Tradition: Beyond 'Add Women and Stir'" 31.

29 Noddings, "The Care Tradition: Beyond 'Add Women and Stir'" 33.

30 Noddings, "The Care Tradition: Beyond 'Add Women and Stir'" 33.

31 UN Women Editors, "The world is failing girls and women, according to new UN report," UN Women, September 7, 2023, https://www. unwomen.org/en/news-stories/press-release/2023/09/press-release-the-world-is-failing-girls-and-women-according-to-new-un-report

32 Organization for Economic Co-Operation and Development, "Employment: Time spent in paid and unpaid work, by sex." OEDC.Stat, 2022, https://stats.oecd.org/index.aspx?queryid=54757

33 More on this in Chapter Four.

34 Eve Rodsky, *Fair Play: Fair Play: A Game-Changing Solution for When You Have Too Much to Do (and More Life to Live)*, (New York: Putnam and Sons, 2021).

35 Peter Brown, "The Silk Road in Late Antiquity," in *Reconfiguring the Silk Road*, ed. By Victor H. Mair & Jane Hickman (University of Pennsylvania Press, 2014).

36 Jennie R. Ebeling, Lynda Garland, Guity Nashat, Eric R. Dursteler "West Asia" The *Oxford Encyclopedia of Women in World History*. Ed Bonnie G. Smith. (Oxford: Oxford University Press, 2008). Brigham Young University (BYU), November 1, 2010. http://www.oxfordreference.com.erl.lib.byu. edu/views/ENTRY.html?subview=Main&entry=t248.e1144-s4

37 British Library Editors, "Women in Medieval Society," *British Library*, https://www.bl.uk/the-middle-ages/articles/women-in-medieval-society

38 Berry and Harris, *Sexuality and Slavery*, 189.

39 Dernoral Davis, "A Contested Presence: Free Black People in Antebellum Mississippi, 1820–1860," Mississippi Historical Society, May 2000, https://www.mshistorynow.mdah.ms.gov/issue/a-contested-presence-free-blacks-in-antebellum-mississippi-18201860

40 "Claudia Goldin wins the Nobel prize in economics: Her work has overturned assumptions about gender equality," *The Economist*, October 9, 2023, https://www.economist.com/finance-and-economics/2023/10/09/claudia-goldin-wins-the-nobel-prize-in-economics

41 Collins. *America's Women*, 250.

42 Collins, *America's Women*, 126.

43 Jeanna Smialek, "Claudia Goldin Wins Nobel in Economics for Studying Women in the Work Force: Her research uncovered the reasons for gender gaps in labor force participation and earnings. She is the third woman to win the prize" *The New York Times*, October 11, 2023, https://www.nytimes.com/2023/10/09/business/economy/claudia-goldin-nobel-prize-economics.html#:~:text=The%20Nobel%20Memorial%20Prize%20in,progress%20in%20the%20work%20force

44 "Claudia Goldin wins the Nobel prize in economics," *The Economist*.

45 Gail Collins. *America's Women*, 250.

46 Gail Collins. *America's Women*, 250.

47 Noddings, "The Care Tradition: Beyond 'Add Women and Stir'" 31–32.

48 Joanna Goodrich, "This Socialite Hated Washing Dishes So Much That She Invented the Automated Dishwasher: Josephine Cochran's machine was the first to use water pressure to clean dishes," IEEE Spectrum, October 16, 2020, https://spectrum.ieee.org/who-invented-the-dishwasher

49 John Thomas McGuire, "'The Most Unjust Piece of Legislation': Section 213 of the Economy Act of 1932 and Feminism During the New Deal," *Journal of Policy History* 20, no. 4 (January 4, 2008): 516–41. doi:10.1353/jph.0.0026.

50 Laura Tobias Gruss and Daniel Schmitt, "The evolution of the human pelvis: changing adaptations to bipedalism, obstetrics and thermoregulation," Philosophical transactions of the Royal Society of London. Series B, Biological sciences vol. 370,1663 (2015): 20140063. doi:10.1098/rstb.2014.0063.

51 Ian Mursell, "Giving Birth was One Big Battle," Mexicolore, https://www.mexicolore.co.uk/aztecs/aztec-life/giving-birth-was-fighting-a-battle

52 Ornella Moscucci, "The Science of Woman: Gynaecology and Gender in England, 1800–1929," Cambridge: Cambridge University Press, 1990.

53 Collins, *America's Women*, 126.

54 Collins, *America's Women*, 118.

55 Collins, *America's Women*, 119.

56 Collins, *America's Women*, 119.

57 Collins, *America's Women*, 119.

58 Brynn Holland, "The 'Father of Modern Gynecology' Performed Shocking Experiments on Slaves: He was a medical trailblazer, but at what cost?" History.com. Last modified December 4, 2018, https://www.history.com/news/the-father-of-modern-gynecology-performed-shocking-experiments-on-slaves

59 Brynn Holland, "The Extraordinary Secret Life of Dr. James Barry. How—and why—did a groundbreaking physician pass as the opposite sex for more than 50 years?" January 17, 2019, https://www.history.com/news/the-extraordinary-secret-life-of-dr-james-barry

60 Mily Mumford, "Dr. James Barry and Recognizing Trans Stories in the History of Science," Westcoast Women in Engineering and Science, August 17, 2021, https://www.sfu.ca/wwest/WWEST_blog/dr--james-barry-and-recognizing-trans-stories-in-the-history-of-.html

61 Collins, *America's Women*, 125.

62 Collins, *America's Women*, 125.

63 Rosalind Miles, *Women's History of the World* (London: Paladin/Grafton Books, 1989) 12.

64 Cynthia Eller, *The Myth of Matriarchal Prehistory: Why an Invented Past Won't Give Women a Future* (Beacon Press: Boston, 2000), pp. 3–104.

65 Rosalind Miles, *Women's History of the World*, 36–45.

66 Tamar Kadari, "Hagar: Midrash and Aggadah," Shalvi/Hyman *Encyclopedia of Jewish Women*, 31 December 1999, Jewish Women's Archive, https://jwa.org/encyclopedia/article/hagar-midrash-and-aggadah

67 David Llewelyn Snellgrove, Donald S. Lopez, Frank E. Reynolds, Hajime Nakamura, Giuseppe Tucci, and Joseph M. Kitagawa, "Buddhism," *Encyclopedia Britannica*, August 23, 2022, https://www.britannica.com/topic/Buddhism

68 Buddhist Studies, "Ananda," Early Disciples of the Buddha, http://www.buddhanet.net/e-learning/history/db_04.htm

69 James Carroll, "Who Was Mary Magdalene? From the writing of the New Testament to the filming of The Da Vinci Code, her image has been repeatedly conscripted, contorted and contradicted," *Smithsonian*, June 2006, https://www.smithsonianmag.com/history/who-was-mary-magdalene-119565482/

70 T. Heffernan, *The Passion of Perpetua and Felicity* (Oxford: Oxford University Press, 2012).

71 Karen Armstrong, *Islam: A Short History* (Waterville: Thorndike, 2002), 4.

72 Armstrong, *Islam*, 34.

73 Shahla Haeri, *The Unforgettable Queens of Islam* (New York: Cambridge University Press, 2020) 61.

74 Miles, *The Women's History of the World*, 130.
75 Gerda Lerner, *The Creation of Patriarchy* (New York, NY: Oxford University Press, 1987) 63.
76 R.W. Allison, "Let Women Be Silent in the Churches (1 Cor. 14.33b-36): What Did Paul Really Say, and What Did It Mean?" *Journal for the Study of the New Testament* 10, no. 32 (1988): 27–60. doi:10.1177/0142064X8801003203, 53.
77 Rosemary Radford Ruether, "Sexism and Misogyny in the Christian Tradition: Liberating Alternatives," Buddhist-Christian Studies 34 (2014): 83–94. http://www.jstor.org/stable/24801355, 85.
78 Mark Cartwright, "The Daily Life of Medieval Nuns," *World History Encyclopedia*, Last modified December 19, 2018. https://www.worldhistory.org/article/1298/the-daily-life-of-medieval-nuns/
79 Miles, *The Women's History of the World*, 130.
80 Joshua J. Mark "Hildegard of Bingen." *Ancient History Encyclopedia*. Last modified May 30, 2019. https://www.ancient.eu/Hildegard_of_Bingen/
81 Joshua J. Mark, "Hildegard of Bingen." *World History Encyclopedia*, May 30, 2019. https://www.worldhistory.org/Hildegard_of_Bingen/
82 Joshua J. Mark, "Hildegard of Bingen." *World History Encyclopedia*, May 30, 2019. https://www.worldhistory.org/Hildegard_of_Bingen/
83 Editors of Encyclopaedia Britannica, "St. Hildegard," *Encyclopedia Britannica*, September 14, 2022. https://www.britannica.com/biography/Saint-Hildegard
84 John Noyce, "Hildegard of Bingen and her Visions of the Divine Feminine," Academia, 2013, https://www.academia.edu/5406213/Hildegard_of_Bingen_and_her_Visions_of_the_Divine_Feminine
85 Joshua J. Mark, "Ten Women of the Protestant Reformation." *World History Encyclopedia*. Last modified March 17, 2022. https://www.worldhistory.org/article/1964/ten-women-of-the-protestant-reformation/
86 National Park Service Editors, "Quaker Influence," National Park Service, April 6, 2020, https://www.nps.gov/wori/learn/historyculture/quaker-influence.htm#:~:text=Followers%20of%20Fox%2C%20Quakers%2C%20believed,with%20God%20and%20the%20Bible
87 Jone Johnson Lewis, "The Woman's Bible and Elizabeth Cady Stanton on Genesis," ThoughtCo, https://www.thoughtco.com/the-womans-bible-excerpt-3530448
88 Marie O'Reilly, Andrea Ó Súilleabháin, and Thania Paffenholz, CHAPTER 03 WOMEN'S PARTICIPATION AND A BETTER UNDERSTANDING OF THE POLITICAL, "Reimagining Peacemaking: Women's Roles in Peace Processes," UN Women, 2015, https://wps.unwomen.org/participation/
89 Margaret Smith Crocco, "The missing discourse about gender and sexuality in the social studies," *Theory into Practice*, 40(1), February 2001, 66.
90 Shocker, J. B. (2014). A case for using images to teach women's history. The History Teacher, 47(3), 448.

91 Garance Franke-Ruta, "When America Was Female," *The Atlantic*, March 5, 2013, https://www.theatlantic.com/politics/archive/2013/03/when-america-was-female/273672/

92 Harley Melzian, No. 31, Artists Victory Exhibit in miniature. Ever Ready Label Corp., 1943, Library of Virginia.

93 Jessica B. Shocker, "A case for using images to teach women's history," *The History Teacher*, May 2014, Vol. 47, No. 3, 425.

94 Shocker, "A case for using images to teach women's history," 426.

95 Shocker, "A case for using images to teach women's history," 427.

96 Jessica B. Schocker, & Christine Woyshner, "Representing African American women in U.S. history textbooks." *The Social Studies*, 2013, 104(1), 23–31.

97 Stephen Gottschalk, "Mary Baker Eddy." *Encyclopedia Britannica*, July 12, 2022, https://www.britannica.com/biography/Mary-Baker-Eddy

98 Mary Baker Eddy Library Editors, "The Life of Mary Baker Eddy," *Mary Baker Eddy Library*, n.d., https://www.marybakereddylibrary.org/mary-baker-eddy/the-life-of-mary-baker-eddy/

99 Amy B. Voorhees, "Mary Baker Eddy, the Woman Question, and Christian Salvation: Finding a Consistent Connection by Broadening the Boundaries of Feminist Scholarship," *Journal of Feminist Studies in Religion*, Vol. 28, No. 2 (Fall 2012), pp. 5–25. Retrieved from Indiana University Press https://www.jstor.org/stable/10.2979/jfemistudreli.28.2.5

100 Mark Twain, *Christian Science: with Notes Containing Corrections to Date* (New York: Harper, 1907), retrieved from Gutenberg Press https://www.gutenberg.org/files/3187/3187-h/3187-h.htm#link2H_PREF

101 Peter A. Wallner's, *Faith on Trial: Mary Baker Eddy, Christian Science and the First Amendment*, (Plaidswede Publishing: Concord, NH, 2014), retrieved from https://www.concordmonitor.com/Archive/2014/11/faithontrial-cmforum-113014

3

Finding Time to Teach Diverse Women's Stories

The most common reason educators give for not including women in the curriculum is not having enough time. Although they may want to include women, they have yet to transition from desire to action, and they are trapped under the illusion that male-centrism is the main narrative all students must know. *Main for whom?* Taken literally, what those educators are saying is that the traditional history, one that is White and male-dominated, takes precedent.[1] They are saying that there is less to learn from the past lives and experiences of women. Women have been denied their history in ways different from other marginalized groups. Women are denied their history as if half of the humanity's existence and nuance is at the bottom of a long to-do list.

What teacher's, schools, or governments put in their course curriculum is an outline of their values as well as what they think students need to be prepared for in college, career, and civic life. The field of social studies in public schools rose from a desire to better integrate and educate the 28 million immigrants joining the American democracy during the Industrial Revolution.[2] Over time, women increasingly attended school beyond elementary grades, and yet the courses changed little to reflect this gender shift. In effect, girls were told that to succeed they needed to learn what men were learning. Yet girls were routinely denied access to colleges, denied jobs at firms despite having the same degrees as their male peers, and so on. Today, girls have caught up to their male peers, they even out-perform them in high school, college, and their early careers, but then something happens: children. The reality is that the workplace has not changed to embrace the highly qualified

DOI: 10.4324/9781003472889-4

adult women who are eager to put their skills to use. Perhaps if we changed the training, new leaders would find innovative ways to improve the workforce. More on this in Chapter 5.

What are we saying if we don't teach equally about half the population? Apparently, students don't need to be prepared for a world that is half female? Apparently, students don't need to research the ways that women have juggled college, career, and civic life? How does one manage a long to-do list? Ask experts on time management: they will tell you not to cut things until you first know how you are *currently* spending your time, which Chapter 2 showed is unconsciously somewhere far less than half about women. *Is there really no wiggle room?*

Sheroification Is Insufficient, Make Time

Background: I Remember Women

The American Revolution history course I took in my junior year of college best illustrates how male history dominated. The course did not broadly cover the events of the revolution; rather, it honed in on the people who most shaped our country during this period: Ben Franklin, Thomas Jefferson, John Adams, and George Washington. For each of these men, we read a book by a male historian such as David McCullough. We were not invited to engage in a discussion of what qualifies someone to gain a place on the list of those who "most shaped our country," and we certainly were not awarded any alternatives to these few men. We did not read any primary accounts of these men, nor did we dive into any criticisms of them. The professor lectured for the entire term with no questions asked by students. It was evident that prominent people were certainly not women and also, notably, not BIPOC (Black, Indigenous, and people of color), poor, or many other differentiating characteristics. This course was "heroification" at its finest.

Of these texts I read so long ago, these are some details I remember: Franklin abandoned his wife and child to go to France; Jefferson had children with an enslaved woman named Sally Hemings, and the consensual nature of this relationship is debated; Abigail Adams wrote letters to her husband while he was away; and women followed the Continental Army that Washington commanded to cook for and nurse the soldiers. I remember these things because I was clinging, as students do, to stories of people like me—in this case: women. This is what students who are denied an education do. Representation not just of women, but of women from diverse backgrounds, matters.

Decades later, now an educator, I've struggled with the challenge of having too many important things to teach and just not enough curricular time;

180 school days is not enough to teach all of US or World history. It's impossible. Obviously, educators pick and choose what they will include and what they will exclude, what they will leave for college, and what is knowable through pop culture.

I was teaching on January 6, 2021; you bet the lesson got tossed out that day. After George Floyd died, most of us redoubled our efforts to teach inclusive histories and critically examine the Black experience in our curriculum. I was teaching the day Russia invaded Ukraine; the next day we learned about the Holodomor and the long history between these two states. I taught world history when the film *Woman King* came out, so I used primary source material to critique the film. I was teaching the week Hamas attacked Israel; I'm sure you see the pattern. Teachers toss and reprioritize the curriculum as it becomes culturally relevant and timely. If there is a time in the history of the world to include women in the mainstream curriculum, it is now.

I love teaching World War II. I know more about World War II than I could possibly ever teach in a single course. One year in my secondary US History course, as I shifted from World War to Cold War, I wanted my students to examine the dichotomy of being a superpower: both a global protector and new-age imperialist. But the whole unit missed the mark because I had placed overemphasis on World War II and not enough on our long history of imperial wars. So, I backed up. Where was I putting my emphasis? What wasn't I covering enough? I looked at all the wars and decided to give each more equal emphasis. We spent just as much time on each of the Mexican, Philippine, and Spanish–American Wars as we did World Wars. After each, I paused and asked them to think about what US actions in that war said about the US and its foreign policy.

I shifted the compelling question for the course to be clear: is the US an imperial nation? Debatable? *Yes*. Important? *Yes*. Researchable? *Yes*. Enduring. *You bet*. I shifted, refocused. I didn't get to go into all the detail I could on World War II anymore. At the end, students had far more profound understandings of our history as a nation, and because we had been debating throughout the course, they had well-argued and different positions on the question. Clearer understandings happened because I moved away from the better-known aspects of the war to more focused instruction on crucial understandings, patterns, and questions. Students listened to speeches from Presidents Frankling D. Roosevelt and Harry S Truman stating plainly that they didn't want anything from the war but peace. We contrasted these claims with the expansion of US military bases during and after the war as well as traced Coca-Cola plants as an example of spreading economic imperialism. Students grappled with and weighed the evidence to form their own perspectives.

I haven't tossed D-Day. No. I teach it differently. I focus on the floating harbor, the landing craft, the aerial bombings: the technology that made Allied victory possible. I emphasize not the horrors of the Holocaust and mass murders of Chinese and Koreans but what was known and the slow action of the international community. I also emphasize heroism and sacrifice. The men who crossed the English Channel knew the predicted death toll. It's important for students to understand their risk, sacrifice, patriotism, and commitment to democratic freedoms.

A strong reflective practice hinges on teachers observing themselves, seeing what's working and what's not, and making changes. It's time we realize that what we are doing is not preparing students for workplaces and marriages that are more gender-equal. Our collective consciousness has shifted, our workplace is more diverse and increasingly female, and we need a curriculum that prepares students for that world. We need to reflect as a profession and reprioritize the history that's important.

Barrier: Too Much Content

Teachers agree that the social studies classroom is the place to talk about women and gender equity.[3] When asked, most teachers claim they are comfortable talking about women and gender-related topics in class, but their rationale for why they don't actually do so illuminates the opposite. In Scheiner-Fisher's study in Florida schools, of the teachers who didn't teach women's history at all, half said it wasn't required, and the other half said there just wasn't enough time.[4] In Chapter 6, we will examine the standards and other methods of understanding what is required in classrooms.

Scheiner-Fisher's study was affirmed by Martell and Steven's study of Massachusetts teachers. In theirs, a majority of teachers (66.1 percent) said they would teach more about gender if they had more time.[5] One teacher said,

> I wish there was more time. It feels like there's always enough time to oversimplify it (Women faced prejudices, then it got better. Gays faced prejudice, then it got better.), but I wish there was more time to REALLY teach it.[6]

If teachers don't make time, students are going into a world, half female, unprepared. The consequence of such limited time on gender resulted in another teacher saying, "I feel it is difficult to keep gender lessons from becoming boys against girls. I wish I had more curriculum support with this."[7] If you watch state legislatures debates women's rights, Title IX, sexual assault, maternity leave and childcare policies, and abortion, it certainly

looks that way there too. Yet women are half of humanity. Women's freedom is human freedom. Women's access to health care is human access to
health care. Teachers must play a role in dismantling this men-versus-women
antagonism.

The problem of curricular time is not unique to the United States. A 2016
study in London by Bridget Lockyer and Abigail Tazzymant gave educators
a forum to discuss their inclusion of women's history. Most expressed exas-
peration with the constraints on their curricular time. One educator in the
London study said,

> I think we do as much as we can crowbar in really. Because the unfortu-
> nate fact is that men have been the people in charge for the last... millen-
> nia, so if you're learning about political history the men are in charge.[8]

These answers reveal a different answer. Setting aside the bits of misogyny
unconsciously present in these comments, if teachers aren't teaching wom-
en's perspectives because of time or a lack of requirement, they don't know
that women *had* perspectives on the things they already teach. They don't
understand that women were entrenched in the historical narrative. They
don't know women's history, and they *certainly* aren't prepared to teach it.

In an effort to acknowledge women in a packed curriculum, many teachers reduce their coverage of women to "pop-up" history, where a woman figure, usually a radical, pops into the curriculum in a sometimes disconnected
and random way. It's tokenism at its finest. It's random to the teacher, and it's
random to the students. It fails to give that woman and her cause (it's usually
a cause) context, and she becomes hard to remember because she isn't well
woven into the story of the past.

Pop-Up History

James Loewen, author of *Lies My Teacher Told Me*, calls traditional history
"heroification," or selecting people to put on a pedestal and honor.[9] This process does not reveal the truth about history—events do not happen in a vacuum. Few leaders act alone. When male historians selected the heroes they
wanted children to read about, they tended to select people who looked and
reminded them of themselves. Loewen called heroification a "degenerative
process" because it distorts the real lives, works, and effects of those historical
figures.[10] To really *see* our leaders is to understand that then, as now, they were
not monolithic; they contained parts we like and parts we don't like. If we
heroify them, it makes our current roundup of leaders difficult to cope with.

As a result of male heroification, women have been left out of the
story. Women were there. Women existed. Women disagreed. Women were
complicated. Women served and took bold action inside and outside the

post-Industrial Revolution "women's sphere." *Why don't we learn about them?* There is something very male about highlighting exemplars and, in effect, putting them on a pedestal. This heroification results in ignoring collaborative efforts, marginalized groups, and parts of the hero's character that might damage their hero status.

The response to heroification of male figures in the past is not sheroification. Women's history must tell diverse women's history in order to explain the depth and breadth of the female experience. Historian Rosalind Miles explained:

> Early women's history was devoted to combing the chronicles for queens, abbesses and learned women to set against the equivalent male figures of authority and ability, creating heroines in the mirror image of heroes... This pop-up... version of women's history, though it had some value in asserting that women can be competent and powerful, had two weaknesses—it reinforced the false effect of male domination of history, since there were always many more male rulers and 'geniuses' than female; and it failed to address the reality of the majority of women's lives who had neither the opportunity nor the appetite for such activities.[11]

Another scholar, Nel Noddings, writing for *Theory and Practice*, critiqued the way women were being added to history textbooks. She explained that the outcomes were somewhat mixed, ranging from positive to absurd. She said that while women were included, it often took some imagination to understand why.[12] In many cases, no white man with such peripheral involvement in an issue would have been included—so why were these women? Although women appeared in illustrations, they were still absent from the written content around the image—illustrations were added of women to say women's history was being taught, but it was less than tokenism.[13]

Women's history, when presented as pop-up history, *sheroifies*, and the biases of the historian are on full display. The most common women taught in school include radical feminists like suffragists, not typical women. Noddings warned that including women in such a way makes an age-old error of measuring female success by a male standard.[14] This approach "obscures contributions" made by women in fields ignored by the social studies curriculum.[15] Noddings argued that women's history should not adhere to traditional approaches, which merely highlights a handful of notable political or social figures as representative. In women's history, these "notable" women do not exemplify the majority of women's history. Their contributions seem like deviations from the norm in a society largely dominated by men.[16]

Many of the women who *do* make history class were radical in their time. As a result, they often advocated for rights and were embroiled in politics—this has left us with the false idea that women's history is about a special interest group. Women are not an interest group—they are half of humanity! Women do not agree, are diverse, and have been present in one way or another throughout history. To better understand women, we need to hear multiple female perspectives.

In 1985, a woman named Alison Bechdel wrote a comic strip satirizing how few women in movies appear as major characters or appear to have lives. The immediate result was something nicknamed the Feminist Movie Test, or the Bechdel Test. Here it is: a film has to have at least two [named] women in it who talk to each other at some point about something besides a man.[17] That's it: two women who exist and talk about stuff. The bar for feminism in film is barely off the ground, and yet, sadly, few films pass the test. Every one of my favorites failed miserably. The only film I show in my history courses that passes the test is *Iron Jawed Angels* (2004), a film about women's suffrage, a film I had never seen until I became a teacher.

This test helped raise awareness of gender discrimination in the industry and also created a rich national dialogue about the absence of women of substance in the media. If women barely exist in the films and don't have friends or meaningful conversations outside of men, what conclusions will people draw about women? It wouldn't be a stretch to suggest they might conclude that girls don't think about important things and are only interested in men.

Sadly, over a decade after Bechdel wrote her comic, little had changed. In most films, women still had token roles. In some, as the climax of the film occurred and the world burned around the characters, the female character came on scene to talk about her relationship with the male character or another domestic affair. Examining the list of the Best Picture winners from the Oscars spanning 1965 to 2003, Allan Johnson concluded,

> Of the almost forty films, only four tell a story through the life of someone who is female—*Chicago, Out of Africa, Terms of Endearment*, and *The Sound of Music*—and only the middle two focus on a serious subject, the other two being musicals.[18]

He argued that this list was proof of the male-centered nature of patriarchal societies. In his analysis, he wrote:

> If you want a story about heroism, moral courage, spiritual transformation, endurance, or any of the struggles that give human life its deepest meaning, men and masculinity are usually the terms in which you must see it. Male experience is what patriarchal culture uses to

represent human experience, even when it is women who most often live it. Films about single men taking care of children, for example, such as Sleepless in Seattle, have far more audience appeal than those focusing on women, even though women are much more likely to be single parents. And stories that focus on deep bonds of friendship—which men have a much tougher time forming than women do—are far more likely to focus on men than women.[19]

Watching your favorite show or film exposes you to some of the toxic stereotypes about women, most notably that they exist to serve men, don't have female friends, and don't have speaking roles.[20] These stereotypes are fueled by an industry dominated by male producers, directors, screenwriters, and agents. Hopefully, our students can distinguish those films from real life, but, sadly, the story of real life, or at least the way it's taught, would not pass the Bechdel Test.

Our traditional teaching of women's history has been satisfied to summarize women's contribution to world history with: *women were meanwhile serving in their traditional role of tending the home.* We have summarized an incredibly diverse half of humanity and, in effect, we have buried the stories of women who did not tend the home and we have devalued those who did—neither is acceptable or reflects much critical thought. *Could one do the same for all of men? "Men were meanwhile…" What is the end of the sentence?*

Women are equally diverse, opinionated, and different. To say *all women* were doing anything in unison fails to acknowledge women as human beings with innate differences. Miles wrote, "There could be as many histories as there are women to write them."[21] Reducing women to what was traditionally valued not only is inaccurate for how many lived but, importantly, gives us an excuse not to acknowledge their contributions, which were greater than they are given credit for. Not all women were wives and mothers—and for those who were, those titles were not all that defined them.

Men have had millennia to craft the field of history, and women's history is only in its infancy. Mistakes will be made, perhaps overemphasis placed on some topics, and ill-fitting definitions developed, but we need more women and men to weigh in for us to find the proper points of emphasis and ways to include women.

Breaker: Inquiry and the Eckert Test
The Inquiry Model
In an effort to teach accurate facts about the past, critical thinking and analysis, empower students in the class, and teach the skills of historians and social

scientists, the National Council for the Social Studies (NCSS) shifted toward a pedagogic approach called the inquiry model or the Inquiry Design Model (IDM). This move also made room for teachers to include more marginalized groups into the curriculum. In 2017, they adopted the C3 (College Career and Civic Life) framework for social studies education.[22] This framework for inquiry introduced one of many approaches for doing inquiry in the classroom. Their approach has four dimensions, which are paraphrased here:

◆ (D1) ask compelling questions;
◆ (D2) use historical thinking skills to examine the question;
◆ (D3) synthesize, analyze, and evaluate the research; and
◆ (D4) take action with this learning.

The framework centers the students, centers questions, and should, in theory, get students to be curious, dive into source material to understand, and help them ask more sophisticated questions.

The C3 Framework has its critics, and its method of implementing the inquiry model is cumbersome, but it is a strong concept. From the right, critics worry about D4, where barely informed students are becoming activists. They worry that students don't have enough information or enough context and that the framework promotes activism over civil discussion.[23] Criticisms from the left interestingly include some of the same criticisms. One scholar pointed to the fact that the inquiries used by the C3 are preplanned, so new sources are predetermined and eliminate student voice.[24] He also critiqued the funders behind the framework, calling them too far right.

When I teach the inquiry model to my pre-service teachers, we read the critiques of the model. I turned whether to use the model into an inquiry itself. Almost always, the conclusion is not to disregard the model but to make it better: to slow it down, give proper context, allow for student selection of source materials beyond those provided, and appreciate the need for civil conversation as well as informed and appropriate activism.

The problem with many inquiries is that while some may include women, they don't center the experiences of women *enough* and thus give zero context to the experience of the woman whose ideas are shared. Take a lesson plan featured on C3 Teachers (the website for the NCSS) about the French Revolution. The question is an appropriate one: *Was the French Revolution revolutionary?* Students will quickly have to define "revolutionary." An adept student will then ask *for whom?* The person who created this inquiry included a number of wonderful primary sources, but only one that featured a woman: Olympe de Gouge. During the French Revolution, women were incredibly active. A woman led the charge on the Bastille. Women marched by the thousands to Versailles to demand bread from the king.[25] Women formed dozens of political organizations to advocate for change in the early years of the revolution.[26] As France was ever more under attack from their neighbors, a group of women formed the Society of Revolutionary Republican Women and began calling for firmer foreign policies and the arming of women soldiers. The Reign of Terror began in September 1793, and political women became a focus. On October 30, 1793, Jean-Baptiste Amar proposed a decree that ceased and silenced all women's political clubs.[27] The decree passed with no discussion. What had been a period of vibrant women's involvement was quickly squashed.

Olympe de Gouge was just one of the many women whom students could discuss. She is, of course, the most radical, and, of course, she's the one who made history. This is the exact reason Dr. Laurel Thatcher Ulrich wrote, "Well-behaved women seldom make history."[28] De Gouge is important, though—she went the furthest, writing the piece they included in the inquiry: *The Declaration of the Rights of Woman and of the Female Citizen*, which advocated for full and equal rights for women in the new French society.[29] Her story is complicated, but like so many others, de Gouge was beheaded during the Reign of Terror for challenging the Republic to hold true to revolutionary ideas.[30] *She was beheaded.* Would students reading this inquiry know that? *No.* The document is presented out of context. The fate of the author is not provided. What a failure! The fact that she asked for equal rights and was beheaded shows how feminism is often met with violence—a function of the hierarchies which the patriarchy is fond of. On this theme, historian Janis MacDonald wrote about the importance of giving women's history proper context:

> I hope… to encourage historians to view different dimensions of women's work and thought in context. Only then will we understand the scope of women's contributions to history as distinct from their appreciation of the limitations of the society in which they operated… In our efforts at rediscovering her story… we may be unconsciously building barriers against the possibilities of new understandings of the past contributions of women in history.

[31]A student could certainly read the document and conclude, "Wow! Women were demanding their rights as far back as 1791!" And that would be only half the story.

Historical inquiries in the classroom must not only ask questions that make central the thoughts of women but help students understand the context in which those women lived. Too often, the questions that are asked of students do little to include the diverse experiences of women and only highlight the de Gouges of the world. They also fail to show how society responds to those women. The Republic banned women's political clubs and involvement. It's not enough to simply show what brave women wrote—we have to show what happened to them. If not, students will be left with the false idea that speaking up is easy. It's not. But women were brave and did it anyway. De Gouge, for example, never backed down and continued writing her critiques of the new republic from her jail cell. She and many other writing women were executed. She called on the crowd at her execution to avenge her.

Living in France during this time was an English woman, Mary Wollstonecraft, perhaps the most famous feminist author of the Enlightenment period. She was inspired by the salons, political discussions, and the boldness with which women engaged in politics. She published her book to advocate for women's rights to education. When the Reign of Terror began, she fled France.

The Reign of Terror ended with the rise of Napoleon, a self-proclaimed emperor of France. He stabilized the violence in France, abolished feudalism, declared equality between men, and codified it into law. Unfortunately for women, what had been an ambiguous position in society was now solidified and traveled wherever Napoleon's armies conquered in Europe. These codes held French women's rights decades behind their peers in the United Kingdom and the United States. A proper inquiry related to French women's experiences of the Revolution is available on the Remedial Herstory Project's website.

The scary part of teaching with inquiry is that teachers may not know all the answers to the questions explored. Good. Push it back on the students. The teacher should transition from expert (which is a false title anyway since most of us are generalists) to facilitator. In this role, teachers model best practices for research methods and show students how to find *real* experts. Teachers transition from being a preacher in front of their class to a coach, supporting their students as they investigate questions. Webquests and project-based learning have long been staples of the social studies curriculum and are gateways for teachers to become practitioners of inquiry. Think of it this way: students who listen to the teacher-expert all class will learn day in and day out that the way toward knowing is through the teacher. When they graduate and are without a teacher-expert, they are lost. Inquiry is helping them be the master of their own education, which goes far beyond high school.

When it comes to better including women in curricular content, the inquiry model allows teachers to ask more inclusive questions and enter the second to last of Tetreault's phases: the Feminist Phase. Here, they can ask questions that include or center women. Here, they can ask questions on male-centric topics but include sources by or about women. Inquiry is the ticket for inclusion. Teachers who are nervous about backlash in their community or school about bringing in more women's voices and topics can fall back on: "What? I'm just asking the question." It's best practice.

The Remedial Herstory Project and other organizations have worked to prepare ready-made inquiries for students that get students debating and discussing history. Inquiries like these guide students through the source materials, which is especially helpful for women's history when so few educators are trained to teach it. In these planned inquiries, documents are collected from archives, databases, and libraries and transcribed to grade level to help student comprehension. These inquiries can be a pathway to stronger inclusion of not just women but all marginalized groups. A teacher could pose a question to the class and include source material from five people from a variety of backgrounds, be that gender, racial, economic, or political, and let students grapple with the ideas presented.

There is ample debate among historians and social studies teachers about what makes up a good research question, but there is a difference between a thesis question and one that makes for good classroom inquiry. Questions for inquiry should ideally be DIRE: *debatable, important, researchable,* and *enduring.* Debates could range from topics that are literally debated in society and politics to topics where the debate is about nuance. Important topics mattered to the people in the past and affected the trajectory of history. Researchable means there are primary sources with which students can explore the answer. Finally, enduring means the answer continues to matter today. These four criteria force students to go through each of the four dimensions of the C3 Framework and demonstrate the skills of social scientists.

Historians caution teachers to be careful with the questions they pose, for "Not all questions are created equal, however."[32] Writing in *Perspectives on History*, Whitney Barrigner, Lauren Brand, and Nichloas Kryczka argued that there is such thing as a bad question. They said:

> Across diverse genres of social studies curriculum, forced choices between moral absolutes, abstract queries of ethical or civic concern, and overly fanciful counterfactuals appear more frequently than they should. Stark and uncomplicated question constructions speed the inquiry process straight to argument, reducing history to a series of positions that one must take and defend. If inquiry is to remain the banner under which history lessons are devised, teachers will need to distinguish good questions from bad ones.[33]

They make clear that there are often good intentions behind the questions teachers pose that may fit that bill. I know I have posed those questions in my classes. When I have posed black-and-white questions, even here, my point has been to help students see, through sources, that the answer isn't black and white; it's usually grey. If it wasn't grey, there wouldn't be a debate and nuance. The question itself matters, as does the depth which students explore the answers.

When I began to consciously add women to my curriculum, I started adding women's sources to the inquiries, or lessons, I already had. I took one lesson on two Black men who cofounded the NAACP but who disagreed on the best path toward Black liberation, and I added the iconic Ida B. Wells-Barnett, another NAACP cofounder. But the problem with this lesson was that I put Wells-Barnett in the position of speaking for all Black women, and there wasn't *women's* diversity. Men get to be diverse and have disagreements in history, but women who pop up in history content don't get that luxury nearly enough.

The Eckert Test

History curriculum serves little purpose if it does not reflect the reality of the world outside the classroom, one that is half female. Patti Lather wrote, "Given the variety of women's experience in relation to culture, class, race, sexual orientation, etc., there are multiple feminist standpoints."[34] I cannot agree more. Copying the model of the Bechdel Test, I created the Eckert Test because I was saddened by how many times I failed to bring a female perspective into my own lessons. The Eckert Test is how I hold myself accountable to a more comprehensive and diverse women's history. The test is this:

1. There are two women in the lesson.
2. Those two women have different opinions.
3. They represent different backgrounds: racial, sexual identity, ethnic, religious, generational, or economic.

Meeting the Eckert Test is possible in every era and region of both US and world history, even as far back as Mesopotamia. Lessons for every period and region of world history are available on the Remedial Herstory Project's website.

When we begin with the assumption that likely not all women agreed on a topic, we can often find more fascinating stories, historic controversies, and compelling classroom discussions. Students learn best when they are empowered to engage in these discussions and take historic examples that help us philosophically examine our own world—one in which controversy and polarization are seemingly everywhere, even among women. Since most teachers are somewhere between compensatory and bi-focal history and many have not found the path to women's diversity, we will break the Feminist phase down over the next few chapters and leave integrating these ideas for the end.

Find Women's Diversity

It's important to remember that it was predominantly white feminists who wrote the first draft of women's history, which biased the field, leaving out the voices of conservative, nonwhite, and lower-class women, among others. Tetreault therefore suggests that teachers examine the broader experiences of women.[35] Congruent with the truly inclusive definition of feminism, Tetreault called this stage "Feminist History," a phase where the diversity of women's experiences could be on full display. She said teachers should ask the following:

- ◆ What were most women doing at a particular time in history?
- ◆ What new categories need to be added to the study of history?
- ◆ What kinds of productive work, paid and unpaid, did women do and under what conditions?
- ◆ How did the variables of race, ethnicity, social class, marital status, and sexual preference affect women's experiences?
- ◆ How have women of different races and classes interacted throughout history?
- ◆ How did women develop a collective feminist consciousness of their distinct roles in the private and public spheres?
- ◆ Who were outstanding women who advocated a feminist transformation of the home and society?
- ◆ What are the appropriate ways of organizing or periodizing women's history?[36]

Moving into this stage, away from compensatory and contribution history, opens up worlds of possibilities. When teachers ask women-centric questions and explore history by and about women, suddenly women's diversity becomes abundantly obvious, interesting, and complicated. I would even add questions like *How did class impact the productive work women did? How did women react to the feminism of the "outstanding" women?*

The American temperance movement, for example, has long been presented as a monolithic movement of like-minded women, if it's presented at all. Sometimes teachers jump to Prohibition and the Progressive era without mentioning the decades-long movement to achieve the abolition of alcohol, which entirely eliminates women's political role. Presented as belonging to an undifferentiated movement, these women had one goal—end alcoholism—and were united in this pursuit. But there are spectrums and layers to the women who joined this movement! Some women were deeply Christian and saw alcohol as sinful. Some were social reformers concerned about women's and children's welfare. Some felt the only way women could reform anything was by having the vote. Others felt women should advocate for change through their men. Some saw alcoholism as a product of poverty. Others saw the compounding effects of racial trauma and wanted the movement to be more intersectional to address lynching.

My favorite example of the spectrum of temperance reformers is Carrie Nation, who famously took to smashing illegal bars in Kansas with a hatchet. Nation garnered a following of equally Christian radicals who simply wanted Kansas law enforcement to enforce the temperance laws. The Women's Christian Temperance Union (WCTU), which Nation belonged to, supported her goals but disapproved of her methods.[37] The WCTU wasn't exactly sure how to respond to such a woman—stand by her sentiment but lament her methods?

The first president of the WCTU, Annie Wittenmyer, wanted to remain strictly focused on temperance work and not be distracted by suffrage or other causes. Frances Willard was a cofounder of the WCTU and succeeded Wittenmyer as president, pivoting the organization to adopt suffrage and a slew of other intersectional reform efforts, yet she didn't include any commentary or reform positions against lynching. So, Ida B. Wells-Barnett called her out on it.

Another great example of women's diversity can be found in the colonial era. Weetamoo was the leader of one of the tribes in the Wampanoag Confederacy and sister-in-law to the Great Sachem in the early years of English colonization in Massachusetts. When she came to power around 1660, the vast majority of Wampanoag had perished from disease. She married many times to form alliances, and when one of her husbands died in English custody, she called foul. Time passed and she remarried, but eventually things between the Wampanoag and the English became too tense, and her sister's husband, Metacom (called Philip by the English), went to war.[38]

Weetamoo's various marriages throughout her life resulted in her commanding the allegiance of every major tribe in the Confederacy. Weetamoo had to decide whether to lead her people to war or try to negotiate. Her new husband sided with the English, but she sided with the Great Sachem: Metacom.[39] She dissolved the political marriage and turned those allied with her against the English.

Yet Weetamoo has been lost to many history books. The war between the Wampanoag and the English settlers was called King Philip's War after Metacom. The rare teacher who remembers to discuss the war typically forgets to mention her efforts to align the tribes of the Confederacy behind Metacom. Weetamoo alone stands as a woman caught in a man's world. Mary Rowlandson is perhaps the best primary source for knowing Weetamoo. She lived during King Philip's War. She was one of many English women who were captured and brought to Weetamoo as prisoners. Many captive women's stories were recorded as anti-Native propaganda during this time. Rowlandson was held for 11 weeks. Years later, she published a book about her experience.

Rowlandson and Weetamoo are fascinating to include because they are two women who were on opposite sides of the bloodiest war in US history (per capita) and disagreed. Rowlandson complained that Weetamoo didn't give her enough to eat. Weetamoo was in charge of a massive war effort in a time of scarcity, Rowlandson's hunger was the least of her worries.[40] Rowlandson was ransomed home, while Weetamoo died during the war. She drowned while crossing a river during the war. Her decapitated head was brought back as a trophy, and when the imprisoned Wampanoag saw it, they wailed in agony over the death of their leader.

Women have differing and diverse perspectives that bring history to life. Without Weetamoo, the teaching of "King Philip's War" is false. It would be like teaching the American Revolution without Alexander Hamilton. Without women's diversity and Mary Rowlandson, women's history becomes monolithic and bland. *With* women's diversity, women's history becomes *juicy* and students love it! Teach juicy history.

Blueprint: The F Word

I'm going to use a dirty word: feminism. Studies show that teachers who identify as feminists are more likely to teach women's history. One study concluded,

> There is evidence that social studies teachers' beliefs on gender influence not only what they see as the purpose of high school sociology classes, but also the time they spend on gender issues in their curriculum… Although sociology teachers may be more aware of the role of gender and sexism in society, due to the course content, this study showed that some sociology teachers might still take a gender-blind perspective.[41]

In another study by the same researchers, they found that feminist teachers shared common practices in their classrooms, including the following:

- ◆ Being skeptical of the representation of gender in traditional textbooks and seeking out supplemental materials that better represented women
- ◆ Being aware of the participation rates of male and female students in class discussions and making efforts to ensure that female students' voices were heard

- ◆ Making connections between past oppression of women and current events to engage students and promote their interest in gender issues
- ◆ Taking initiatives beyond the classroom to support and empower female students.[42]

How the teachers came to their approaches was driven by their personal life experiences.[43] Each of the participants felt marginalized in some way, perhaps because of their race, gender, or life experiences. Marginalization played a significant role in aligning their ideology with feminism. For example, Alex, a biracial man who participated in their study, felt like an outsider and wanted to change the educational experience for students who were like himself. Tina grew up in a male-dominated community and experienced sexism, which led her to teach about gender equity. Liz faced sexism in her previous career and wanted to break stereotypes about assertive women. These personal experiences shaped their teaching philosophies and fueled their passion for feminism. The teachers' beliefs influenced their lessons and teaching practices.

The notion that one has to personally experience marginalization to have enough empathy with the female experience and feminism to teach about these subjects would make me laugh if it wasn't so sad and horrifying: I do not have to identify as a men-ist to teach about men in my curriculum, yet it seems that one has to personally experience oppression and explicitly value the improvement of women's rights and equality in order to acknowledge that half of the population is worthy of critical study. To motivate educators to reprioritize and make space for women in their course content, feminism must become more appealing. We must talk about the F word.

Pragmatically, for my purposes, since almost 60 percent of secondary social studies teachers are men and the gender gap is worse at the college level, men in particular must embrace feminism if women's topics and history are ever going to be taught in schools. Men must identify with the need to advance the lives and rights of women. But this is harder than it sounds because the status of men in society is not great.

So many times when I discuss the status of women in society, I hear the rebuttal, "but the male suicide rate." My response is always, "I am concerned about that, too." This debate tactic is called "switch tracking," where you dismiss the point made about one track or idea and jump to a completely different topic. The effect is that neither issue is really discussed. One stumbles into a logical fallacy which argues that since men commit suicide at higher rates, the pay gap just doesn't exist? No. Those are two different topics. When discussing gender issues, we must resist the desire to switch tracks. Both are true and concerning. Gender equality is not a one-way street. One can be concerned about girls and women as well as the status of boys and men. Society can hold two concerns at the same time: teachers can too.

More social studies teachers need to identify as feminists, and they need to understand that they can and should *also* care about boys and men. Further, feminist ideas and solutions benefit many of the problems facing men, like suicide. The problem is not the ideas but the politicizing of the F word. To articulate this breaker, I'm going to break down feminism, how men benefit, why men should be feminists, and lastly (and perhaps confusingly) what studies show and why I think we should stop using the F word.

What Is Feminism?

People have debated feminism for decades. So, here's what I mean by feminism: bringing an end to sexism.[44] It's not about ending men, it's about ending norms, structures, and systems that disadvantage and exploit women. The word "féminisme" was first used by French socialist philosopher Charles Fourier in the 1830s; it wasn't added to the *Oxford English Dictionary* until 1894.[45] Women before or immediately after that would not likely have used the term to describe themselves, especially because there was less intersectionality between movements.

Feminism made significant progress in combating sexism and patriarchal norms in the mid-twentieth century. Title IX in particular has completely changed the landscape for women. It was arguably the most effective piece of legislation to create equalities that protected both men and women. That progress came because of the activism of feminists.[46]

The forces working against feminism have done a number on progress in the last 30 years, claiming that feminism is hurting men, when the reality is the exact opposite. Studies have shown that young people are turned off from feminism but also that their understanding of feminism is misled. In a study, eighth-graders described feminists as "women who think men aren't equal."[47] Scholars concluded that "students uniformly agreed that the term 'feminist' was a problematic and often uncomfortable label… 'It means you hate men,' at least one student in all but one group said."[48] Teachers in the study too were found distancing themselves from those they deemed "women's libbers."[49] This shows the effect of conservative backlash against feminism in the last several decades.

Everyone should be a feminist. Shouldn't we want equal opportunities for our sons and daughters? It should be shameful to not be a feminist, but the forces working against the feminist movement in promotion of outdated and oppressive traditional gender roles have been working hard. In the current climate, feminism can be a powerful force.[50] Feminism offers tools to understand inequalities between the sexes and resist oppressive systems that impact both men and women. Feminism prompts us to question how these systems shape our realities and challenge women and men's marginalization. Teaching women's history is important for feminism. We cannot tell women they are equal in society and then also say that people like them aren't worthy of historical study. We must all be feminists, anti-sexists.

How Do Men Benefit from Feminism?

Men benefit from feminism because it allows them to break out of social boxes that most men don't fit in anyway, boxes that hold men back financially, romantically, and socially. What is the box? The patriarchy. The patriarchy is not men, it's a social system. Allan G. Johnson, a sociologist and author of *The Gender Knot: Unraveling our Patriarchal Legacy*, argues, "Patriarchy is a kind of society, and a society is more than a collection of people. As such, 'patriarchy' doesn't refer to me or any other man or collection of men, but to a kind of society in which men *and* women participate."[51] As such, feminism is an alternative system: not one where women dominate men, but where hierarchies perpetuated by the patriarchal system are dismantled and men and women are more equal and free. Removed from the boxes that the patriarchy stuffs men into, the majority of men will benefit from such a system, but they need direction.

Many people don't know the full definition of misogyny. They end their understanding with "hatred of women." But misogyny is also weaponized against men, or "men perceived as effeminate."[52] Men hide qualities they deem too feminine, like their emotions, certain tastes, and preferences because they are so often associated or marketed to women. Misogyny prevents men from living a full life and being true to themselves. I have many manly friends who work in schools. Some held other "manly" jobs before they worked in schools, or they work as contractors in the summer for some extra cash. Teaching, coaching, counseling, nursing, and other jobs men do in schools have been seen as "women's work" to some people. I'll never forget the look of defeat on the face of one of my colleagues when an irate mother stormed into his office and said that *because* he was a wrestling coach, he was a pedophile. Beyond being illogical, she was weaponizing misogyny against him. I imagine other men who work in schools have had similar experiences.

Rigid definitions of masculinity and the emphasis on non-emotional stoicism have fueled a male suicide rate that should concern everyone. In 2021, the suicide rate among US males in 2021 was approximately four times higher than the rate among females.[53] Repurposing my own phrasing, men are half of the population but nearly 80 percent of suicides. This rate has been steadily climbing for the last two decades. It is not feminism that created a rising male suicide rate, it is the insistence on an old definition of manhood that does not serve the modern man coupled with a natural tendency toward impulsivity. Feminism is not a zero-sum game. Asking for rights does not take away rights from men.

Asking for women to be included in the curriculum, though perhaps nuanced, isn't different. It may mean minimizing some men, but it also allows for the adding of others. I've loved the men women's history has introduced me to. Deep study into Susan B. Anthony gave Frederick Douglass more depth and introduced me to her father, a champion for women's education, and Henry R. Seldon, her lawyer who passionately defended her in court. Those men give boys examples of how men can support women.

The patriarchal norm enforces a hegemonic masculinity where men dominate not only women but other men. This is a system that serves few and simultaneously traps men in a constant fear of a masculinity crisis. It's also a total scam for men of lower classes. Men who are not powerful themselves are dominated by other men, but they still feel a certain connection to the patriarchal norm of dominance because it rewards their social position over women, regardless of a woman's class dominance over them. This helps explain why a construction worker—it's a stereotype yet too often true—may feel entitled as a man to sexually harass a well-dressed professional woman who is his class superior as she passes by. The scam is that both the construction worker and the woman are subordinate to other men within the system. The same scam was used to empower poor whites as slave catchers in Antebellum America. Rather than seeing how their conditions and those of the enslaved were similar, poor white men relished their little bit of power and helped oppress those who were only just below them in status. The patriarchy feeds lower-class men scraps rather than real power. The patriarchal system not only suppresses lower-class men but marginalizes male minority groups based on their races and sexual orientations. Men not at the top of the hierarchy are left with few resources to manage their anxieties and stressors. The liberation of women benefits men because it fights against the same forces oppressing the vast majority of men.

Why Must Male Teachers Join Feminism?

Men must join feminism not just to integrate women and gender history and issues into the mainstream social studies curriculum but also to practically aid men in understanding, defining, and strengthening an improved vision of manhood fit for a modern world. Old models of masculinity were arguably necessary when we physically fought one another for resources and land, where one's family and the honor of your wife were threatened by other men, but that is not the 21st-century world we are living in. It's time for manhood to evolve, keeping the same heroism and risk-taking that are characteristic of males but using a model defined by abundance, not scarcity.

High school boys have already been conditioned in the hierarchy of the patriarchy. They have an idea of what it is to "be a man" and it's limited due to their maturity, yes, but also by what the culture of the patriarchy feeds them. I've observed boys who tough it out only to fail. I've also seen boys exploit maternal figures, like teachers, in their life in a version of learned helplessness which causes them to fail. These norms aren't helping boys; they are struggling and failing all around us.

The most vocal supporters of boys and men on these issues are not feminists but those who blame feminism and want to return women to a state of abject dependence. Women will not go back to the Dark Ages. This is not a viable policy solution. Further, supporting men should be central to conversations about gendered impacts. Where gender inequality exists and women are given privileges denied to men, feminists should be the first to point this out, not the sexists. Instead, too often, feminists stay silent and let the voices that want to advance men at the expense of women lead the way. This holds not only men back but women, which circularly hurts men, who are often partnered with women.

Feminism has improved women's status considerably, and that has put men used to unearned privileges or surviving on scraps of dominance in a seeming state of shock. Even though women are not oppressing men, the shift from unearned privilege to a state closer to equity feels like oppression for them.[54] Studies show that "relative deprivation" or the feeling that your group is doing worse than it used to creates "outgroup prejudice."[55] This explains why those concerned about boys and men, or the challenges facing men, struggle to see how those issues are tangential to those impacting women. Things are harder than they used to be for men, but to advocate for backward trends is to show unmerited preference for men *over* women. Instead, society must continue to champion progress for women *and* offer men new solutions, new social scripts, and new models of masculinity.

One of the biggest places boys need our help is in schools where feminine qualities, skill sets, and neuro-capabilities thrive. Girls are 14 percentage points more likely to be school-ready by kindergarten because of the way girls' brains mature more quickly.[56] This advantage widens the gap through elementary school, where girls outperform male peers on standardized exams across many subject areas.[57] Girls outperform boys in high school across most areas of measuring performance, dominating class ranks and earning an average grade of an A across subjects, while male grades average a B.[58] In recent years, women in the US earned 57 percent of college degrees across all subjects, a pattern replicated around the world.[59]

Richard Reeves, a Senior Analyst at the Brookings Institute, believes these data are evidence that schools are structurally biased toward girls. Prior to Title IX, men were 13 percentage points more likely to go to college. Since then, it has swung in the complete opposite direction, with girls 15 percentage more likely to attend.[60] Black and poor boys are the most at risk and least receptive to traditional policy interventions aimed to improve learning outcomes. Studies of implicit bias, criminal sentencing, and even cultural issues around masculinity show how much Black men are uniquely stigmatized, Reeves said. He referred to data showing a wider gender gap between Black boys and girls than White ones. The gap between girls and boys widens the further down the socioeconomic ladder one goes. By almost every measure of disadvantage, boys are doing worse than their female counterparts.[61] Middle- and upper-class parents, he surmised, have the resources and the knowledge to help their boys overcome their disadvantages.

Policies should be designed to do what these wealthier families are doing to help their boys already. Reeves proposes redshirting, or delaying, all boys in K–12 schools for one year.[62] Research has shown girls' prefrontal cortexes develop earlier than those of boys, giving them impulse control earlier, which in turn helps them to do better in school. So, holding boys back one year would allow them to be the developmental equals of girls in their classes and perform better overall.

Other solutions that Reeves proposes to *men's problems* are the exact policies that feminists have been advocating for decades! Men and women should cease seeking traditional partners as the social conditions that made those relationships function no longer exist. Further, men should be encouraged to go into fields like health care and teaching currently dominated by women workers, social studies education being the only exception. He suggested promoting boys-only scholarships like those to encourage girls to go into STEM (science, technology, engineering, and mathematics) fields, but instead to encourage men into what Reeves calls "pink collar" or HEAL fields: health, education, administration, and literacy.

Divorce rates skyrocketed during the feminist movement of the mid- twentieth century. Why? Because a society where women are not dependent on men as providers means that men have to provide family value beyond income. They need to be emotionally available, caregivers, and life part- ners, but there are few models for this version of masculinity. They need to share in domestic duties and contribute to parenting children.[63] Feminism has allowed women to have diverse expressions of their femininity: they can work or not, they can play sports or not, they can wear pants or not. Women have many identities: daughter, wife, mother, employee, volunteer, coach, and friend. Men too often identify with their job. When one's entire identity is contained in a single area, problems in that area have high impact.[64] When women struggle at work, they can fall back on their roles as mothers. For men, there has not been this kind of widespread change.

Despite huge changes for women, men's roles have stayed largely the same in the last half-century. This is not the fault of feminism, but the so-called men-ists who want to support men by holding to a version of manhood that harms the vast majority of men. Society can hold two ideas at the same time. Feminism has improved the conditions of women, and men need help finding their feet in a world where women don't *need them* but want them. Unfortunately, the loudest voices for men's issues have come from the dark corners of the internet and political spheres, not feminists. Social media phenomena like Andrew Tate and scholars like Jordan Peterson purport to support men but offer few positive solutions other than cheering them back into the box. Instead, they use their position to promote misogyny. The problems facing men have solutions that don't hurt women's progress. These men cannot hold two ideas at the same time: that men need help and so do women. It's not black and white. This is not a zero-sum game. Some of what they tell their mostly male audience is helpful and empowering. Tate teaches his millions of followers to take hold of their destiny and be accountable. In the case of Peterson, the ideas are often grounded in sound psychological studies. But in both cases, those nuggets of good messaging are buried behind backward, sexist, and misogynist messaging that is trumpeted either for clickbait or because that too holds their appeal. Although I am alarmed by *what* they say, I'm more often alarmed by *how* they say it: aggressively and angrily. They are the antithesis of the stoic, non-emotional, masculine: posturing falsely, weakly.

What will happen if male teachers don't? Tate got the attention of teachers early because school-aged boys found him online and were parroting his ideas in classrooms. Tate is openly hateful toward women, appearing shirtless in his videos and teaching a young generation of boys how to be "men" by offering boys the old box of masculinity. This includes coercing girls into having sex with them, faking intimacy to convince girls to be videotaped doing sexually explicit things, and committing sexual violence.[65] On webcams and social media, Tate built an empire, charging his audience for online classes that gave them the tools to emulate him. Unfortunately, this advice is geared toward a world that no longer exists. Owing to his behavior and regular run-ins with the law, he was removed from mainstream paths to fame, now most social media platforms have banned him, and he was arrested in Romania in late 2022 on allegations of rape and human trafficking.[66] But *this* is where the next generation is turning for a model of masculinity because adult role models have failed.

Kids are desperate for guidance on women, gender, and sexuality, and if they don't find it through mainstream outlets like school, they will look for it elsewhere, and men like Tate are eager to fill the gap and monetize it. Interviewed by *Education Week*, a teacher from Texas said,

> The younger boys, they're so impressionable. They're definitely at an age where they're trying to figure out, what does it mean to be a man? What kind of man will I become? It seems like the whole Andrew Tate thing captures them.[67]

In Hawaii, another teacher said, "There's been a huge increase in rape jokes that the boys are making... I've been teaching for 17 years, and that's not really a topic that comes up, especially in a joking matter."[68] These teachers are not alone. Tate is forcing us to have these conversations. Education should be timely and relevant and prepare students for a world where Tates exist.

Male teachers and role models play an important role in countering Tate's limited thinking. Jake White, a male teacher in London, published an article in *Newsweek*. He said, "Tate has flipped the narrative around sexual assault, so many young male students are saying things like: 'Well what about these innocent men who haven't actually raped someone, but are in the public eye so are targeted by women who want money.'"[69] This idea is perpetrated by the right to stoke a fear of women: misogyny. White and his colleagues started by handling student comments one at a time, but the volume continued to increase. So he and his colleagues, Jack Glass and Tom Wiltshire, decided to do a school-wide assembly to talk about masculinity. They told students, "We want to show you the other side of what it means to be a man. To be kind and compassionate to everyone."[70] He said he could see the shift in student expression in the assembly as the male teachers spoke out about this. Boys want to be good men. Teachers need to show them how.

While Tate is on teachers' radar, Peterson scares me more because he is a polished, former Harvard professor and psychologist who propounds basically the same ideas. Where Tate discussed accountability, Peterson says that most of his patients need to "grow the hell up, accept some responsibility, live an honorable life."[71] This is probably a good message for some people, but similarly it's the gateway to pretty demeaning messaging about women.

According to Peterson's worldview, masculinity represents order, while femininity represents chaos, the same ancient idea that Confucius promoted with yin and yang. Peterson likes ancient messaging and traditional ideas. He suggests that an excessive presence of femininity is a new problem, and his solution is to return men to positions of power over women. If we knew women's history, we would all roll our eyes because that argument is millennia old. He points to his male-centric history to argue that men held positions of power due to their merit, not privilege. He is also not a historian. He said, "The people who hold that our culture is an oppressive patriarchy, they don't want to admit that the current hierarchy might be predicated on competence."[72] Some women's history would do him good.

He feels a sort of gendered anxiety and loss, which he uses to fuel his rhetoric. He said, "The masculine spirit is under assault."[73] Feminism is attacking the hierarchies and systems that have promoted men at the expense of women's autonomy and liberty. Peterson is not a visionary. He is unable to see a way forward that supports both men and women, and he champions backward movement toward male hierarchy over women as the solution to male problems. He believes that humans are wired for hierarchy. To support his arguments, Peterson relies heavily on the influence of biology, which he sees as a type of fate predicting gendered behavior.[74] He frequently references ancient myths, invoking tales of witches, biblical allegories, and ancient traditions.[75]

He's dangerous because he twists data to support his skewed worldview. For example, he uses studies that show women are twice as likely as men to reproduce to show women's dominance over men and then argue that men need marriage to ground them. Studies show that where men outnumber women or men have fewer marriage prospects, there are higher rates of crime. Under China's one-child policy, for example, in addition to rising rates of female infanticide, violent crime rates doubled as the majority-male population aged.[76] This biological tendency is nuanced and can be curbed by social policy. Marriage certainly benefits men in a variety of ways, but he believes that male violence is the effect of not having romantic or sexual partners. He thinks social policy should be designed to ensure men are married. I don't disagree that men need to be active in family life, but as a cure for male violence women need to be sacrificed to these men? It's not what he's saying, but *how* he proposes to achieve it: "The cure for [male violence] is enforced monogamy. That's actually why monogamy emerges," he says.[77] He flatly believes that forcing women into marriages is a rational solution. To him, women hold all the power in relationships and without "enforced monogamy" would only choose men of higher status, abandoning less socially successful men. Again, this is not a zero-sum game. Challenges facing men should not be resolved by trapping women, literally, in marriages. That *is* in its very essence the definition of misogyny: preference for men *over* women. Society instead must ask: how can we help both men *and* women?

Old models and rhetoric are not helping men. Reeves says, "Without the clear direction and social incentives of the old provider-protector model of manhood, many men are left rudderless, underpowered, drifting."[78]

People like Tate and Peterson are the old "Custodians of the Patriarchy" fighting to maintain their dominance as others work to reimagine the system.[79] Testosterone, like estrogen, has profound impacts on our lives and development. Yet for boys, testosterone-fueled masculinity has been something to punish. A mostly female teaching force has tried to temper toxic masculinity instead of teaching masculinity. Reeves adds that there is "a desperate need for some positive, male-specific guidance, which is now missing in mainstream culture."[80]

One challenge that feminists, me included, have struggled to articulate is that these traps of masculinity, sometimes called "toxic" masculinity, do not mean that masculinity itself is bad. In fact, quite the opposite. The qualities of masculinity should be cherished. These include decisiveness, rationality, control, toughness, coolness under pressure, strength, competitiveness, logic, forcefulness, autonomy, self-sufficiency, and emotional regulation.[81] We need to coach young men to harness these qualities in service of their communities, not at the expense of various members of the community, including women.

Feminism, advocacy for gender equality, helps boys. Like girls, boys need a new narrative and model for their role in society. The answer is not backward toward oppression, but forward. But we must welcome these conversations into our classrooms. We have had decades to discuss and debate women's new roles, keeping the bits we liked about the old (empathy, compassion, etc.) and tossing what we don't (weakness, dependence, etc.). Now we need to do it in our schools and give young people direction. We need to help hold the social fabric together, families together, through a new view of womanhood and manhood. There will inevitably be debates about solutions, but we can't solve the problem if we aren't having the conversation and preparing young people.

There are so many people talking about gender in the world, but it's chaotic, toxic, and fueled by political rhetoric. Students need trusted adult role models trained in discussing controversial pedagogy and gender studies to talk about gender issues in schools. There, in a rigorous academic setting, studies can be presented, causality examined, and students can form their own conclusions.

Finally, I'm a purist when I read Title IX. This section of the Civil Rights Law of 1972 prohibits sex-based discrimination in schools and education programs receiving federal funding. How can we honestly look at a curriculum that is 5 percent or even 20 percent centered on male experiences and say it isn't discriminatory? That is the essence of discriminating: discerning, separating women out, biased toward men, prejudiced against the female experience. All those issues are caked in the present coverage of women's lives in primary and secondary classrooms. Teachers must teach women's history to give women equal educational opportunity and the chance to know their history, and if we are to get all social studies teachers on board, we are talking about mostly men.

Should Teachers Use the F Word?

Gender is greater than any other social condition in its impact on human life, expression, and experience.[82] It impacts men and women equally, daily, individually, and intimately. So why aren't we teaching it? Should teachers use the F word? A teacher could try to teach women's history in a substantive way, but how will that help her if her students complain about her feminism and biases? Will her administration have her back? Can she defend herself using state standards and textbooks as a reference? Will her students still test well on subject exams? Is the community ready to look our historical biases and sexism in the eye?

In 2022, four scholars did two experiments to test male responses to people who "challenge or legitimize societal gender inequality." Their conclusion was mixed and rather confusing:

> Men respond more negatively toward women who challenge, compared to legitimize, the gender hierarchy. Conversely, men respond more negatively toward men, compared to women, who legitimize the gender hierarchy on an explicit level. It thus can be beneficial for women to legitimize the gender hierarchy and, in fact, they seem to "get away with it," while for men this is socially undesirable. Although legitimizing the gender hierarchy might have personal benefits for women, it results in maintaining the gender hierarchy… While challenging the gender hierarchy comes with a cost for women personally, it can have great impact to effectively elicit social change by activating men to pursue gender equality.[83]

In other words, for women it's better to stay silent on gender inequities to protect friendships, but practically they benefit from feminism. For men, promoting women's status in society helps them. So should teachers use the F word? It depends on their gender and the gender of the people they are talking to.

Outside of the classroom, activists have studied the best ways to market feminism to a male audience and bring them on board with pro-feminist perspectives. One study examined the aftermath of the #MeToo Movement in China. A Chinese woman died from arson burns inflicted by her male partner. This invigorated dialogues about women's rights all over social media, especially a popular app called WeChat where scholars studied commentary in the public accounts. Studying these discourses, scholars found that men were more persuaded by ideas that centered women's humanity, and the universality of freedom, rather than this being a "women's issue". The scholars explained,

> Human interest was the most frequently used frame by all types of WPA [WeChat public accounts] authors (79.8%). Without touching political controversy, human interest became the safest means of persuasion, through which social media influencers intended to arouse emotions applicable to all human beings, such as empathy, caring, and outrage, by illustrating women's specific sufferings.[84]

So if that is what is palatable, is that not what teachers should do? Teach women's history from within the frame of universally agreed upon human needs and values? Essentially, the answer is stop using the F word. Instead, use inclusion. Instead, point out that women's exclusion is inaccurate history.

Some scholars have pointed out that this is "skirting" around feminism to make it more digestible. I wonder if the end justifies the means? Mardi Schmeichel examined published lesson plans and articles used in social studies curriculum about women. In her study, she found that while women and divisive ideas were discussed, there was an almost complete absence of controversial vocabulary. In the 16 lesson plans that met the selection criteria, only one explicitly stated that the purpose was to promote gender equality.[85] The majority (8) justified the inclusion of women's history by offering a technical focus like examining primary sources. Five aimed to "offset" the lack of focus on women, which Schmeichel didn't consider an explicitly feminist purpose (Table 3.1).[86]

She also selected 33 articles published in social studies journals and magazines with at least one descriptor about both instruction and gender. She wanted to find articles that were essentially describing lesson plans or activities for students that centered on gender. She then evaluated them for the

Table 3.1 Mardi Schmeichel Finds That Most Teachers Skirt around Feminism In Their Expressed Purposes For Their Lessons on Women

Purpose of the Lesson	Total
Technical focus	8
Offsetting deficit of attention to women in curriculum	5
Working toward gender equity	2
No rationale	1

Source: Eckert's table with data from Mardi Schmeichel, "Skirting around critical feminist rationales for teaching women in social studies," *Theory & Research in Social Education*, 2015, 43(1), 7.

"degree" to which they emphasized women's history or women's issues. In 33 articles, she said, "there are no references to gender bias, feminism, patriarchy, or sexism in these articles. The word 'feminist' appears twice but only in references. In one instance, it is within the title of a book about Alice Paul, and in the other, it is embedded within a citation of a publication produced by the Feminist Press publishing house."[87] Schmeichel found and worries that the teachers are shying away from critical feminist discussions. This article about suffrage, for example, was framed as promoting civic values rather than women's agency against the patriarchy. Aren't both true? She writes:

> [T]he absence of these terms from the lesson plans is conspicuous. Although there may be a range of ways to work against gender inequity without using the words 'feminism' or 'sexism,' for example, the use of these words, as well as the feminist label, and the invitation to a critical stance they offer, does matter. Their absence points to the work of politics, power, and identification and leads us to question the connection between the absence of these terms and the lack of attention in the lesson plans to systemic political, economic, and cultural structures and potentially uncomfortable explorations of women's status in society. These concerns, which reflect feminist arguments for including women in curriculum, would seem to be salient in lesson plans that promote attention to women in a field that has largely ignored these topics. Yet these ideas are not present in the texts.

[88]Ultimately, getting students to see, question, and evaluate gender in their own contexts is the goal. Are teachers failing if they don't address them?

In the UK, Richard Stopford also studied the challenges of what he called "teaching feminism." He wrote that

> [F]or some students, learning about feminism can be a confounding, confusing and hostile experience. While likely true, it is too quick and obvious to point out that this is because the student is, in some way or other, committed against feminism. After all, one can learn something and yet disagree with it.[89]

Schools open students to ideas and points of view that are new to them, and they may not agree with all of them. But feminism in particular poses particular challenges because, as he puts it, "feminist claims can clash with students' sense of self and world."[90]

From my own experience of teaching in a conservative school district, I know teachers are trying to subtly insert conversations about gender without politicizing the classroom. In many cases, they are not ready to take on the F word. I may be copping out here, but I think, at least initially, this is an okay step in the phases of implementing women and gender studies into social studies curriculum. Teachers are skirting around it because they are in the trenches of political discourse. Scholars and professors of women's studies and women's history often speak from privileged positions at universities where they have academic freedom and/or disconnect it from the realities of public schools. Having taught in rural public schools, I know firsthand how challenging it is to teach with feminist pedagogies and ideologies. Sadly, when I dropped the F word, I felt the ideas were better received.

But teachers should have Schmeichel in the back of their head when she says,

> In P–12 and social studies teacher education practice, the silence on feminism is deafening. The women's and feminist movement and the explosion of scholarship in women's and gender studies in the rest of academia have had very little impact on the traditional social studies curriculum in the United States.[91]

She's not wrong. I will explore this further in Chapter 5, but we aren't there yet.

Resources for Feminist History
Recommended Reading: Books About Feminism and Women's Publications

Not all feminist writing is written for the public. In fact, a lot of it is written for a scholarly audience already accustomed to certain terminology. Sometimes that space can be an echo chamber. I was thrilled when I read *Feminism is for Everybody* by bell hooks (she purposefully leaves her name lowercase to emphasize her ideas). To me, she made feminism approachable and included women and men of all classes in the struggle while breaking down complex topics.

It's also incredibly helpful to stay current on women's issues and ideas. Subscribing to a women's news outlet will help you take that perspective. Consider *The Lilly*, the *Washington Post's* women's publication, *Ms. Magazine*, the *19th*, or get news summarized for you by *The Skim*. These are just a few of the news outlets that produce news and information about the world from a women's lens with women figures at the center of it. Reading from these sources, bringing their authors and contributors into your repertoire of perspectives to consider, will help you better include half of the world. Tackling the barriers that persist for women today means staying current with the world as it impacts and is impacted by women.

Sample Inquiry: Should Social Reform Movements, Like Temperance, Be Intersectional?

Most Americans would fail a basic test of the temperance movement, including perhaps the most important fact: that this was the largest, most successful movement in US women's history. Teaching the temperance movement is often done poorly. Few teachers I've encountered, let alone Americans, can name any of the major players in the movement. Teachers often fail to explore the nuances and debates *between* women about laws, enforcement, and intersectionality. Centering the people, not prohibition, brings the story to life. When those people are centered, the "moral crusade" is no longer monolithic and women's diversity is on full display. This is juicy history. When an opportunity exists for women's voices to be heard and read, and their diversity acknowledged, *shouldn't we be capitalizing on it?*

The WCTU thrived in a time before women had the right to vote. Women and their allies had to puzzle through how to use their power as citizens, women, and mothers to draw attention to drunkenness and its impact on women as well as productive and domestic life. The WCTU had epic debates: Should they also endorse suffrage? Or would suffrage distract from the issue they cared most about?

While the WCTU eventually decided to endorse suffrage under the leadership of Frances Willard, she was unwilling to back other intersectional issues.[92] Ida B. Wells-Barnett, an avid reformer, anti-lynching advocate, and journalist, asked Willard to take an anti-lynching position, but she refused. The two took to the press.[93] Eventually, under mounting pressure, the WCTU made statements against lynching, but the damage was done. Neither Willard nor Wells-Barnett redacted their earlier comments.

The intersectionality of reform movements gives students context for the complexity of reform efforts and the pattern of division by people who should be allies. It also gives students examples of women like Willard who are remarkable leaders and heroes but complex, flawed, and wrong in other respects. Students need to see more examples of women being complicated to understand the real complicated women in their lives today. And how amazing is it that we can examine these issues using quotes and sources from the women themselves?!

To reach the feminist stage of history, teachers need to include the ideas, lives, and experiences of women outside the radical women who so often dominate history classes. Finding the experiences of non-feminist and poor women can help make this interesting. Teachers can also look at how the layers of race and sexuality impact people's perspectives. The following inquiry reexamines the overarching white narrative and asks questions to highlight women's diversity. It was built using an outstanding online guide from the Frances Willard Museum that is also worth exploring. It is downloadable on the Remedial Herstory Project's website.

Should social reform movements, like temperance, be intersectional?

Intersectional means the interconnected nature of social categorizations such as race, class, and gender. Temperance was largely a reform movement for women; should it also take a stand for issues of white violence effecting the Black community? In this inquiry, students will examine contrasting primary source accounts and form their own conclusions on whether temperance reform should have been intersectional. And was lynching an issue that temperance reformers should consider speaking out on? This inquiry will also expose students to harmful stereotypes from the late 1800s about Black men. Students will expose the claim that Black men were a threat to white women in the South.

Document A: Frances Willard "Do Everything"

Frances Willard was the second president of the WCTU and a vocal supporter of entwining women's suffrage and temperance reform. During her tenure, she made the temperance movement the most powerful women's political movement of the period.

"When we began the delicate, difficult, and dangerous operation of dissecting out the alcohol nerve from the body politic, we did not realize the intricacy of the undertaking nor the distances that must be traversed by the scalpel of investigation and research... The "Do Everything Policy" was not of our choosing but is an evolution as inevitable as any traced by the naturalist or described by the historian... A one-sided movement makes one-sided advocates. Virtues, like hounds, hunt in packs... An all-round movement can only be carried forward by all-round advocates; a scientific age requires the study of every subject in its correlations. It was once supposed that light, heat, and electricity were wholly separate entities; it is now believed and practically proved that they are but different modes of motion. Standing in the valley we look up and think we see an isolated mountain; climbing to its top we see that it is but one member of a range of mountains many of them of well-nigh equal altitude."

Willard, Frances. Address before the Second Biennial Convention of the World's Woman's Christian Temperance Union, and the Twentieth Annual Convention of the National Women's Christian Temperance Union. London: White Ribbon Publishing Co., 1893.

Source
1. Who is the source of this document and what position are they in?

Document
2. What does the author mean by "do everything"?
3. What does the author mean by "all-round"?

Analysis
4. What sorts of things do you think would be helpful in achieving these goals?
5. Would an intersectional effort fall under her vision of "Doing Everything?"

Document B: Ida B. Wells

Willard's "Do Everything" policy required some persuasion to include issues that most affected Black people in the South, namely lynching. Despite claiming that she had "not an atom of race prejudice" because her family were abolitionists, Willard stated, "We ought to have put an educational test upon that ballot from the first. The Anglo-Saxon race will never submit to be dominated by the Negro so long as his aptitude reaches no higher than the personal liberty of the saloon." After these remarks were published, Ida B. Wells, a fellow temperance reformer and a fierce anti-lynching advocate and suffragist, called foul.

All things considered, our race is probably not more intemperate than other races. By reason, though, of poverty, ignorance, and consequent degradation as a mass, we are behind in general advancement...

Miss Francis E. Willard, president of the National Women's Christian Temperance Union, lately told the world that the center of power of the race is the saloon; that white men for this reason are afraid to leave their homes; that the Negro in the late prohibition campaign, sold his vote for twenty-five cents, etc.

"Miss Willard's statements possess the small pro rata of truth of all such sweeping statements. It is well known that the Negro's greatest injury is done to himself."

Wells-Barnett. "Temperance and Race Progress." AME Church Review. Last modified 1891. Retrieved from https://scalar.usc.edu/works/willard-and-wells/ida-b-wells-temperance?path=timeline.

Source
6. Who is the source of this document and what position are they in?

Document
7. Why is the author critical of Willard?
8. In the context of temperance reform, what does she mean by "the Negro's greatest injury is done to himself"?
9. Does this disagreement move the temperance movement forward? Explain.

Analysis
10. What do you think would be the best way for Willard to respond to this critique?

Document C: Ida B. Wells

Wells traveled in Europe giving speeches that publicly called out Willard and others for doing nothing about lynching.

"I find wherever I go that we are deprived the expression of condemnation such hangings and burnings deserve, because the world believes negro men are despoilers of the virtue of white women. … Unfortunately for the negro race and for themselves, Miss Frances E. Willard and Bishops Fitzgerald and Haygood have published utterances in confirmation of this slander."

Wells, Ida B. Alfreda M. Duster, Ed. Crusade for Justice: The Autobiography of Ida B. Wells. *Chicago: University of Chicago Press, 1970.*

Analysis
11. What do you think would be the best way for Willard to respond to this critique?

Document D: Frances Willard

Willard encourages the WCTU to pass an anti-lynching resolution, but the word lynching is removed from it after pushback by white southern members of the WCTU. Wells did not stop criticizing her in the press. Willard and her friends defended their characters against Wells's attacks. Wells accused them of caring more about their reputations than the plight of Black people. At subsequent annual convention, Willard proposed a new anti-lynching resolution. This was her letter to the WCTU leadership encouraging this resolution. Does she seem to care about lynching or her reputation?

I feel sure it will do much to silence the absurd outcry against us that is made by those who have heard only one side of the question and hence have received an entirely false impression concerning the attitude of the W.C.T. U. You know, dear friend, of the difficulty in which I have been placed by those most unjust controversy and I feel sure that you will do all in your power to help secure the unanimous adoption of the resolution. Let me say that it is my earnest hope to make a trip through the South in company with Lady Henry Somerset as soon as possible. Just when I cannot say but it is more on my mind than any other one line of work in "my own my native land."

Frances Willard responds to Ida B. Wells and proposes a draft resolution against lynching for the WCTU. Retrieved from https://scalar.usc.edu/works/willard-and-wells/letter-from-frances-willard-july-3-1895-2.

Analysis
12. Does she seem to care about lynching or her reputation?

Overall, do you think the temperance movement should have been intersectional and include an anti-lynching position, or does that deter from their overall aims?

Notes

1 Martell and Stevens, "Perceptions of Teaching Race and Gender: Results of a Survey of Social Studies Teachers," 284.

2 Margaret Smith Crocco, "The Missing Discourse About Gender and Sexuality in the Social Studies," *Theory Into Practice: Rethinking the Social Studies*, Vol 40, No. 1, February 2001, 66.

3 Martell and Stevens, "Perceptions of Teaching Race and Gender: Results of a Survey of Social Studies Teachers," 280.

4 Scheiner-Fisher, "The Inclusion of Women's History In The Secondary Social Studies Classroom," 42.

5 66.2 gave the same excuse for teaching about race.

6 Martell and Stevens, "Perceptions of Teaching Race and Gender: Results of a Survey of Social Studies Teachers," 283.

7 Martell and Stevens, "Perceptions of Teaching Race and Gender: Results of a Survey of Social Studies Teachers," 283.

8 Bridget Lockyer and Abigail Tazzymant, "'Victims of History': challenging students' perceptions of women in history," Teaching History (165): 8 Historical Association 2016 0040-0610, 12.

9 Loewen, *Lies My Teacher Told Me*, 9.

10 Loewen, *Lies My Teacher Told Me*, 9–10.

11 Miles, *Women's History of the World*, 12.

12 Noddings, "The Care Tradition: Beyond 'Add Women and Stir'" 29.

13 Noddings, "The Care Tradition: Beyond 'Add Women and Stir'" 29.

14 Noddings, "The Care Tradition: Beyond 'Add Women and Stir'" 30.

15 Noddings, "The Care Tradition: Beyond 'Add Women and Stir'" 30.

16 Noddings, "The Care Tradition: Beyond 'Add Women and Stir'" 30.

17 Alison Bechdel, "Bechdel Test," Bechdel Test, n.d., https://bechdeltest.com/

18 Johnson, *The Gender Knot*, 10.

19 Johnson, *The Gender Knot*, 5.

20 Jocelyn Nichole Murphy, "The role of women in film: Supporting the men -- An analysis of how culture influences the changing discourse on gender representations in film" (2015). *Journalism Undergraduate Honors Theses*, 2, http://scholarworks.uark.edu/jouruht/

21 Miles, *The Women's History of the World*, 15.

22 The National Council for the Social Studies, *The College, Career, and Civic Life (C3) Framework for the Social Studies*, (Silver Spring, MD: NCSS, 2017) retrieved from https://www.socialstudies.org/sites/default/files/c3/c3-framework-for-social-studies-rev0617.pdf

23 Robert Pondiscio, "The Not-So Great Society," *Heritage*, April 15, 2020, https://www.heritage.org/curricula-resource-initiative/research/the-not-so-great-society

24 Alan Singer, "How the NCSS Sold Out Social Studies and History," *History News Network*, December 16, 2014, https://historynewsnetwork.org/article/157845

25 Harrison W. Mark, "Women's March on Versailles," *World History Encyclopedia*, June 28, 2022. https://www.worldhistory.org/Women's_March_on_Versailles/

26 Hollie McDonald, "Social Politics of Seventeenth Century London Coffee Houses: An Exploration of Class and Gender" Honors Projects, 2013, 208, http://scholarworks.gvsu.edu/honorsprojects/208

27 "Discussion of Women's Political Clubs and Their Suppression, 29–30 October 1793." LIBERTY, EQUALITY, FRATERNITY: EXPLORING THE FRENCH REVOUTION. https://revolution.chnm.org/d/294

28 Laurel Thatcher Ulrich, *Well-Behaved Women Seldom Make History*, *1st Ed* (New York: Alfred A. Knopf, 2007), xiii.

29 Kathleen Kuiper, "Olympe de Gouges," *Encyclopedia Britannica*, October 30, 2022, https://www.britannica.com/biography/Olympe-de-Gouges

30 Rosalind Miles, *Women's History of the Modern World: how radicals, rebels, and every woman revolutionized the last 200 years* (New York : William Morrow, 2021), 22.

31 MacDonald, "The Need for Contextual ReVision," 214.

32 Whitney Barrigner, Lauren Brand, and Nichloas Kryczka, "No such thing as a bad question?" *Perspectives on History*, Vol. 61: 6, September 2023, 28.

33 Whitney Barrigner, Lauren Brand, and Nichloas Kryczka, "No such thing as a bad question?" *Perspectives on History*, Vol. 61: 6, September 2023, 28.

34 Patti Lather, "Critical frames in educational research: Feminist and poststructural perspectives," *Theory into Practice*, 1992, 31(2), 87–99.

35 Tetreault, "Integrating Women's History," 216.

36 More on this in Chapter Six.

37 Kansas Historical Society, "Carrie Nation" *Kansas Historical Society, Kansaspedia*, August 2017, https://www.kshs.org/kansapedia/carry-a-nation/15502

38 Women and the American Story, "Life Story: Weetamoo (c.1635-1676)," *New York Historical Society*, October 16, 2020, https://wams.nyhistory.org/early-encounters/english-colonies/weetamoo/

39 Lisa Brooks, *Our Beloved Kin: A New History of King Philip's War* (New Haven: Yale University Press, 2018), https://doi.org/10.2307/j.ctt1z27jbr, 169.

40 Brooks, *Our Beloved Kin*, 255.
41 Kaylene M. Stevens and Christopher C. Martell, An avenue for challenging sexism: Examining the high school sociology classroom, *Journal of Social Science Education*, 15(1), 2016, 70.
42 Stevens and Martell, "Feminist Social Studies Teachers," 8.
43 Stevens and Martell, "Feminist Social Studies Teachers," 8.
44 bell hooks, *Feminism is for Everybody* (Cambridge, MA: South End Press, 2000), viii.
45 Karen Offen, "On the French origin of the words feminism and feminist," *Gender Issues*. 8 (1988). 45-46. 10.1007/BF02685596.
46 Mardi Schmeichel, "Skirting around critical feminist rationales for teaching women in social studies," *Theory & Research in Social Education*, 2015, 43(1), 2.
47 L. S. Levstik and J. Groth, "Scary thing, being an eighth grader": Exploring gender and sexuality in a middle school U.S. history unit." *Theory & Research in Social Education*, 30, 2002, 244. doi:10.1080/00933104.2002.1047 3193.
48 Levstik and Groth, "Scary thing, being an eighth grader," 249.
49 Levstik and Groth, "Scary thing, being an eighth grader," 197.
50 Schmeichel, "Skirting around critical feminist rationales for teaching women in social studies," 2.
51 Johnson, *The Gender Knot*, 5.
52 Margaret Smith Crocco, "The missing discourse about gender and sexuality in the social studies," *Theory into Practice*, 40(1), February 2001, 65.
53 CDC, "Suicide Data and Statistics," Center for Disease Control, May 11, 2023, https://www.cdc.gov/suicide/suicide-data-statistics.html.
54 Gordon Hodson, Megan Earle, and Maureen A. Craig, "Privilege lost: How dominant groups react to shifts in cultural primacy and power," *Group Processes & Intergroup Relations* 2022 25:3, 628.
55 Hodson, Earle, and Craig, "Privilege lost," 628.
56 Reeves, *Of Boys and Men*, 5.
57 Reeves, *Of Boys and Men*, 5.
58 Reeves, *Of Boys and Men*, 6-7.
59 Reeves, *Of Boys and Men*, 11.
60 Reeves, *Of Boys and Men*, 7.
61 Reeves, *Of Boys and Men*, 51.
62 Reeves, *Of Boys and Men*, 135.
63 Eve Rodsky, *Fair Play: Fair Play: A Game-Changing Solution for When You Have Too Much to Do (and More Life to Live)*, (New York: Putnam and Sons, 2021).
64 Reeves, *Of Boys and Men*, 32.

65 EJ Dickson, Adam Rawnsley, and Stefania Matache, "Andrew Tate Built an Empire on Bullshit: Here's the real story," *The Rolling Stone*, March 15, 2023, https://www.rollingstone.com/culture/culture-features/andrew-tate-empire-real-story-1234696706/

66 Jenny Gross, "Andrew Tate Is Released From Jail and Placed Under House Arrest," *The New York Times*, April 3, 2023. https://www.nytimes.com/2023/04/03/world/europe/andrew-tate-house-arrest-romania.html?login=smartlock&auth=login-smartlock

67 Madeline Will, "Misogynist Influencer Andrew Tate Has Captured Boys' Attention. What Teachers Need to Know," *Education Week*, February 2, 2023, https://www.edweek.org/leadership/misogynist-influencer-andrew-tate-has-captured-boys-attention-what-teachers-need-to-know/2023/02

68 Madeline Will, "Misogynist Influencer Andrew Tate Has Captured Boys' Attention. What Teachers Need to Know."

69 Jake White, "I'm a Teacher. Andrew Tate Is Dangerous, So I'm Doing Something About it," *Newsweek*, February 28, 2023, https://www.newsweek.com/andrew-tate-teacher-school-misogyny-1783709

70 White, "I'm a Teacher."

71 Nellie Bowles, "Jordan Peterson, Custodian of the Patriarchy: He says there's a crisis in masculinity. Why won't women — all these wives and witches — just behave?" *New York Times*, May 18, 2018, https://www.nytimes.com/2018/05/18/style/jordan-peterson-12-rules-for-life.html

72 Bowles, "Jordan Peterson, Custodian of the Patriarchy."

73 Bowles, "Jordan Peterson, Custodian of the Patriarchy."

74 Reeves, *Of Boys and Men*, 123.

75 Bowles, "Jordan Peterson, Custodian of the Patriarchy."

76 Reeves, *Of Boys and Men*, 91.

77 Bowles, "Jordan Peterson, Custodian of the Patriarchy."

78 Richard V. Reeves, "Andrew Tate and the Wests Lost Boys," Unheard. October 30, 2022. https://unherd.com/2022/10/andrew-tate-and-the-wests-lost-boys/

79 Bowles, "Jordan Peterson, Custodian of the Patriarchy."

80 Richard V. Reeves, "Andrew Tate and the Wests Lost Boys," Unheard. October 30, 2022. https://unherd.com/2022/10/andrew-tate-and-the-wests-lost-boys/

81 Johnson, *The Gender Knot*, 7.

82 Robert Strayer and E. Nelson, *Ways Of The World, 3rd ed* (Boston: Bedford/St. Martin's, 2016).

83 Ilona Domen, Daan Scheepers, Belle Derks, and Ruth Van Veelen, "It's a man's world, right? How women's opinions about gender inequality

affect physiological responses in men," *Group Processes & Intergroup Relations*, 25:721.2022. 10.1177/13684302211042669.

84 Xinying Yang, Hongfeng Qiu, and Ranran Zhu, "Bargaining with patriarchy or converting men into pro-feminists: social-mediated frame alignment in feminist connective activism," *Feminist Media Studies*, 12, 2022. 10.1080/14680777.2022.2075909.

85 Schmeichel, "Skirting around critical feminist rationales for teaching women in social studies," 7.

86 Schmeichel, "Skirting around critical feminist rationales for teaching women in social studies," 7.

87 Schmeichel, "Skirting around critical feminist rationales for teaching women in social studies," 13.

88 Schmeichel, "Skirting around critical feminist rationales for teaching women in social studies," 13–14.

89 Richard Stopford, "Teaching feminism: Problems of critical claims and student certainty," *Philosophy and Social Criticism*, 2020, Vol. 46(10), 1204.

90 Stopford, "Teaching feminism," 1204.

91 Schmeichel, "Skirting around critical feminist rationales for teaching women in social studies," 3.

92 Frances Willard House Museum, "Introduction," Truth-Telling: Frances Willard and Ida B. Wells, n.d. https://scalar.usc.edu/works/willard-and-wells/introduction?path=index

93 Frances Willard House Museum, "The WCTU and Lynching, 1893," Truth-Telling: Frances Willard and Ida B. Wells, n.d. https://scalar.usc.edu/works/willard-and-wells/1893-wctu-anti-lynching-resolution?path=timeline

4

Representation Matters

When we remember these women we can become inspired, empowered, and enlightened. History helps us to learn about ourselves and reminds us to continue to strive for greatness.[1]

—Ann Varner

Think of the irony of being a young girl in school who is regularly told that you are "equal now" because some laws have been passed in the last century, but entire lessons go by in your history class in which not one woman is mentioned. In our economy, women remain burdened with the challenge of balancing career with family. Some try and do it all, but in most cases, family responsibilities and domestic labor disproportionately impact women. The repercussions of this ripple through our economy, impacting the available labor force and couple's purchasing power. Women remain the vast minority of political leaders despite being the majority of voters. So, whom are teachers preparing for college, career, and civic life?

The C3 Framework for the Social Studies aims to prepare students for College, Career, and Civic Life. Those three areas tend to dominate the focus of most social studies standards, but college, career, and civic life for whom? By omitting explicit conversations about women's historical exclusion from these spaces, girls are less equipped to make wise career decisions. Further, by excluding family life from this list, the National Council for the Social Studies (NCSS) has made frank that these standards are for those unburdened by childcare, elderly care, and other social responsibilities that often

DOI: 10.4324/9781003472889-5

fall to women. They have defined the social studies to exclude the "social" epicenter: the home.

Shifting what teachers discuss in social studies could not be more pressing. There is evidence that 60 percent of the economic growth experienced since World War II was due to the growing numbers of women in the workforce. Therefore, how family life impacts women's careers is worthy of academic study in the classroom. Women have come so far, but as Helen Reddy put it, "I'm still an embryo with a long, long way to go."[2]

They say, "If you can see it, you can be it." In this chapter, I add that you need women civic leaders to make structural changes for girls to "achieve it." Women are more likely to champion women-friendly policy in politics and on the job. We need more women in those positions of power. Helping girls see themselves in leadership positions in history books and at the front of classrooms can be an important first step in social progress.

As discussed in Chapter 3, there are particular and difficult challenges facing men. Here we will discuss those impacting women. Let's not switch tracks. Intellectuals can hold two ideas at the same time: men have challenges and so do women. When one reads from women scholars, you'll notice that almost all take a moment to state the facts. In a 2015 article for *Theory & Research in Social Education*, Mardi Schmeichel wrote, "If you think we are living in a post-sexist world, you are wrong."[3] She continued:

> Gender inequality is not something we have moved beyond... Although contexts have changed, very similar conversations emerged in the domain in the Women's Rights Movements of the 1960s and 1970s. What is different now is that these conversations, and the negative attitudes regarding women that have surfaced because of them, are rearing their heads at a time in which the feminist stance that could empower women and girls to push back against this rhetoric has been positioned as unpalatable and irrelevant.[4]

Feminist theories fall in line with broader approaches in social science, yet the sexist forces have worked hard to make feminism disagreeable and exclude women's topics from curriculum.

It's impossible to discuss representation for women without exploring the ways in which economies restrain the choices for mothers specifically. The fallacy that women are equal now or have equal opportunity permeates our culture and perpetuates the barriers to women's inclusion—and it just doesn't stand up to fact. Much more must be done to dismantle the hurdles that women face, and teachers aren't even starting the conversations in their classes. How can we be *social* studies teachers if we aren't discussing social issues that impact every family? This chapter will explore the challenges facing women today by using data and fascinating case studies. It will consistently come back to the idea that how money is invested reflects society's value systems and that the failure to adequately compensate women for their labor reflects society's devaluing of women's contributions. We need inquiries that address these issues in our classrooms yesterday.

It's Not Just History

Background: Being a Woman With a Career

Although I am a teacher, I was a teacher in a male field. I was also a varsity soccer coach; around 30 percent of all high school varsity coaches are women, which means that most girls who play sports have male coaches.[5] The challenges I faced in my career were not unique: they are represented in study after study. My life and career are emblematic of the problems facing women and families everywhere.

When I began my career as a social studies teacher, I had very few female role models—even as a millennial. All my social studies teachers in high school were men. In undergrad, the entire history department was male. I sometimes wonder if that's why I declared Political Science, where there were female professors, and my male advisor went out of his way to tell me I belonged in the all-male freshman class. It was only in graduate school that I encountered women historians. As I moved toward teacher certification, there were few women social studies teachers in the state to observe. In my first job, I joined a predominantly male social studies department, led by a male department head, under a male principal. *Does the maleness that dominated my experience matter?* No—it shouldn't! Generally, I had a great deal of support from the school and community. At times, though, it was hard to discern whether challenges I faced were just the normal challenges of public education, working on a team of unique people, because I was new, young, or a woman. It could have been any or all of them.

Although everyone faces challenges in the workplace, I faced those *and* those driven by sexism. The most egregious offense occurred during a soccer game I was coaching. I used an offside trap, and the referee was slow and out of position and routinely missed that players on the other team were offsides (meaning they are out of bounds and shouldn't be allowed to play the ball). When an opposing player scored from way offsides, I was indignant. If you've never watched a soccer game before, coaches yell sometimes. Most of my male coaches yelled when I was a player. So, I yelled from the sidelines, "She was offsides!" It was a fact. The referee, who happened to be the head assigner for referees in the state, ran from where he was on the field directly at me, yellow card raised. He berated me for what felt like minutes. He was challenging me to "Say it again! Say it again! You know what's coming!" and bullying me with the threat of a red card and game expulsion. It was sickening. I stepped backward, away from the pitch, in a gesture to show that I was stepping down and stood with my hands at my side silently and took it to model how I would like my players to behave in their interactions with refs. Satisfied that he had dominated me into submission, he swaggered away. I watched silently the rest of the game as the opposing male coach's challenges to the referee went unthreatened.

After the game, I privately asked the other coach, who was a nice guy, what the referee's name was so I could report the incident. He widened his eyes to say, "Yeah, that was bad" and gave me his name. The referee saw us talking and again crossed the pitch to yell at me. It is hard to describe how puffed up, red-faced, and aggressive he was to convey just how scary the threat of violence was. He was so hostile toward me, fathers of my players on the sideline crossed to stand between us. He was escorted off the field by the other referee all while threatening to get me fired and calling me gendered and belittling things like "a bad little girl!" as he went. I was 31 at the time. I must restate for the sake of understanding the absurdity that this incident happened at a high school soccer game over a coach yelling a fact from the sidelines. Thankfully, the Athletic Director's daughter was on my team and had witnessed the entire thing. My school filed a complaint. We never saw him at games again.

I had to deal with the fear of physical violence *at my workplace*. I had to decide whether this incident would change the way I talked with referees. I also had to deal with the reality that I was one of the *only* woman coaches whom players on the two teams would see all season. Some of those girls may want to be coaches one day. The bus ride home from the game and the practices that followed were haunted by the incident. Players brought it up as scary and uncomfortable. *What did my players learn? When you are a strong woman, you get threatened and verbally abused by men? Were they inspired by my resilience or scared by the scenario?* If I changed how I acted, I would be showing my girls that strong women cower to powerful men. I had a few days to sit with it before our next game and decided that I had to be myself and coach the way I always did. I couldn't let sexism change the way I did my job. I had to be brave. That season, our team made school history, going further in the end-of-season tournament than ever before.

This guy was a bad egg, for sure. The male leaders in my school and even dads on the sidelines rallied to my defense. This incident was the worst of the kinds of everyday sexism I dealt with on my job. Very little was done about the many times I was called a "bitch" and a "whore" by students or talked down to or over in meetings. In all these incidents, no action was taken by the administration, because these behaviors are *normalized in our culture*. Certainly, these incidents could actually be commentary on ineffective administration. I was often praised by my superiors for how well I handled tough cases and got through to kids. So maybe from their perspectives I didn't need help handling it. Either way, managing the sexism of the community fell on me. Since it was kids, I had to adopt an attitude that these are just words and these young men desperately need my love and support. I was able to shift my thinking and not take offense. I was on my own to cope with it, and I developed some thick skin.

All in all, things were fine, and I was dealing with it—then everything changed when I became a mom. I went from finishing my third ironman triathlon in August to being in the worst physical condition I'd ever been in by June. What had previously been questionable sexist experiences or chalked up to bad eggs was now systemic and all-encompassing. The inequity of all of it was palpable. My husband and I both became parents that year, but I had to endure a three-day labor which ended in an emergency delivery and two surgeries over the next year and half. It's no one's fault that women are the ones to have babies—it is our society's fault for what we do next. I had to deal with an out-of-the-ordinary painful recovery while caring for a baby alone. *I* needed a caregiver, but my husband was given only a couple weeks of parent leave by his school. I wasn't even cleared to sit up on my own before he went back to work.

I was able to piece together five months of paid leave, small fractions of what I would have had in other countries but still much more than most mothers in the US. During that time, I developed postpartum depression (PPD). PPD is common in complicated birth situations. One in ten women develops it. For me, it was the combination of a difficult birth, a recovery that lasted many months instead of weeks, a colicky baby, and being *completely* out of any routine. I had never had depression before. When people describe me, energetic and enthusiastic are usually in the top five descriptors. Not during that period. I was lethargic, moody, and angry; I cried constantly, and every single day I thought about dying. I couldn't imagine going back to work, but I also knew that nothing about my thoughts sounded like me. I started to jokingly make decisions based on "What would old-Kelsie do?" I decided she would have gone back to work, so I did. Work saved me. Work gave me purpose, and I slowly became myself again.

Why is PPD important? It's no one's fault if a woman gets PPD; it is the government and health-care system's fault that there aren't better procedures in place. PPD is underdiagnosed—I diagnosed myself and on my own sought a therapist to help me cope. She confirmed that this was PPD. *Why was I diagnosing myself?* Pregnant people have doctor appointments every single month slowly shifting to every week the closer they come to term. *After* birth is when most maternal deaths occur due to complications postpartum. *After* birth is when PPD develops and around 13-33 percent of maternal deaths are due to suicide.[6] Standard practice postpartum is to have a doctor appointment 6 weeks after birth to check if everything is healing well. In my case, that six-week appointment revealed I had retained placenta which required surgery. Could we not have dealt with this sooner? It would have saved me weeks of heavy, heavy bleeding. Why aren't there equal numbers of appointments postpartum as prebirth? Why aren't counselors recommended to families when they have a child, to help them with the transition from no kids to the life-altering experience of having kids? These are structural choices that leave women feeling alone—like they were the first one to ever give birth.

In college, I tore my ACL playing soccer. I often contrast the support I had with that inquiry to the support postpartum. I had regular check-ins, I was referred to weekly physical therapy and told not to run for six months. At six weeks postpartum with my second child, I remember the doctor "clearing" me to have sex again. I hadn't slept in weeks, seven layers of my abdomen had been sliced 10 cm open for the second time in two years, and I could barely sit up without support. *Was that a joke?* The difference in care was alarming.

The structural failures were ever-present when I returned to work after my first child. I had to pump breastmilk during my preparation periods, and there wasn't a designated room or time, which meant I had to prepare for my classes after school while caring for my son. There may be other medical comparisons that affect men, like a wound that needs hourly care. A longer maternity leave would have given me more time to wean my son while getting closer to the two years of breastfeeding recommended by the American Pediatric Association. I pumped in my classroom. I would routinely have students come to my room and jiggle the lock or even shout to me on the inside, creating a stressful environment, which apparently impacts the quality of the milk produced. It wasn't sanitary, and the refrigerator was too far to get there and back before my classes started. Thankfully, it was winter, and I was able to store the milk bottles outside my window in the snow (graciously, no students ever asked about it). I decided to switch to formula, not because I couldn't produce milk but because zero effort was made to support me as a new mom and the stress of juggling all of it became too much. I'm sure someone at the school would say that if I had asked for things they could have accommodated, but I was not the first teacher ever to have a baby. *Were there really no policies or procedures in place to support young moms?* When I had my second child, I decided not to breastfeed at all, because the whole experience had been so stressful. The second time around, I made every effort to protect my mental health.

It wasn't just the physical stuff I endured; it was also economical. There I was juggling home and work life, and immediately I felt the pay penalty new moms around the world face. I was forced by my principal to quit three stipend positions, costing my family over $5,000. I resisted giving up the roles and was told the only option was to work through maternity leave. The Family Medical Leave Act applied only to my teaching job—not stipend roles. I was going to miss only a couple months. I asked if we could prorate the stipend with a sub or push off my work until January—there was no wiggle room.

The challenges I had aren't out of the ordinary, and sadly the lack of support and lack of flexibility were choices made by those in power. The challenges I faced as a new parent on the job could have been solved by anti-sexist policies, basic infrastructure, better childcare, and even a single person in human resources who checked on me when I returned to the job. I eventually applied to be a professor at the nearby state university. It was a dream job, but when it came to sexism, the grass was not greener on the other side. By then, I had thicker skin and was older and wiser. What I learned was that the problem wasn't with just one school. The problems were so normalized they were everywhere. What should have been beautiful early years with my growing family were made difficult by policy. *Why aren't these issues hurting half of us and our families a top priority? Why are we repeating this history?*

Barriers: The Glass Ceiling

A barrier to teaching women's history is the pervasive belief that sexism is behind us and women are equal now. If women were equal, they would be seen and heard and their stories would be told equally—not just in history class but everywhere. They are not, and the insinuation is an insulting form of gaslighting. As recently as 2020, women made up 7 percent of Fortune 500 CEOs, 6 percent of Nobel Prize winners, and only 24 percent of "heard, read about or seen in newspaper, television and radio."[7] Women reported 37 percent of news stories, and this trend is also true in the "democratized" digital media. In film, women represented 31 percent of speaking characters, 23 percent of protagonists, and 21 percent of filmmakers.[8] In sports, "Despite progress, women still continue to be excluded… and are paid far less than men in wages and prize money globally."[9] Women's self-expression, ideas, and personhood remain visible at a small fraction of those for men. *Why?* (Figure 4.1)

Women's Public Representation

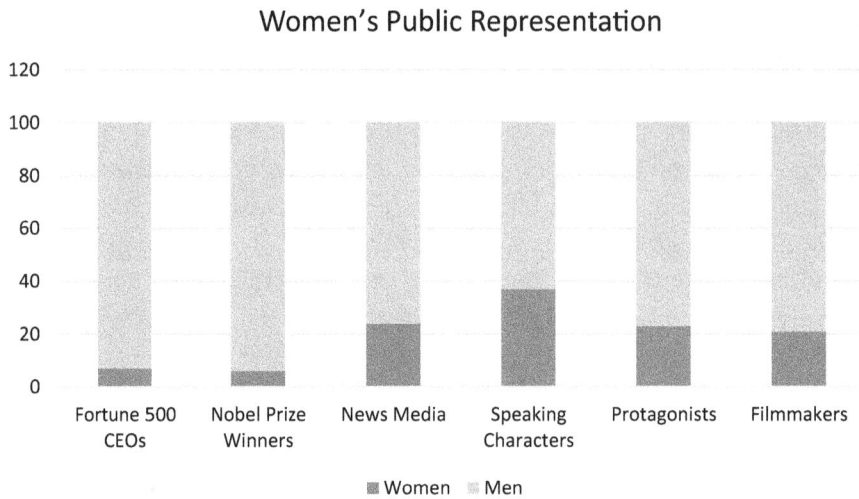

Figure 4.1 Women's Public Representation.

Source: Eckert's table with data from UN Women Editors, "Visualizing the data: Women's representation in society," UN Women, February 25, 2020, https://www.unwomen.org/en/digital-library/multimedia/2020/2/infographic-visualizing-the-data-womens-representation.

Although women are earning more degrees, they remain less visible as characters and experts. This chart shows that society has not yet found a way to combat sexism and allow women to coexist in public life.[10]

The Pay Gap

If sexism were over, there wouldn't be a substantial pay gap, and teachers should be teaching about it. Women are just as capable as men in these fields. In high school and college, on average, women outperform their male peers. In their early careers, women also outperform their male counterparts. It is not until the middle of their careers when women are having children that there's a shift.[11] Many people, like Jordan Peterson, blame the challenges that women face in workplace advancement on women and their choices. He says women are less cutthroat in their careers and that elite women often give up their wages when they marry wealthy men.[12] He believes women are choosing to make less—women are the reason for the pay penalty. In his scathing article about recent pay gap research by the Institute for Women's Policy Research (IWPR), John Phelan of the Foundation for Economic Education (FEE) claimed that the pay gap between men and women was flawed because it was calculated using the average salaries of men and average salaries of women but with no consideration of degree, experience, or professional field.[13] He said that looking at the data this way does not account for choices women make, asserting that women, on average, work 7 hours a day to the

8 hours the average male worker puts in. He said that anyone who works less than someone else should expect to earn less. *Do women work less than men?*

Phelan and Peterson need women's history. Phelan argues that businesses should not be responsible for paying for women's domestic labor, and that seems fair. However, when we examine the early history of capitalism and the shift from cottage industries to salaried factory work, it becomes obvious how this system was designed to reward the patriarchy. The Industrial Revolution moved the Western world from an agrarian to an industrial society—a shift that was perhaps most profound for women. During this time, people left farms, where men and women had shared the burden of labor, and moved to cities and factories. Men's work, as it was labeled, became salaried, and women's work became invisible and unpaid—even though women continued to hold full-time jobs. This period marked a turning point in the rigid separation between domestic work and salaried work. This change happened only a short time ago, yet our perception is that women's work has always been undervalued. Phelan and others need to study women's labor history, which reveals that industrial unions often barred women's inclusion to protect men's work at the expense of women. This was conveniently left out of my history lessons.

Women do make choices that contribute to their own invisibility and lower income, but the notion that this is a free choice rather than a constrained and economic one is simply not true. When one adds layers like race, these choices are even more difficult. In their salaried roles, obviously the answer is yes. But if all things were equal, why would women work less? The answer is that all things are not equal.

Harvard researchers, for example, examined data collected from the highly unionized and regulated Massachusetts Bay Transportation Authority (MBTA), where wage differences between men and women were virtually unthinkable. The union contract was written in a way to bar a sexist boss from favoring male employees. Workers had access to the same choices that could advance their careers. Here is Phelan's analysis of the study:

> They find that male train and bus drivers worked about 83 percent more overtime than their female colleagues and were twice as likely to accept an overtime shift—which pays time-and-a-half—on short notice and that around twice as many women as men never took overtime. The male workers took 48 percent fewer unpaid hours off under the Family Medical Leave Act each year. Female workers were more likely to take less desirable routes if it meant working fewer nights, weekends, and holidays. Parenthood turns out to be an important factor. Fathers were more likely than childless men to want the extra cash from overtime, and mothers were more likely to want time off than childless women.[14]

His conclusion is actually very similar to those of IWPR, but their analysis of the implications is different: "Women's 'choices' are not necessarily choices."[15] Families at the peak of their professional careers are also often raising children, and this family choice has a disproportionate impact on the woman's career: a pay penalty. The Center for American Progress explains:

> Today, many families with young children must make a choice between spending a significant portion of their income on child care, finding a cheaper, but potentially lower-quality care option, or leaving the workforce altogether to become a full-time caregiver. Whether due to high cost, limited availability, or inconvenient program hours, child care challenges are driving parents out of the workforce at an alarming rate. In fact, in 2016 alone, an estimated 2 million parents made career sacrifices due to problems with child care.
>
> Child care challenges have become a barrier to work, especially for mothers, who disproportionately take on unpaid caregiving responsibilities when their family cannot find or afford child care. In a 2018 survey conducted by the Center for American Progress, mothers were 40 percent more likely than fathers to report that they had personally felt the negative impact of child care issues on their careers.[16]

Why is it difficult for young families to find childcare? Answer: we have a long history of expecting women's work to be free and thus underfunding the people who do this vital work.

Underfunding "Women's Work"

If sexism had ended, the type of work women that have traditionally done and continue to choose to do would be valued and paid equally. Teachers should be teaching about this and fostering respect for jobs in health, education, administration, and literacy (HEAL).[17] Childcare workers, almost all women, earn the equivalent of a cashier or food service worker on average.[18] In fact, across the board, jobs traditionally held by women are lower paid. When traditional women's work is underpaid across industries, it becomes obvious that neither the difficulty of the job nor the risk involved or the training required predicts pay differences—it's about the gender of the people who have traditionally done the work.

Teachers are a prime example of women's jobs being paid less. Teacher posts in the nineteenth century advertised publicly that female teachers were paid one third the salary of male teachers![19] Schools were filled with brilliant and highly educated women whose other respectable alternatives were factories or domestic servitude. Educated women became teachers when other jobs were denied to them. Despite being paid less than men, female teachers into the mid-1990s benefitted from a wage "premium" compared to women in other fields. But in the 1990s, women were welcomed into other higher-paying fields in greater numbers, which changed their circumstances. As more fields opened to women, many women left teaching, but they remained the primary labor behind education—still 75 percent today. Men, meanwhile, took a major hit in their salaries by becoming teachers. Today, that penalty remains high at 35 percent.[20] The expectation that teachers' salaries remain low persists in both public and private schools. In 1960, female teachers had a 14.7 percent wage premium; by 2021, they had a 17.1 percent wage *penalty*. In those six decades, there was a huge negative shift for women teachers. In 2021, teacher salaries reached an all-time low since the Economic Policy Institute (EPI) began tracking their data at the turn of the millennium. Factoring in the vast benefits public employees tend to receive, the EPI found that teachers earn about 20 percent less nationally than those with similar degrees in other fields, though it varies considerably by state.[21] Nowhere in the United States do teachers earn more than their counterparts in other fields (Figure 4.2).[22]

Women in various fields routinely request equal pay but are denied because of comparisons to similar jobs within that field, a flawed comparison that perpetuates the wage gap. When jobs are compared between comparable "male" and "female" fields, however, the pay gap is significant. The IWPR compared elementary school teachers, the most common female occupation, to software developers, the most common male occupation.[23] Both jobs require similar degrees, risks, and burdens. On average, elementary school teachers earned $982 per week, while software developers made $1,894 per week, not to mention the fact that female software developers make $200 less per week than their male peers on average.

Discrimination Fuels Pay Gap

If sexism were over, the pay gap would not be fueled by discrimination notably and flagrantly within fields, and teachers should be teaching about this. The IWPR concluded in their expansive study and research into the data of more than 125 occupations that "women's median earnings are lower than men's in nearly all occupations, whether they work in occupations predominantly done by women, occupations predominantly done by men, or occupations with a more even mix of men and women."[24] This was true between men and women of the same race as well. Perhaps the most famous example is that of the US national soccer teams, where women earn substantially less than men. The argument is that the women's game generates less revenue than the men's. The US women's team actually earns a higher percentage of revenue than the men's team does, but the women argue that the commitment

% State Teacher Wage Penalty

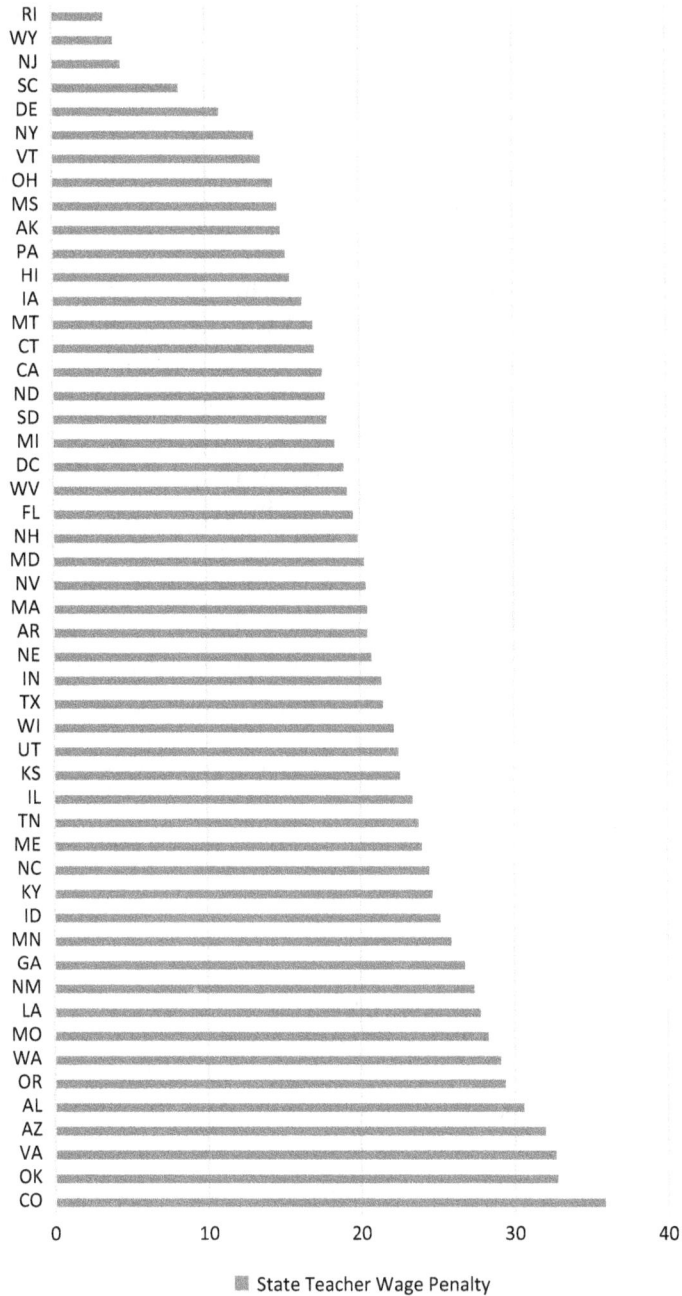

Figure 4.2 Teacher Wage Penalty by State.

Source: Eckert's table with data from Sylvia Allegretto, "The teacher pay penalty has hit a new high: Trends in teacher wages and compensation through 2021," August 16, 2022, https://www.epi.org/publication/teacher-pay-penalty-2022/.

and labor are equivalent and should garner equal pay.[25,26] The argument is about value: how do we as a society value the people who work in it? When people put in equal effort, risk, and time, shouldn't they be paid similarly?

The wage gap is closing in part because women are earning more and male wages are stagnating—this is not how anyone wants the gap to close. In 1979, only 13 percent of women earned more than the median man.[27] Today, it's 40 percent, which is not perfect equality, but it is incredible change in such a short amount of time. Men, by contrast, have seen wages stagnate, and with fewer going to college, their career prospects are limited. Since 1980, median earnings for men with only a high school diploma have decreased by 28 percent![28] As Reeves puts it, "male jobs have been hit by a one-two punch, of automation and free trade," not feminism.[29]

In her work which won her the Nobel Prize for Economics, Dr. Claudia Goldin found that while in the past, gaps in wages could be explained by men earning more degrees or working in fields that were paid better, those excuses are no longer valid. Dr. Goldin showed that "most of the earnings difference is now between men and women in the same jobs… [and occurs] after the birth of a woman's first child."[30]

The Motherhood Penalty

If sexism wasn't a problem, the "Motherhood Penalty" would be addressed through social policy, and teachers should be teaching about this. In the last quarter century, despite feminism, mothers stayed home at essentially the same rate because the apparent penalty of having children falls primarily on mothers and childcare is an enduring problem that society has not yet solved.[31] Many lament the declining "American family" and the fact that young Americans are increasingly choosing not to have children, but isn't that just a wise economic choice? The cost of living continues to rise, many families depend on two incomes, and the way society treats mothers leaves a lot to be desired. The comedian Michelle Wolf said it best in her bit performed at the Apollo in 2018:

> I don't want to have a baby or a family. I want a career that's what I want and I know there's a lot of people out there that are like… you don't have to choose you can have it all. "Women can have it all." Yes, stop saying that! You act like act like all is good. All does not mean good… Even if a woman out there definitely wants it all we've put up too many obstacles in your way to make it possible it's like, "Oh congratulations you're having a baby! Great, couple things, we're gonna need you to get that car accident of a body back to work as soon as possible because this is America and we don't think you need time to

recover. Also, you should breastfeed it's what's best for the baby but don't do it in public you pig!... Your salary is just enough to cover the cost of childcare and we know you're exhausted you don't really know who you are anymore... And sweetie smile! [Applause][32]

In less than a minute and a half, she spoke the sad and hilarious truth about how women are screwed over in this system that demands so much from them and somehow makes every problem their fault. It went viral and received millions of views.

There are generational differences between women in when they get married, what careers they choose, and whether or not they choose to have children. These career and family choices changed due to structural changes and had major impacts on birth rates and divorce rates. Sixty percent of 20th-century economic growth can be traced back to women entering the work-force in greater numbers and the expansion of the qualified labor pool.[33]

Women and families are making economic choices, and students should study them. A Pew Research Center study saw a huge surge in stay-at-home parents, especially dads, in the wake of the Great Recession, but that growth, due largely to the fact that they couldn't find work that would offset the cost of childcare, then growth plateaued.[34] The stagnation of stay-at-home parent-ing could reflect both the continued desire of many parents to make the care of their children their life's work and how few options parents have for sup-port. While governments debate policies that either would make workplaces more mother-friendly or send them back to the home, having the next gen-eration of students discuss and debate policy solutions would be a worthy exercise for a classroom of students who may one day want to have children.

The socialized default to mom as the parent, rather than a gender-neutral view of parenting is holding back not only women but, by default, men too! When women earn more than men, isn't it logical that they should work and dad stay home? While dads stay home more frequently than they did in the 1980s, only 7 percent of dads stay home to care for their kids.[35] So while some refer to this problem as the "Parenthood Penalty," let's call a spade a spade: it's a motherhood penalty. Reshma Saujani, the founder of Moms First, addressed this issue head-on. She said women do two thirds of the caregiv-ing and lose an average of four percent of their income per child.[36] For men, the experience is the opposite: they gain six! Some call this the "Fatherhood Bonus." She explained that women do the physical reproductive labor and are forced into the workforce weeks or months before they are ready, sometimes just two weeks after birth and before they are cleared by a doctor. It would be unfair to blame the patriarchy for biological aspects of child-rearing, but after recovery and breastfeeding, there seems little reason that the pressure and responsibility of child-rearing could not be shared between parents. Gloria Steinem, in her essay "The Importance of Work," reminded everyone that we all had two parents.[37]

In the United States, only 9 percent of workplaces offer paid paternity leave, and 76 percent of fathers return to work within a week of their child's birth, leaving new mothers to fend for themselves.[38] After birth, doctors recommend a whole slew of limitations on women's activity, especially for women who give birth by cesarean section. After the birth of a baby, fathers are caregivers not only to their children but also to their recovering wife. Usually the woman is not cleared for normal activity by her doctor for six to twelve weeks. *How is he supposed to support his partner if he's back at work?*

Richard Reeves, a senior analyst at the Brookings Institute who focuses on the challenges faced by boys in society, aims to address occupational segregation. This phenomenon refers to the social expectation that men and women should pursue certain types of jobs. For instance, teaching, nursing, and psychology are predominantly female-dominated fields, which means that men have few male role models in teaching, limited access to counselors who understand their unique challenges, and few examples of male caregivers.[39] Men are less than 25 percent of K-12 teachers, down to only 20 percent in the lower grades. They are only 9 percent of nurses and 6 percent of personal assistants.[40] Both men and women benefit from diverse representation, so it is crucial to see more men actively engaged in caregiving roles.

The Welfare Mom

If sexism were a thing of the past, stereotypes like that of the "Welfare Mom" wouldn't insult and degrade poor women in impossible circumstances. The pay gap is narrowing among elite women and men, but class barriers and the types of jobs that poor women hold perpetuate the pay gap. Class, race, and gender together paint a much better picture of the problem.[41] In the 1980s, Ronald Reagan popularized this idea of a "Welfare Mom," a single mom who mooches off of government programs to care for her children.[42] His stigmatizing of women not only was hurtful, by mocking women most in need of support, but also illustrates the false belief consistent throughout women's economic history: women's work is supposed to be free.

Reagan's portrayal of a, usually Black, woman who exploited the welfare system by collecting checks to support numerous children without holding a job suggested that she strategically had multiple children to maximize benefits and manipulate the system for her advantage. This narrative, many argue, covertly played on racial biases, subtly perpetuating conscious or unconscious racism and re-enshrined the idea that homemaking is not work. Though Reagan never explicitly named a specific individual, he utilized this term to advocate for his economic policies, aiming to reduce government spending. The real-life inspiration for this characterization was Linda Taylor, a woman who defrauded the government of substantial sums and engaged in multiple simultaneous marriages. Although Taylor was white, she became envisioned as a Black woman in the public's perception, adding to existing racial prejudices. She was an exception, not the norm—a falsehood said enough times that it became memorable.

The reality is that women more than men live in poverty. Globally, 70 percent of the poor are women.[43] If sexism didn't thrive, poverty wouldn't be so strongly tied to gender. In 2020, the Center for American Progress found that "Women have higher rates of poverty than men across almost all races and ethnicities."[44] Women of color are disproportionally represented in these data, showing that women's issues are also issues of race and that if white women like myself are serious about ending sexism, then we must also fight to end racism.

This is the system our government has created. Poor mothers must choose between low wages, men, or the government for financial support. Given that many of these women are in relationships with men of the same social class, who too have unreliable jobs and low wages, those men, when out of work, can be seen as yet another mouth to feed.[45] If we care about family values, shifting our cultural reliance on the default parent as mom and helping everyone see the vital role men play as caregivers will give those men purpose in families. More equitable family policies will not only keep qualified women in the workforce but help close the childcare gaps.[46]

We also need to understand more deeply how awful these choices are for poor mothers. I lost my dad to a heart attack at age 10. I know firsthand the choices that single mothers make. My mom chose to be with us, to support us through grief, rather than to work. Can anyone really condemn her for that impossible choice? She chose a basic social security income which was not enough to maintain our middle-class lifestyle, so that she could be there—to parent. Thankfully, my upper-class grandparents supplemented the government support she received; it is only because of generational wealth that I lived a middle-class life. Sadly, so many people are empathetic to my situation and not to those of women whose partner is gone for another reason. *Does it really matter why the breadwinner is gone?* But morally, and in the eyes of the 31 percent of people in poverty who are minors, should it really matter *why* the father is gone?[47] The reality is he's gone, and again society treats mothers with scorn and condemnation. The term "welfare mother" is essentially ridiculing women for using the cards the system dealt her and trying to care for her family.

The solutions to the challenges facing lower-class women are embroiled in the competing economic philosophies of democratic capitalism and more socialist ideas. These data speak volumes about how the present system has failed women. In any debate about competing global or even national solutions, the needs and challenges facing women of color should be centered so that solutions that help more of us are sought.

Women in Power

Studies show that change won't happen, sexism won't end, until there are more women in positions of power in government and business. And in case you were going to point to the increasing number of women in politics, it's nowhere near half. Globally, in 2020, 24.9 percent of parliamentarians were women, and only 23 women held a position as head of nation state or government.[48] In the 2018 US midterm elections, women made up only 20 percent of Congress, and only six out of 50 governors were women.[49] If women had an equal opportunity to participate, that figure could easily be 50 percent.

Researchers have proven the importance of women in politics for the well-being of women and families. Political scientist Jessica Saracino used data from the Institute of Women's Policy Research to show that "Women legislators in the United States are more likely than their male counterparts to include legislation concerning women, children, and families among their top priorities... [and] are more successful in their efforts to pass these bills into law."[50] She concluded that her data indicate a "strong relationship between the status of women and the number of women legislators in that state."[51] Saracino's work was backed by the work of many others.[52] Amy Caiazza's research found that while left-leaning politicians were more likely to support bills related to women's rights, gender was a stronger predictor of that position.[53] Caiazza also found that high levels of women's turnout at the ballot box resulted in increased attention to women's issues across genders.[54] Therefore, work at the state level to raise women's status leads to greater representation, cyclically producing greater everyday results for women.

A 65-year longitudinal study by the Gallup Poll showed that, over time, Americans have shifted their perspective on whether they would vote for a well-qualified woman for president.[55] In 1937, just 33 percent said yes. By 1999, 92 percent said yes. This sounds optimistic, and it is: feminism has a major impact. However, a poll by Ipsos in 2019 compellingly found that of those who said they would vote for a woman, 33 percent believed their neighbor would not.[56] This concept has been dubbed "sexism by proxy," in which people change their voting behavior and pick someone they perceive to be electable on the basis of outdated sexist standards that they don't even believe themselves. It also could be a convenient way to disguise sexism and create an invisible barrier for women in politics.

So what role do teachers play in ending sexism? They do what they are trained to do: teach about it. The solution to all of these problems is directly teaching about sexism as it impacts the economy and government and ending sexism in the cultural training that students get in our classrooms.

Breaker: Teach About Sexism

In a personal communication to me about teaching women's history, Laurel Thatcher Ulrich wrote, "It is very important to ground history (including political history) in economics. It is also important for students to understand how laws explicitly excluded women from many benefits that allowed men to dominate both the economy and politics."[57] To do this, economic definitions that teachers already use need to be investigated from a gendered perspective. Teachers need to examine women's labor, paid and unpaid, and discuss its significance in our economy. They must look at the layers of race and class and how those impact women.

Teachers need to turn each of the items briefly summarized in this chapter into lessons for investigation in the government and economics classrooms. While my writing makes clear where I stand on all of these issues, they are hotly debated in our politics: replicate those in your classroom. That is what inquiry is about! Take each one of the topics and have students do online research. Make them pull from multiple and diverse sources using current data and information. You can point them to some of the studies I have cited and referenced here or pull in ones you've found. Make a model congress or business executive board and have them decide if they should and how they could make more equitable policies. Consider the following:

- What should be done about the pay gap? Consider stagnating male wages as well as race and class data.
- Should health, education, administration, and literacy (HEAL) jobs pay more? Consider the role that gender plays in who chooses these jobs.
- Should men be incentivized through scholarship programs into HEAL educational programs like women are into STEM (science, technology, engineering, and mathematics)?
- What should be done about wage discrimination? Consider the balance between personal privacy and equity.
- What should be done about the Motherhood Penalty and Fatherhood Bonus? Consider the impact any policies would have on children and the cost–benefit analysis that families make.
- Should the government adopt universal healthcare? Consider the strengths and weaknesses of the present system as well as alternatives.

As students hash out these arguments, they will be more prepared for a world that is half female and involved in finding solutions to make the world a place where more people can fulfill their potential.

Questions posed for inquiry should be debatable. Note that the question is not "Is there a pay gap?" There is. That's a fact. What we should *do about it* is the question. There are debates where people pose a hurtful question, and when protest inevitably occurs, they rebut, "What? I was just asking." There are questions about women and the economy that are offensive. They involve any question that strips women of choice, personhood, or freedom. For example, the question "Should women stay at home?" The *only* fair answer to that question in a democracy built on the notion of personal freedom is: if she wants to. Now, "Should government funding support single mothers?" This question is about a society's collective finances and is a fair question. Of course, in a society where the government subsidizes loads of industries, it is also fair to conclude that a government that does not subsidize mothers and gives preference to male-dominated fields like farming and the military is sexist. The rebuttal might then be that farms provide food to families and the military protects them, so those *are* investments in women and family. On and on it can go with students becoming more informed and thoughtful as they discuss.

Having these discussions in a classroom is crucial to ending sexism but only if it's actually a discussion. True inquiry comes from both the questions posed and the culture built around the way we answer them. If students are resistant to the ideas I've shared here, they should feel safe to vocalize those feelings. If discussion departs from being productive, perhaps a break or a cooling-off could occur so that conversation can return to facts and empathy. Therefore, to really teach women's topics well, teachers must adopt inclusive pedagogies.

Blueprint: Inclusive Pedagogy

Making room for women in the curriculum is only half the battle. Young women need to know they have a place in the field in order to encourage more women to join the field. Inclusive, or feminist, pedagogy includes any teaching practices that empower *all* students to speak and engage in the class-room. These include student-centered practices that remove the teacher from the podium and share the airwaves with students.

Although women represent 75 percent of teachers across K-12 education, gender bias in the classroom is well documented. In in their book *Failing at Fairness: How America's Schools Cheat Girls*, Myra Sadker and her husband David Sadker explained, "Every day in America little girls lose their independence, achievement, and self-esteem. Subtle and insidious, the gender biased lessons result in quiet catastrophes and silent losses. But the casualties of tomorrow's women are very real."[58] They looked at standardized test data, which showed that girls outperformed their male peers in elementary school but that, by high school, SAT and ACT scores fell behind.

Inclusive pedagogies help to dismantle hierarchies. Teaching practices that encourage only confident extroverts to engage reinforce the cycle of girls not feeling they have a place in the history classroom, as those outspoken students are often boys.[59] Teachers in Sadker and Sadker's study explained that they gave boys more attention because they "need it more. Boys have trouble reading, writing, doing math."[60] The more attention given to boys, the worse girls did, and most teachers had no idea they were doing it. This implicit bias can be treated with attention to inclusive pedagogies.

Schools are full of hidden curriculums, and reinforcing gender norms is one. Sadker and Sadker found that girls were more frequently praised for conforming to gender norms and rules. Compliance makes great workers but less great innovators and contributes to the crisis of low self-esteem among young girls. Martell and Stevens wrote:

> By praising young women for their appearance and for following the rules, teachers are presenting a hidden curriculum, one which sends the message that boys need to be smart and girls need to be pretty. This type of hidden curriculum in schools can be very dangerous for women, especially at an age when young women are beginning to understand the social pressure to look or behave a certain way… What is particularly troubling is that the social studies classroom can and should be a place of social change, rather than a place that reinforces women are not equal partners. Yet, many social studies teachers and curriculum developers are not fighting for gender equity.[61]

Gendered behaviors are present in preschool through secondary. Boys speak up even when they are not called on. Methodologies that encourage and leave space for marginalized students to find their voice are crucial for gender equity. Mixed-gender groupings can sometimes be detrimental to female engagement, as boys and men have a tendency, in both the class and the workspace, to ignore girls' contributions and ideas.[62] Teachers also tend to give boys more attention in the classroom, which reinforces the message that they belong.[63] Beyond the history classroom, schools at large reinforce traditional binary gendered expectations that are not only white, Christian, and settler but also cisgender (when a person's gender expression corresponds to their sex at birth), heteronormative, and patriarchal.[64] Reflecting on my own experience as an educator, I noticed that almost all the end-of-year class awards I gave in history went to male students.

Crocco begins her article "The Missing Discourse About Gender and Sexuality in the Social Studies" with vivid and grabbing examples that help us understand how urgent it is to address gender dynamics in schools. Citing acts of violence that had made national headlines, such as the gang rape of a girl by a football team, the Columbine shooting, and the murder of a gay student, she writes, each of these tragedies has been 'explained' in a variety of ways: easy-to-access firearms, distracted parents, and broken families—her list went on. While any and all can be true, she notes, "sexist and homophobic slurs have been implicated in each violent incidents."[65] A piece of these topics, usually unaddressed by the media in the aftermath of these events, is the toxicity of strict gendered expectations and scripts that deny opportunities to girls and freedom of expression to boys.[66]

When I work with students, I make overt these problems and the need to listen to one another, rather than allow loud voices to dominate. It's not just gender, it's also the education system's preference for extroversion. Our job as teachers is also character development and molding. After I know my students well and have strong relationships with them, I might even introduce a discussion or debate and call out some of my extroverts. The dialog might go, "We all know _____ is super smart. But today I want to hear from all of you, and _____ is going to need to practice listening."

In a 2018 study of feminist teachers who used inclusive pedagogies, a variety of approaches were used to mitigate gender norms from outside the classroom that may permeate behavior inside it.[67] Most teachers monitored the participation rates of male and female students to ensure that female students' voices were heard in the classroom. For instance, Alex recognized that women are often socialized to be submissive, which could lead to less active participation. He adjusted for this by incorporating online conversations and written reflections and deliberately calling on girls during class discussions. Tina, for example, reflected on which students she called on and how often. She acknowledged that boys tend to be more talkative and louder, which can result in their being called on more frequently. To address this, Tina made a concerted effort to ensure that both male and female students had opportunities to contribute to class discussions. Her goal was for every student to be engaged at least once during each period, whether it was through reading or sharing their opinions.

My colleague, Sarah Achorn, used tokens to regulate how much certain kids spoke in the space. Kids would be given a cup and a certain number of tokens, each representing the quantity of student contributions to the discussion. After students contributed, they would move a token into their cup.

This made them conscious of how much they were talking or not talking. While that really worked for her, there are many well-researched strategies for inclusive instruction. Here are a few classroom strategies that create space for all learners:

- *Think, Pair, Share*: In this strategy, a student first examines a source or question independently. This allows students who, for a variety of reasons, may not be the first to speak up to form their thoughts. They then group up with students who looked at different documents and teach the group about their source while learning about others.
- *Four-Corner Debate*: In the corners of the room, teachers tack up a piece of paper with four different possible answers to the inquiry question. After students examine sources and consider questions and possible theories, pose the inquiry question to the room at large and ask students to move to the corner of the room (or in-between locations) that represents their answer. This method does not necessarily force students to speak, but it does force them to take a stand, literally. From there, call on students representing different perspectives to explain their choice. As students discuss the topic, they are allowed to move closer or farther from ideas. This is a great strategy for kinesthetic learning. By consciously framing the intention of the moving debate as a way to hear multiple perspectives, it creates space for marginalized students to find their voice.
- *Socratic Seminar*: This strategy extends the learning and gets students to question what they still don't know or understand. Start with the inquiry's question. Students should be encouraged to answer one another's question directly but also to answer the question with another question. This continues the conversation and gets at richer ideas. The teacher should try to say as little as possible and let the students lead the dialogue. One strategy for this is to seat students in a circle. Give each of them a cup and two or three tokens. When a student makes a substantive contribution to the discussion, the teacher walks over and places a token in the cup, signaling that they have contributed. Students will become aware of who has spoken and who has not, which encourages them to leave space for one another.
- *Structured Academic Controversy*: In this strategy, teachers take the overarching question and turn it into a "debate." Students can choose or be assigned to a side in the debate and use the documents provided to argue their "answer" to the overarching question. They can argue over interpretations and credibility of some documents. Teachers can

build structures into the Structured Academic Controversy to ensure that all students have a space to engage.

◆ *Reacting to the Past*: This strategy is a type of active learning through role-playing. In Reacting to the Past games, students are assigned characters from the past and must communicate, collaborate, and compete effectively to advance their objectives. This is helpful in encouraging students to speak up and engage because they are not sharing their own ideas but rather those of people from the past. Students must stay in character throughout the role-play. Students are encouraged to use sources to inform their character development and to generally stick to the philosophy of the character, but the games do not have a fixed script or outcome.

Teachers shy away from these strategies most often when they feel they must prove their competence. New teachers tend to lecture more than veteran ones because the former are afraid to surrender the learning to students and want the class to know they are intelligent. Teachers must let students learn by diving into facts and data, doing research, thinking critically, and having the space to make mistakes and be corrected by the classroom expert.

Feminist teachers reject the linear approach to teaching and learning and instead embrace a multifaceted and social process of knowledge creation that involves interaction, collaboration, and negotiation. They aim to create an inclusive learning environment where students are active participants and valued members of a community of learners rather than being positioned as passive recipients. Within this framework, each learner brings their unique perspective, shaped by their specific experiences within various social contexts and groups. Therefore, the ideal learning dynamic involves a reciprocal exchange between students and teachers. In this type of learning environment, knowledge is co-constructed.

Additionally, Schmeichel argued that feminist research requires "responsiveness to positionality," where one considers the identity, location, and time of the sources one is investigating.[68] She explains that these are "the same kinds of understandings, upon which implementation of multiple perspectives in history education realized."[69] Feminist practices should question the status quo and get students doing social scientific or historical research. Feminist practices should de-centralize the teacher and put the pressure back on the students to think.

As states around the country moved to ban or restrict abortion prior to *Roe v. Wade* being overturned in June 2022, I doubled down on my teaching of abortion rights and history in my classes. This is the type of controversial subject that would lead marginalized students to clam up. I used the above methods to decentralize instruction and put students—*all students*—at the center. I pulled diverse sources from across the political spectrum and designed a multiday inquiry. Then I let my students and the evidence do the talking. I never shared my personal feelings with students about abortion access. In fact, I said very little over the three class periods. The data speaks for itself, and that's what I want to teach my students to do—to be objective observers of evidence. It was a powerful student-centered lesson. Powerful because students were working with difficult documents, analyzing data on maternal, fetal, and infant mortality rates, and powerful because the students learned *more* because I said very little. The class dynamic was 17 boys to four girls from across the political and economic spectrum—a recipe for female silence. Despite the ratios, my use of feminist pedagogy made space for the girls to speak up equally.

Resources for Inclusive Pedagogy
Recommended Reading: Books That Gender the Economy
For a deeper understanding of the economy and the gendered shifts it has undergone in the last century or more, it's important to read books by economists and social science researchers. Data is persuasive and can speak for itself when it comes to how the economy effects certain groups of people. Nobel Prize-winning economist Claudia Goldin's book *Career and Family* is a must-read. She expertly analyzes the career choices of several different generations of women across the previous century in US history to illustrate how structural changes and scientific discoveries allowed these women to make decidedly different choices. I also really valued reading *Of Boys and Men* by Richard Reeves, the analyst mentioned above. Since many educators are concerned about the plight of boys in schools, this book is a practical guide to data-backed solutions that will help boys—notably not at the expense of girls. I also highly recommend Eve Rodsky's *Fair Play*, which helps couples better understand domestic labor and the "mental load" while giving couples a toolkit for sharing domestic responsibilities.

Sample Inquiry: Was, or Is, the ERA Good for Women?
Women don't agree on the path forward. Economic security for women through the ability to work in well-paying jobs and fairer workplaces has meant that women are working both for a wage and for their families. The caregiving role remains under- or unfunded and devalued in society. What to do about that is a huge debate among women and has been for the last century. Do women want or need equality? Or do they need equity? And what does equity look like? How involved should the government be in social reform?

These questions were raised by Alice Paul almost immediately after women won suffrage—the only acknowledgement of women in the US Constitution. The Equal Rights Amendment (ERA) has a long, complicated history in the US and would make a great lesson on how a bill becomes a law. But the substance of the law itself and how it is rolled out are also important. Women stood on both sides of this issue as the amendment went from state to state in the 1970s to be ratified. Its feminist proponents, like Betty Friedan, were met with a fierce conservative women's backlash under the leadership of Phyllis Schlafly (who notably made a whole career out of telling women not to have careers) and her STOP ERA organization. The following inquiry explores their differing perspectives on the ERA. It is downloadable on the Remedial Herstory Project's website. There is also a video version of this inquiry using footage from when Betty Friedan and Phyllis Schlafly debated each other on television.

Is the ERA good for women?
Below are differing documents in favor of and against the ERA from women. Read the documents provided and respond to the questions. Then consider the question: was the ERA good for women?

1. As you read, record sentences or ideas that show the ERA is good for women or bad for women in the middle columns.
2. After you finish the two middle columns, look back at the evidence. Which information is most persuasive to you? Mark that #8. Which evidence is least persuasive to you? Mark that #1.

Rank	Evidence that ERA is GOOD for women	Evidence that ERA is BAD for women	Rank

Overall questions for analysis
1. Add up the rank on each side. Which side weighed more? Why do you think it worked out that way?
2. In conclusion, was the ERA good for women?

Document A: Equal Rights Amendment

The following amendment to the US Constitution was proposed by woman suffragist Alice Paul in 1923 to extend to women legal protections not covered by the vote and to end sex discrimination. It passed in Congress in 1973 but was not ratified by all 38 states needed.

Equality of rights under the law shall not be denied or abridged by the United States or by any state on account of sex.

Equal Rights Amendment, 1923.

Document B: NOW Position Statement

In 1967, the National Organization of Women (NOW) published the following position statement on the ERA. Betty Friedan was then the president of NOW.

NOW's Statement of Purpose endorses the principle that women should exercise all the privileges and responsibilities of American society in equal partnership with men... The Fourteenth Amendment to the United States Constitution provides that no State shall "deprive any person of life, liberty or property, without due process of law; nor deny to any person with its jurisdiction the equal protection of the laws." The Fourteenth Amendment restricts the States and the "due process" clause of the Fifth Amendment similarly restricts the Federal Government from interfering with these individual rights.

However, the Civil and Political Rights Committee of the President's Commission found in 1963 (Report, p. 34): "The courts have consistently upheld laws providing different treatment for women than for men, usually on the basis of the State's special interest in protecting the health and welfare of women. In no 14th Amendment case alleging discrimination on account of sex has the United States Supreme Court held that a law classifying persons on the basis of sex is unreasonable and therefore unconstitutional. Until such time as the Supreme Court reexamines the doctrine of 'sex as a basis for legislative classification' and promulgates the standards determining which types of laws and official practices treating men and women differently are reasonable and which are not, it will remain unclear whether women can enforce their rights under the 14th amendment or whether there is a constitutional gap which can only be filled by a Federal constitutional amendment."

...Constitutional amendments, like statutes, are interpreted by the courts in light of intent of Congress... Therefore, the probable meaning and effect of the Equal Rights Amendment can be ascertained from the Senate Judiciary Committee reports (which have been the same in recent years):

1. The amendment would restrict only governmental action, and would not apply to purely private action. What constitutes "State action" would be the same as under the 14th amendment and as developed in the 14th amendment litigation on other subjects.

2. Special restrictions on property rights of married women would be unconstitutional; married women could engage in business as freely as a member of the male sex; inheritance rights of widows would be the same as for widowers.
3. Women would be equally subject to jury service and to military service, but women would not be required to serve (in the Armed Forces) where they are not fitted any more than men are required to so serve.
4. Restrictive work laws for women only would be unconstitutional.
5. Alimony laws would not favor women solely because of their sex, but a divorce decree could award support to a mother if she was granted custody of the children. Matters concerning custody and support of children would be determined in accordance with the welfare of the children and without favoring either parent because of sex.
6. Laws granting maternity benefits to mothers would not be affected by the amendment, nor would criminal laws governing sexual offenses become unconstitutional.

Support of and opposition to the Equal Rights Amendment

The National Woman's Party, which continued to carry on the feminist movement following the adoption of the Nineteenth Amendment, has led the fight for an Equal Rights Amendment. Other organizations which have supported the amendment include the National Federation of Business and Professional Women's Clubs, the General Federation of Women's Clubs, National Association of Women Lawyers, National Association of Colored Business and Professional Women, St. Joan's Alliance, American Federation of Soroptimist Clubs, and various women's professional and civic organizations. Strong opposition to the amendment has come from the labor unions. Other organizations opposing the amendment have included the Americans for Democratic Action, National Council of Jewish Women, National Council of Catholic Women, National Council of Negro Women.

…Women have been seeking equal rights under these [the 14th Amendment] since 1872… Women can and should continue to do so until discrimination in laws and official practices is eliminated…

Supporters of the Equal Rights Amendment believe that the potential of the 14th amendment is too unclear and that women's constitutional rights to equality are too insecure to rely exclusively on the possibility of getting more enlightened court decisions under that amendment.

NOW. "ERA Position Paper." 1967. Retrieved from https://feminist.org/resources/feminist-chronicles/part-iii-the-early-documents/era-position-paper-1967/.

Document C: Phyllis Schlafly

Phyllis Schlafly was a conservative politician and the leader of the organization STOP Era, which worked to combat feminist social reconstruction. She was the most prominent opponent to the ERA.

Of all the classes of people who ever lived, the American woman is the most privileged. We have the most rights and rewards, and the fewest duties. Our unique status is the result of a fortunate combination of circumstances.

1) We have the immense good fortune to live in a civilization which respects the family as the basic unit of society. This respect is part and parcel of our laws and our customs. It is based on the fact of life—which no legislation or agitation can erase—that women have babies and men don't.

If you don't like this fundamental difference, you will have to take up your complaint with God because He created us this way. The fact that women, not men, have babies is not the fault of selfish and domineering men, or of the establishment, or of any clique of conspirators who want to oppress women. It's simply the way God made us...

The institution of the family is advantageous for women for many reasons. After all, what do we want out of life? To love and be loved? Mankind has not discovered a better nest for a lifetime of reciprocal love. A sense of achievement? A man may search 30 to 40 years for accomplishment in his profession. A woman can enjoy real achievement when she is young—by having a baby... Children are a woman's best social security—her best guarantee of social benefits such as old age pension, unemployment compensation, workman's compensation, and sick leave. The family gives a woman the physical, financial and emotional security of the home—for all her life.

2) The second reason why American women are a privileged group is that we are the beneficiaries of a tradition of special respect for women which dates from the Christian Age of Chivalry. The honor and respect paid to Mary, the Mother of Christ, resulted in all women, in effect, being put on a pedestal. This respect for women is not just the lip service that politicians pay to "God, Motherhood, and the Flag." It is not—as some youthful agitators seem to think—just a matter of opening doors for women, seeing that they are seated first, carrying their bundles, and helping them in and out of automobiles. Such good manners are merely the superficial evidences of a total attitude toward women which expresses itself in many more tangible ways, such as money. In other civilizations, such as the African and the American Indian, the men strut around wearing feathers and beads and hunting

and fishing (great sport for men!), while the women do all the hard, tiresome drudgery including the tilling of the soil (if any is done), the hewing of wood, the making of fires, the carrying of water, as well as the cooking, sewing and caring for babies. This is not the American way because we were lucky enough to inherit the traditions of the Age of Chivalry. In America, a man's first significant purchase is a diamond for his bride, and the largest financial investment of his life is a home for her to live in. American husbands work hours of overtime to buy a fur piece or other finery to keep their wives in fashion, and to pay premiums on their life insurance policies to provide for her comfort when she is a widow (benefits in which he can never share). In the states which follow the English common law, a wife has a dower right in her husband's real estate which he cannot take away from her during life or by his will. A man cannot dispose of his real estate without his wife's signature… In Illinois, as a result of agitation by "equal rights" fanatics, the real-estate dower laws were repealed as of January 1, 1972. This means that in Illinois a husband can now sell the family home, spend the money on his girlfriend or gamble it away, and his faithful wife of 30 years can no longer stop him.

The Real Liberation of Women

3) The third reason why American women are so well off is that the great American free enterprise system has produced remarkable inventors who have lifted the backbreaking "women's work" from our shoulders. In other countries and in other eras, it was truly said that "Man may work from sun to sun, but woman's work is never done." Other women have labored every waking hour— preparing food on wood-burning stoves, making flour, baking bread in stone ovens, spinning yarn, making clothes, making soap, doing the laundry by hand, heating irons, making candles for light and fires for warmth, and trying to nurse their babies through illnesses without medical care.

The real liberation of women from the backbreaking drudgery of centuries is the American free enterprise system which stimulated inventive geniuses to pursue their talents—and we all reap the profits. The great heroes of women's liberation are not the straggly-haired women on television talk shows and picket lines, but Thomas Edison who brought the miracle of electricity to our homes to give light and to run all those labor- saving devices—the equivalent, perhaps, of a half-dozen household servants for every middle-class American woman… Thus, household duties have been reduced to only a few hours a day, leaving the American woman with plenty of time to moonlight. She can take a full or part-time paying job, or she can indulge to her heart's content in a tremendous selection of interesting educational or cultural or homemaking activities.

The Fraud of the Equal Rights Amendment

In the last couple of years, a noisy movement has sprung up agitating for "women's rights." Suddenly, everywhere we are afflicted with aggressive females on television talk shows yapping about how mistreated American women are, suggesting that marriage has put us in some kind of "slavery," that housework is menial and degrading, and—perish the thought—that women are discriminated against. New "women's liberation" organizations are popping up, agitating and demonstrating, serving demands on public officials, getting wide press coverage always, and purporting to speak for some 100,000,000 American women. It's time to set the record straight. The claim that American women are downtrodden and unfairly treated is the fraud of the century. The truth is that American women never had it so good. Why should we lower ourselves to "equal rights" when we already have the status of special privilege?… This Amendment will absolutely and positively make women subject to the draft. Why any woman would support such a ridiculous and un-American proposal as this is beyond comprehension. Why any Congressman who had any regard for his wife, sister or daughter would support such a proposition is just as hard to understand. Foxholes are bad enough for men, but they certainly are not the place for women—and we should reject any proposal which would put them there in the name of "equal rights."…

Another bad effect of the Equal Rights Amendment is that it will abolish a woman's right to child support and alimony, and substitute what the women's libbers think is a more "equal" policy, that "such decisions should be within the discretion of the Court and should be made on the economic situation and need of the parties in the case." Under present American laws, the man is always required to support his wife and each child he caused to be brought into the world. Why should women abandon these good laws—by trading them for something so nebulous and uncertain as the "discretion of the Court"? The law now requires a husband to support his wife as best as his financial situation permits, but a wife is not required to support her husband (unless he is about to become a public charge). A husband cannot demand that his wife go to work to help pay for family expenses. He has the duty of financial support under our laws and customs. Why should we abandon these mandatory wife-support and child-support laws so that a wife would have an "equal" obligation to take a job?… Do women really want to give up this special privilege and lower themselves to "equal rights", so that the mother gets one child and the father gets the other? I think not…

What "Women's Lib" Really Means

Many women are under the mistaken impression that "women's lib" means more job employment opportunities for women, equal pay for equal work, appointments of women to high positions, admitting more women to medical schools, and other desirable objectives which all women favor. We all support these purposes, as well as any necessary legislation which would bring them about. But all this is only a sweet syrup which covers the deadly poison masquerading as "women's lib." The women's libbers are radicals who are waging a total assault on the family, on marriage, and on children. Don't take my word for it—read their own literature and prove to yourself what these characters are trying to do. ...

In intellectual circles, a New York University professor named Warren T. Farrell has provided the rationale for why men should support women's lib. When his speech to the American Political Science Association Convention is stripped of its egghead verbiage, his argument is that men should eagerly look forward to the day when they can enjoy free sex and not have to pay for it. The husband will no longer be "saddled with the tremendous guilt feelings" when he leaves his wife with nothing after she has given him her best years. If a husband loses his job, he will no longer feel compelled to take any job to support his family. A husband can go "out with the boys" to have a drink without feeling guilty. Alimony will be eliminated.

Women's Libbers Do Not Speak for Us

...If the women's libbers want to reject marriage and motherhood, it's a free country and that is their choice. But let's not permit these women's libbers to get away with pretending to speak for the rest of us. Let's not permit this tiny minority to degrade the role that most women prefer. Let's not let these women's libbers deprive wives and mothers of the rights we now possess.

Phyllis Schlafly Report 5, no. 7 (February 1972). "WOMEN'S LIBERATION AND OTHER MOVEMENTS." America in the Sixties—Right, Left, and Center: A Documentary History. Westport, CT: Praeger, 1998. Last modified January 1, 1972. *https://awpc.cattcenter.iastate.edu/2016/02/02/whats-wrong-with-equal-rights-for-women-1972/.*

Notes

1 Ann Varner, "March: Women's History Month," University of Missouri Kansas City Women's Center, March 5, 2018, retrieved on March 11, 2018 from https://info.umkc.edu/womenc/2018/03/05/march-womens-history-month/

2 "I Am Woman," *I Don't Know How to Love Him*, Capital Records, 1972, Record. Helen Reddy and Ray Burton.

3 Mardi Schmeichel, "Skirting around critical feminist rationales for teaching women in social studies," *Theory & Research in Social Education*, 2015, 43(1), 2.

4 Schmeichel, "Skirting around critical feminist rationales for teaching women in social studies," 2.

5 Zippia, "HIGH SCHOOL COACH DEMOGRAPHICS AND STATISTICS IN THE US," Zippia, July 21, 2023, https://www.zippia.com/high-school-coach-jobs/demographics/

6 Kathleen Chin, Amelia Wendt, Ian M Bennett, Amritha Bhat, "Suicide and Maternal Mortality," *Current Psychiatry Reports*, 2022, 24(4), 239–275, https://doi.org/10.1007/s11920-022-01334-3

7 UN Women Editors, "Visualizing the data: Women's representation in society," UN Women, February 25, 2020, https://www.unwomen.org/en/digital-library/multimedia/2020/2/infographic-visualizing-the-data-womens-representation

8 UN Women Editors, "Visualizing the data."

9 UN Women Editors, "Visualizing the data."

10 Heidi Hartmann, Ariane Hegewisch, Barbara Gault, Gina Chirillo, Jennifer Clark, "Five Ways to Win an Argument about the Gender Wage Gap (Updated 2019)," Institute for Women's Policy Research, last modified September 11, 2019, https://iwpr.org/publications/five-ways-to-win-an-argument-about-the-gender-wage-gap/

11 Brandon Long, "Is Jordan Peterson Right About Agreeable Women? (No)," Medium, February 14, 2019, https://medium.com/slightly-educated/is-jordan-peterson-right-about-agreeable-women-no-d30eb6f319e

12 Nellie Bowles, "Jordan Peterson, Custodian of the Patriarchy. He says there's a crisis in masculinity. Why won't women — all these wives and witches — just behave?" New York Times, May 18, 2018, https://www.nytimes.com/2018/05/18/style/jordan-peterson-12-rules-for-life.html

13 John Phelen, "Harvard Study: 'Gender Wage Gap' Explained Entirely by Work Choices of Men and Women: The 'gender wage gap" is as real as unicorns and has been killed more times than Michael Myers," Foundation for Economic Education, December 10, 2018, https://fee.org/articles/harvard-study-gender-pay-gap-explained-entirely-by-work-choices-of-men-and-women/?gclid=CjwKCAjw26H3BRB2EiwAy32zhZKsF45zDh2P22RHSXgHrfc-hthCcA1Xh1hyUhN3A9XFwvx9XP6u6hoCXokQAvD_BwE

14 Phelan, "Harvard Study."

15 Hartmann, Hegewisch, Gault, Chirillo, Clark, "Five Ways to Win an Argument about the Gender Wage Gap."

16 Leila Schochet, "The Child Care Crisis Is Keeping Women Out of the Workforce," Center for American Progress, last modified March 28, 2019, https://www.americanprogress.org/issues/early-childhood/reports/2019/03/28/467488/child-care-crisis-keeping-women-workforce/

17 A term coined by Richard Reeves.

18 Gillian B. White, "Why Daycare Workers Are So Poor, Even Though Daycare Costs So Much: They can't even afford child care for their own kids," *The Atlantic*, last modified November 5, 2015, https://www.theatlantic.com/business/archive/2015/11/childcare-workers-cant-afford-childcare/414496/

19 Gail Collins, *America's Women*, 107.

20 Sylvia Allegretto, "The teacher pay penalty has hit a new high: Trends in teacher wages and compensation through 2021," August 16, 2022, https://www.epi.org/publication/teacher-pay-penalty-2022/

21 Sylvia Allegretto, "The teacher pay penalty has hit a new high."

22 Sylvia Allegretto, "The teacher pay penalty has hit a new high: Trends in teacher wages and compensation through 2021," August 16, 2022, https://www.epi.org/publication/teacher-pay-penalty-2022/

23 Ariane Hegewisch and Adiam Tesfaselassie. "The Gender Wage Gap by Occupation 2018," The Institute for Women's Policy Research, April 2, 2019, https://iwpr.org/publications/gender-wage-gap-occupation-2018/

24 Hegewisch and Tesfaselassie, "The Gender Wage Gap by Occupation 2018."

25 Gajanan, Majita. "The USWNT Seeks Nearly $67 Million in Damages In Equal Pay Lawsuit Against U.S. Soccer. Here's What to Know About the Case." Time Magazine. February 21, 2020. https://time.com/5653250/uswnt-equal-pay-lawsuit/

26 Andrew Das, "U.S. Women's Players and U.S. Soccer Settle Equal Pay Lawsuit." *New York Times*, May 22, 2022, https://www.nytimes.com/2022/02/22/sports/soccer/us-womens-soccer-equal-pay.html

27 Reeves, *Of Boys and Men*, 24.

28 Richard Reeves & Isabel V. Sawhill, "Men}s Lib," The New York Times, November 14, 2015. https://www.nytimes.com/2015/11/15/opinion/sunday/mens-lib.html?_r=0

29 Reeves, *Of Boys and Men*, 21.

30 Smialek, "Claudia Goldin Wins Nobel in Economics for Studying Women in the Work Force."

31 Gretchen Livingston, "Stay-at-home moms and dads account for about one-in-five U.S. parents," PEW Research Center, last modified September 24, 2018, https://www.pewresearch.org/fact-tank/2018/09/24/stay-at-home-moms-and-dads-account-for-about-one-in-five-u-s-parents/

32 Michelle Wolf, "Nice Lady," Performance at the Apollo, 2018, retrieved from The Female Lead, uploaded on September 3, 2023, https://www.youtube.com/watch?v=HRA8LsMNqTQ

33 Claudia Goldin, *Career and Family: Women's Century-long Journey Toward Equity* (Princeton, New Jersey, Princeton University Press, 2021).

34 Livingston, "Stay-at-home moms and dads account for about one-in-five U.S. parents."

35 Livingston, "Stay-at-home moms and dads account for about one-in-five U.S. parents."

36 Jennifer Chowdhury, "Woman of Impact: Reshma Saujani," In Style, November 1, 2023, https://www.instyle.com/reshma-saujani-moms-first-woman-of-impact-8385201

37 Gloria Steinem, "The Importance of Work," *Outrageous Acts and Everyday Rebellions*, 3rd Edition (New York, NY: Henry Holt and Company, 2019).

38 Kathy Gurcheik, "Availability, Use of Paternity Leave Remains Rare in U.S.," SHRM: Better Workplaces Better World, last modified August 16, 2019, https://www.shrm.org/resourcesandtools/hr-topics/behavioral-competencies/global-and-cultural-effectiveness/pages/availability-use-of-paternity-leave-remains-rare-in-us.aspx

39 Richard V. Reeves, *Of Boys and Men*, 24.

40 Richard V. Reeves & Isabel V. Sawhill, "Men's Lib," *The New York Times*, November 14, 2015. https://www.nytimes.com/2015/11/15/opinion/sunday/mens-lib.html?_r=0

41 Hooks, *Feminism is for Everybody*, 43.

42 Amanda Marcotte, "Nancy Reagan's anti-feminism might be her most lasting legacy," Salon, March 7, 2016, https://www.salon.com/2016/03/07/nancy_reagans_anti_feminism_might_be_her_most_lasting_legacy/

43 Tshiamo Mobe, "10 Women Scientists Leading the Fight Against the Climate Crisis: These incredible women in STEM fields are working towards a greener future," *Global Citizen*, April 11, 2022, https://www.globalcitizen.org/en/content/women-scientists-climate-change-solutions-stem/#:~:text=The%20Reuters%20Hot%20List%20of,reaching%20implications%20of%20climate%20change

44 Center for American Progress, "The Basic Facts About Women in Poverty: Women, especially women of color, in the United States are more likely to live in poverty than men, and they need robust, targeted solutions to ensure their long-term economic security," *Center for American*

Progress, August 3, 2020, https://www.americanprogress.org/article/basic-facts-women-poverty/

45 Reeves, *Of Boys and Men*: Why the Modern Male Is Struggling, Why It Matters, and What to Do About It Washington, D.C.: Brookings Institution Press, 2022.

46 Reeves, Of Boys and Men: Why the Modern Male Is Struggling, Why It Matters, and What to Do About It Washington, D.C.: Brookings Institution Press, 2022.

47 Center for American Progress, "The Basic Facts About Women in Poverty."

48 UN Women Editors, "Visualizing the data."

49 A.W. Geiger and Kim Parker, "For Women's History Month, a look at gender gains – and gaps – in the U.S.," PEW Research Center, last modified March 15, 2018, https://www.pewresearch.org/fact-tank/2018/03/15/for-womens-history-month-a-look-at-gender-gains-and-gaps-in-the-u-s/

50 Jessica Saracino, "The Effect of Socioeconomic Status on the Number of Women in State Legislatures," *Public Purpose: An Interdixciplinary Journal American University's Graduate School of Public Affairs*, Vol. 6. Issue 1 (Spring 2008), https://www.american.edu/spa/publicpurpose/upload/the-effect-of-socioeconomic-status-on-the-number-of-women-in-state-legislatures.pdf, 125.

51 Saracino, "The Effect of Socioeconomic Status on the number of women in State Legislatures," 125.

52 Amy Caiazza, "Does Women's Representation in Elected Office Lead to Women-Friendly Policy? Analysis of State-Level Data," Women & Politics, 26:1, 37, DOI: 10.1300/J014v26n01_03.

53 Caiazza, "Does Women's Representation in Elected Office Lead to Women-Friendly Policy?" 41.

54 Caiazza, "Does Women's Representation in Elected Office Lead to Women-Friendly Policy?" 45.

55 Frank Newport, David Moore, and Lydia Saad, "Long-Term Gallup Poll Trends: A Portrait of American Public Opinion Through the Century," last modified December 20, 1999, http://news.gallup.com/poll/3400/longterm-gallup-poll-trends-portrait-american-public-opinion.aspx

56 Mary McGrath, "Opinion: Are Americans ready for a female president? Yes. In fact they might prefer one," last modified November 24, 2019, http://www/latimes.com/opinion/story/2019-11-24/elect-woman-president-warren

57 Laurel Thatcher Ulrich, Personal Communication, August 22, 2022.

58 Myra Sadker & David Sadker, *Failing at fairness: How America's schools cheat girls*, New York, NY: Simon and Schuster, 2010, 76.

59 Lumen Learning, "Gender Differences in the Classroom," Educational Psychology, N.D., https://courses.lumenlearning.com/suny-educational psychology/chapter/gender-differences-in-the-classroom/

60 Myra Sadker & David Sadker, *Failing at fairness: How America's schools cheat girls*, New York, NY: Simon and Schuster, 2010, 5.

61 Kaylene M. Stevens & Christopher C. Martell, "Feminist social studies teachers: The role of teachers' backgrounds and beliefs in shaping gender-equitable practices," *The Journal of Social Studies Research*, 2018, https://doi.org/10.1016/j.jssr.2018.02.002i, 4.

62 Karen Zittleman and David Sadker, "Gender Bias in Teacher Education Texts: New (and Old) Lessons," Journal of Teacher Education 53, no. 2 (March 2002): 168–80. https://doi.org/10.1177/0022487102053002008, 178.

63 Marina Bassi & Mateo Diaz, Mercedes & Blumberg, Rae & Reynoso, Ana, Failing to notice? Uneven teachers' attention to boys and girls in the classroom, IZA Journal of Labor Economics, 2018, 7. 10.1186/s40172-018-0069-4, 16.

64 Elizabeth J. Meyer, "Sex, Gender, and Education Research: The Case for Transgender Studies in Education," Educational Researcher 51, no. 5 (June 2022): 315–23, https://doi.org/10.3102/0013189X211048870, 316.

65 Margaret Smith Crocco, "The missing discourse about gender and sexuality in the social studies," *Theory into Practice*, 2001, 40(1), 65.

66 Crocco, "The missing discourse about gender and sexuality in the social studies," 67.

67 Stevens & Martell, "Feminist Social Studies Teachers," 9.

68 Schmeichel, "Skirting around critical feminist rationales for teaching women in social studies," 2.

69 Schmeichel, "Skirting around critical feminist rationales for teaching women in social studies," 2.

5

Learning to Embrace Controversy

Why should a democratic people dedicated to equality not apply the attention now given to the roles in history of women?... Is this the voice of 'political correctness' or a recognition of the link between a democratic society anymore historically complete and accurate rendering of the past?[1]

— Gary B. Nash, Charlotte Crabtree, and Ross E. Dunn, *History on Trial*

Don't Patronize Our Youth

Our students of all genders need comprehensive women's history. Since "doing" history, which means developing the knowledge and skills of budding historians and social scientists, is a desired outcome for secondary graduates, inclusive and diverse women's history aligns perfectly. It is important that, as teachers learn, they give women's history the chance to be equally complicated, as his-story is. In the study of women's history, where the patterns of the past reoccur in strong cycles, it is important to do the story justice. When discussing the subordination of women in power, Mary Beard wrote, "The long view will help us to avoid the simple diagnosis of 'misogyny' that we tend to be a bit lazy to fall back on."[2] She said, "If we want to understand—and do something about—the fact that women, even when they're not silenced, still have to pay a very high price for being heard, we need to recognize it it's

DOI: 10.4324/9781003472889-6

a bit more complicated and that there is a long backstory."[3] Teachers have the power to explore this complexity with students—to understand women's agency amid oppression. Doing this will allow women from the past, and therefore women in the present, to be seen, heard, and complicated.

Making students, and sometimes their families, aware of hardships that women have faced and still face may challenge worldviews. If one's definition of feminism is "anti-men," then giving feminism any airtime would be difficult. Those students are the hardest to teach and guide through discussions of women and gender. Even sympathetic students are hard to manage, because the worldview of most adolescents is pretty black and white. They have yet to see the grey areas and nuance. A classmate who questions whether men should be denied opportunities to take overtime pay in order to close the pay gap, for instance, may be called "sexist" by other students who see themselves as "champions" of women's rights. Having and leading these conversations are hard.

It is made even more difficult in a polarized political climate that demonizes public educators for teaching the most current scholarship and bans books about diverse people and experiences. Teachers are in the trenches of a struggle for freedom, democracy, and intellectualism. They daily defend the First Amendment and are creating the spaces where students can talk across political, social, race, and class difference. Teachers are saving our democracies and training a new generation to battle extremism. Teachers should be proud of what they do to build relationships, create little intellectuals, and teach tolerance. Talking about women's topics remains controversial, and teachers who try *will* face push back. Unfortunately, dealing with challenges is part of the mission, as all worthy missions are. It's time that teachers embrace the controversy, expect it, and not be worn down by it.

Background: They Tore Up My Books

I have been accused by students and parents of being too conservative, too liberal, too moderate, not enough of an activist, or too much of an activist. The feedback has sometimes been hurtful and malicious. All I want to do is teach kids. One student walked into my class and saw a quote from Ida B. Wells-Barnett on the wall with a fist next to it, said it was too "Black Lives Matter," and refused to take my class. Once students trashed my classroom, ripping up and tossing copies of a classroom set of books they politically disagreed with—not the other books, just that one. Did I have two different class sets? Yes. Did I teach both sides? Yes, they just didn't want to hear the other one—but that is my job. My colleagues helped me clean up the room before the first class, and I taught with a fire under me like never before. This is what teachers do.

In my early years teaching US history, I used a collection of primary sources, an online textbook, *A People's History of the United States*, and *A Patriot's History of the United States*, a book written in reaction to the former. For almost every topic, we would examine these various sources to come to a deeper understanding of the events. One day, my principal came to me with a letter from a parent who claimed I was having them read from a "known anarchist." By this, the parent meant Howard Zinn, a professor of history at Spelman College and later political science at Boston University, a World War II veteran, and the author of *A People's History of the United States*. Being new to the profession, I was nervous. *Am I in trouble?*

My meeting with the principal took a mere 30 seconds. He said, "Send an email to the parent explaining your use of the text in the class." That was it. Good teaching can be defended, and he knew that. I wrote my email and the case was closed.

Every year for the rest of my career, I faced these types of criticisms from parents. And every year, I would write an email explaining how I used that source. That was the crux of it—it's not what sources are used in the class-room but *how they are used*.

Navigating the challenging political climate is part of being a teacher. A few years later, a parent exempted their child from my course for a week because I was teaching about the LGBTQ+ movement. I had started the unit by teaching students the definition of sodomy and exploring religious and legal histories that influence present sentiments about the issue. The mother did not want her daughter learning about that. I prepared an alternative cur-riculum on Black civil rights activists. Months later, I finally had a chance to talk to that mother. Too much is lost in translation between a student's interpretation of what happens in the classroom and what the parent hears at home. When I was able to explain my methods, the mother said, "If I had known that is how you intended to teach it, I might have let her stay." I learned a good deal that day about how to bring parents and other stake-holders in.

The hardest feedback I ever got was from a bold and openly gay student I had during my second year of teaching. He told me how hurtful it was to have to debate his right to marriage, in my classes. He was not wrong. And yet the only unit I ever had parents remove students from was the LGBTQ+ unit. People were debating it on the Supreme Court, and my classroom needed to provide a space for honest discussion and understanding of the issues at hand. This happened at his (and likely other students') expense in order to build deeper understanding with their peers. Part of having a strong reflec-tive practice is hearing critiques that are valid. Hearing this kid's pain caused me to change my tone and approach.

I've been criticized a great deal—but most frequently from people on the right. No one ever criticized my use of *A Patriot's History of the United States*, whose introduction includes an explicitly conservative intention. No one criticized me for having students explore the platform of the America First Committee or reading the anti-Semitic speeches by Charles Lindbergh. Not once did anyone ever complain that I had students read excerpts from Adolf Hitler's book *Mein Kampf*. Not one criticism. *What does this tell me?* The criticisms of my classroom tell me more about the politics of the criticizer than they do about what I'm doing.

Grounding my pedagogy in sources, inquiry, and evidence, I grew thick skin and confidence that I could withstand the culture wars which were brewing around me. I developed a strong sense of mission and loved the work of teaching tolerance, challenging frameworks, and making strong thinkers.

Then the pressure shifted from outside the education profession to the top. In the wake of the 2016 election, the Governor appointed an extreme Education Commissioner who had never held any position in education and chose to home-school his own kids. He set about promoting a voucher program which reduced funding to public schools and seemed to seek opportunities to de-professionalize the work we did in schools.[4] After Republicans won both the House and the Senate in the New Hampshire legislature in 2020, they increased their efforts to restrict the professional decisions of teachers. Their target was Critical Race Theory (CRT).

While I knew that many K–12 teachers talked about systems theory, I didn't know a single teacher who taught CRT in their high school classes—it's a legal theory taught in law schools. I was not familiar with it and had to look it up when the press began reporting that other states were passing laws hostile to it.

Then the national iteration of the culture wars became local. In 2021, as I drove to the high school where I taught, I started to notice huge blue printed signs lining the road that read "Save Our Children." A couple of loud folks in that community were worried about the teaching of CRT in US history classes. Not one of the people who showed up to the school board meetings to rail against what we were teaching knew that I was the only US history teacher. None of them knew my name. None of them knew that I was an award-winning history teacher. Or that my students tested above state averages on AP exams. Or that our school led more students to the national contest for National History Day than any other school in the state. None came to observe my classes and actually *see* what I was doing—and I did invite them. None asked my kids, who were confused and scared by the political climate, what it was like to take my classes. It wasn't personal. It was political. I was the invisible teacher in the middle of the culture wars. This was the world that teachers were teaching in and still are. Classrooms have become politicized, teachers demonized, and curriculum scrutinized.

The anti-CRT law did pass, but only after revisions which took the teeth out of it.[5] Essentially, teachers could teach Black history, they just couldn't tell kids that because they were white, they were racist. *Was that even happening in schools?* The law was so frustratingly vague that it put everyone in a panic. *If I talk about Frederick Douglass, am I going to be accused of violating the CRT law and lose my teaching license?* Ten of the seventeen members of the Governor's Advisory Council on Diversity and Inclusion resigned.[6] Teachers everywhere stood somewhere between terrified and indignant. I was indignant.

In the summer of 2021, as the President of New Hampshire Council for the Social Studies (NHCSS) and having just accepted a teaching position at Plymouth State University as Coordinator of Social Studies Education, I was thrust into the local spotlight. I spoke out against the Commissioner's silencing tactics.[7] I championed the inquiry model as a solution to the culture wars over this topic. To me it's not about the books or the primary material that is read in the classroom but about *how* it is presented, analyzed, and discussed.[8] I also explained my concerns about *how* a state would actually enforce the law. I know from my own experience that students regularly misinterpret things that happen in the classroom. Some students lie to protect themselves. I regularly taught classes in which no other adult witnesses were present. So how exactly would one prove that a teacher taught in a way that violated this law? But I also knew that the law was weakly written at best. No one was going to get fired.

At our state's annual social studies conference, I addressed a room of teachers and I think I spoke to the moment we were in. Teachers, many of us with graduate degrees, were being criticized by laypeople over content we've spent our careers studying. I challenged them all to be brave in the face of the climate we are in. I told them what I've told you, that I'm in it too and we can support each other through it. It received an ovation and applause. Years later, it is still referenced at the annual conference.

Fear is a great tactic. If teachers became afraid that they "might" be challenged and "might" lose their teaching license, they might stop teaching controversial topics altogether. Some did. Then a New Hampshire chapter of Mom's for Liberty created a fund—a reward for the first person to successfully get a New Hampshire teacher fired.[9] This bounty made national headlines.

No one lost their job. So the commissioner got ugly and did what bullies do—he used his platform and power to scare teachers. He wrote an opinion piece in which he blasted "advocate teachers" for "bias" and teaching about sensitive topics like sexuality and gender. He provided a link to a PDF of "real evidence" submitted to the Department of Education, including a mention of a nonbinary teacher who asked the class to address them by their preferred pronouns "they/them." He was lambasted by the press for bigotry.

One of the people on his PDF had been in the audience at my presidential address that fall. A substitute teacher took a picture of a chart in her classroom that showed the various systems of government and conveniently cropped it to show only "socialism" and its definition. She was investigated over an issue that should have been immediately dismissed as absurd. Her investigation was unknown to the NHCSS, this teacher was on our short list for the 2022 Teacher of the Year. She won. In her speech, she referenced my address and reminded everyone to be brave, "you might just win Teacher of the Year."

All around the country and world, battles over what gets taught in schools are being fought by people who aren't often experts in education or content areas. The recent iteration is just inflammation of the culture wars that have long plagued public education. They are old and need to be treated as such. These laws are part of a larger agenda to delegitimize and de-professionalize the public schools. Teachers have the degrees and coursework in child development, not legislators. Teachers have the background in their content area, not legislators. They had to meet a minimum GPA, not legislators. Teachers have passed qualifying assessments to hold their posts. They are the certified, local professionals—they are the best and the brightest of local workforces. *What is the point of all that rigor if we are going to then harass them while they do the work?*

Being brave does not mean being unafraid or not frustrated. It does not mean that things around you are fine. Being brave is feeling the fear and doing it anyway. Women's history is heartbreakingly controversial. Making room for women may mean less on x and suddenly we are back in the culture war. Failure to be brave benefits the status quo, one that is woefully absent of diverse figures and ideas.

Barrier: Women's History Is Controversial

Controversy touches every subject of the social studies, and educators need to hone their craft of delicately mediating controversy. Most history and teacher education programs provide educators with sociological tools for analyzing race and class in their curriculum—but too few teachers are prepared to discuss gender and sexuality. Within women's history, it is impossible not to encounter topics about power and the patriarchy, rape and sexual assault, gender expression, diverse sexual preferences, and abortion. Paradigms and frameworks for analyzing women in history are absent from many teacher training programs, causing some to shy away from deeply integrating these topics in the curriculum. Writing in 2001, Margaret Smith Crocco made plain that these issues are not new and should not deter us from teaching diverse children in our classrooms. She said:

> Not only do teachers risk significant resistance to their efforts at broaching these topics due to the entrenched attitudes of an essentially conservative profession and within many parent communities, but also because of the pressures in terms of curriculum coverage emanating from today's standards/high stakes testing movement.
>
> No doubt, many teachers themselves lack depth of understanding of these issues or bring religious and personal objections to certain aspects of this subject. Furthermore, few teacher education programs in the social studies tackle gender, much less sexuality. At the secondary teacher preparation level, the focus is often on creating subject matter specialists rather than teachers concerned with caring for the whole child.[10]

Discussing Rape and Sexual Assault

Our textbooks and teachers fail to do justice to the violence against women in all parts of the world and, in so many ways, cover it up through omission. One in every handful of women we know has been sexually assaulted. As a woman, I was privy to stories from friends who had been sexually assaulted by their babysitters, strangers, or some guy at a party in college. These are stories that friends told me in confidence: quietly. Women whispered about these things before the #MeToo movement, when speaking about sexual harassment and assault became more widespread. I watched as each of these friends came forward. And I watched as, one by one, they were doubted, shamed, and harassed. *Why don't people believe women? Is it the heroification of men? Is it the high burden of proof within our legal system? Is it years of indoctrination into a patriarchal structure that favors men?* Or is it that we don't know our own history—that sexual assault and rape were pervasive throughout it?

This is incredibly common in the way war is discussed. Histories written by the victors rarely discuss how the vanquished are treated and even more rarely discuss the impact on women. Rape and war go hand in hand, but talking about rape in the secondary classroom is intimidating if not impossible because of school policies. But to ignore rape as an effect of war is to not really teach war and to cover up women's history, intentionally or unintentionally. The covering up of rape denies children very important contexts for understanding global conflicts and relationships between certain peoples.

In World War II, for instance, Japanese soldiers raped thousands of Chinese women during their assaults on their cities. These women were often referred to as "comfort women," a terrible term to explain their plight. French and Polish women found themselves in difficult positions without suste-nance for their families and needing kindness and favor from Nazi soldiers. Discussions and debates about this dynamic and the meaning of the term *con-sent* in these situations are essential to helping students understand concepts of consent today. French women who "collaborated" with Nazis were labeled as whores following the war; their hair was chopped off, and they were often brutalized in public. Learning about Soviet armies marching on Berlin to end the war without discussing the topic of rape leaves students without con-text for German women's behavior. Many committed suicide rather than be gang-raped by Soviet soldiers. One primary account stated, "Red Army soldiers don't believe in 'individual liaisons' with German women... Nine, ten, twelve men at a time—they rape them on a collective basis."[11] A female journalist based in Berlin, Natalya Gesse, observed, "The Russian soldiers were raping every German female from eight to eighty."[12] Russian soldiers denied the accounts, insisting that women were asking for it or deserved it. Allied soldiers in the West, American, British, Canadian, French—they too raped women in their march across Germany.[13] Women who had collaborated with the Nazis or Japanese faced immeasurable social shame. Their heads were shaved, and they were paraded as whores and ostracized—worse, they were physically assaulted by their countrymen.[14] Whatever the reason for its absence, the coverage is factually inaccurate.

One would think that, further back in history, coverage of these atrocities would be more common, as the people and nations discussed are further and further removed, but in some cases, the coverage is actually worse. The spread of the Mongol Empire, for instance, was rapid and vast, accomplished largely by the wholesale slaughter of the conquered, something common throughout world history. Often not mentioned is the plight of women, who were raped or taken as concubines after the men they knew and loved were murdered. These women, in many cases, were forced to bear the children of their cap-tors. A genetic study in 2003 found that about 16 million people living today are directly related to Genghis Khan, the Mongol leader.[15] He had four legiti-mate sons, who would go on to father dozens of illegitimate children. One was known to welcome 30 new virgins to his harem every day.[16] Women were ranked by beauty, the prettiest sent to him and the less attractive to his sons. How are the rape and trafficking of these women discussed? Almost all the world history texts I examined omitted these details. Of the books that I've found, the AP world history textbook *Ways of the World* is the most inclusive of women, but even this book, in its chapter on pastoral peoples, shies away from rape. The authors discuss the Mongols' treatment of women and note that the Chinese, Arab, and European neighbors found the more egalitarian treatment of women unseemly, but they fail to mention the plight of women conquered by the Mongol army. They offer two sentences on the subject: "City after city was utterly destroyed and enemy soldiers were passed out in lots to Mongol troops for execution, while women and skilled craftsmen were enslaved" and "Historians continue to debate the extent and uniqueness of the Mongols' brutality, but their reputation for unwavering harshness proved a military asset."[17] The authors seem perfectly fine with traumatizing students with the vision of mass execution, but of the thousands of women sent on for perpetual rape, they remain silent.

If it's possible to do worse than omission, contemporary media accomplished it. *The Guardian* titled an article about Khan's mass rapes "We owe it all to superstud Genghis,"[18] and the *National Geographic* titled their Valentine's Day article "Genghis Khan a Prolific Lover, DNA Data Implies."[19] Genghis Khan was a serial rapist who used polygamy, rape, and military prowess to conquer the world—love and attraction had nothing to do with it. These article titles are examples of the persistent rape culture that plagues not only our culture but also our history.

War is not the only place where rape is ignored. Rape is ignored in our history curriculum when it offends our own history. One cannot teach about slavery, Reconstruction, or the civil rights movement without centralizing rape. The children of enslaved women were destined for slavery as prescribed by state laws, so white masters were given legal permission to rape and "breed" Black women at their mercy. Harriet Jacobs was an escaped slave who wrote that her motivation to flee her master was because he had prepared an outbuilding that he planned to use as a rape house for her. At the time, she was still a child.[20] During Reconstruction, countless Black women were raped to "put them in their place" and to show Black men how powerless they were to stop it.

This dynamic in the South continued through the civil rights movement of the 1950s and 1960s, highlighted by the Montgomery bus boycott. Recy Taylor was one of many women who were sexually harassed and assaulted in the Montgomery area. She was gang-raped by seven white men in 1944 while walking home from church with a friend and her son.[21] Recy survived the encounter and reported her case to the sheriff, including a description of the car.[22] The sheriff interrogated the owner of the car, who confessed to the crime, also naming the men who were with him. The sheriff then released the confessed rapist. The next evening, Recy Taylor's home was burned down. Not one person was charged for these heinous crimes. The National Women's History Museum explained, "Even though Taylor reported the crime, witnesses confirmed her story, and one of the men confessed, the men were not brought into custody."[23] She and her family fled. The NAACP and notable activists like Rosa Parks, Mary Church Terrell, Langston Hughes, and W. E. B. Du Bois flooded the area to address this grievous wrong. Despite two grand juries being convened, no one was prosecuted for the crime. You won't find Recy Taylor's story in a history textbook. It wasn't until 2011 that historian Danielle L. McGuire told Taylor's story in her book, *At the Dark End of the Street*, which highlighted her story and those of countless other women who lived in the Montgomery area. To tell the story of the Montgomery bus boycott and ignore the women raped and assaulted by white officials in that community is to completely deny children the context as to *why* they were boycotting to begin with!

As a result, Rosa Parks is perhaps one of the most misrepresented women in history, mostly because of the emphasis on race equity rather than her work for gender too. Her "sheroification" has erased the other crucial women in the movement. Taylor's case was just one of many rape cases that Parks investigated on behalf of Black families. Another notable case was a woman named Gertrude Perkins, who was raped by two police officers in uniform.[24] A decade later, tensions over the Montgomery bus system rose not only because the drivers were racist but because they were sexually harassing women who rode the bus.[25] JoAnn Robinson was the head of a Black women's organization in Montgomery that was working to address the treatment of Black women. She wrote petitions to the mayor months before the boycott to try to bring about a change, to little avail. Resolved to finally do something about the situation, Parks sat down very intentionally in December of that year and refused to move when the bus driver asked her to. Upon her now infamous arrest, JoAnn Robinson printed flyers and distributed them to the women of Montgomery, calling for a one-day strike that ended up lasting a year.[26] It was *after* the strike was under way that the male clergy became involved.[27]

To accurately teach the history of the boycott requires teachers who both know this information and are willing to tackle those topics in their classrooms. To look at Parks only in relation to her race ignores that she was also a woman living in a world that gave white men unbelievable privilege. Is it the sexual nature of rape that keeps it out of the secondary history classroom? Is rape worse than lynching? Worse than torture? Genocide? We teach about all these things in history classes. The only obvious difference is that rape happens to women at the hands of men. The patriarchy justifies itself as necessary to protect women. Is this dark side of women's history not taught because rape is evidence of the ultimate failure of the patriarchy to protect women's interests?

History teachers do not hold back on violence that men face, and this double standard in the classroom contributes to the double standard outside of it. If people were aware of how common rape has been throughout history, few would be surprised by sexual assault statistics or that the United Nations has deemed patriarchal violence against women the most pressing human rights of our time.

Discussing Abortion

There is no "women's topic" more controversial and yet more important than abortion in contemporary society. Women's lives hang in the balance of an educated public and the officials they elect. While the school health teacher may understand the science and process behind an abortion, they are not skilled in teaching across differences: *the social studies teacher is.*

If social studies teachers are not teaching abortion, who is? Where are students learning about the women who get an abortion and why? Where are they learning about the procedure and about fetal and maternal health rates? Where are students forming their opinions about it? Where are they learning that women across the political spectrum disagree on abortion? And where are they learning that not everyone agrees with their perspective? Whether pro-abortion or anti-abortion, we should want our citizens to understand the issue and take evidence-based positions that save as many lives as possible. If teachers don't address critical lines of questioning on abortion, where will students be challenged to value women for their full humanity and right to their bodies?

The inequitable experience and burden of reproduction that have been placed on women throughout time have led to complicated legal battles over competing rights in society. Important questions need to be both understood and answered:

- ◆ Do women deserve privacy in healthcare decisions related to their bodies?
- ◆ When should the government be allowed to intrude on those conversations?
- ◆ Is it possible for nonmedical professionals like the police and government to decide what is a health emergency?
- ◆ Do the unborn have rights over the mother's rights? If so, at what point?
- ◆ Do fathers have rights over their unborn offspring?
- ◆ Can the government force women to carry out a pregnancy?
- ◆ What role should medical science play in legal policy?
- ◆ What comparisons can be drawn between pregnancy and other health conditions?
- ◆ Is there an equivalent comparison where the government intervened with men's bodies or healthcare?

Any or all of those could be discussion questions for the classroom.

In a government class, a proper question for inquiry could be *What should be done about abortion?* I like this question because it is grounded in the reality of abortion. I built a three-day inquiry available on the Remedial Herstory Project's website with my colleague Dr. Alicia Gutierrz-Romine, a medical historian and professor who specializes in 20th-century illegal abortion. We broke the issue down using polling data from Gallup and Pew Research Center, historical documents, moral and religious perspectives, medical fact sheets, and more.

Before the inquiry should even begin, we lay some groundwork and rules for decorum:

> This inquiry is understandably difficult for students to discuss and teachers to facilitate because of the highly charged political climate that surrounds the issue of abortion. Before beginning the inquiry, the teacher should lay some ground rules to moderate students and establish decorum. Consider the following:
> Objective: to better understand the abortion debate.
>
> **Rules for Decorum**
> 1. We will assume everyone values the lives of both women and babies.
> 2. We will assume everyone tries to respect women.
> 3. We will assume everyone acts with morality.
> 4. We will not accuse each other of misogyny or murder, although we might read it.
> 5. We will avoid personal examples and strive for hypothetical ones.

In the next section, I will discuss the problem of insisting on civility in discussion, but for now, humor me. These ground rules make clear that the teacher is looking for evidence-based practices that do the most good.

In the inquiry, day 1 is a fact-finding mission. *What is an abortion, and is it a safe and humane procedure?* Students learn about the different types of abortions and at what stage in pregnancy they occur. The sources debunk the fallacies promoted by the right in the propaganda film *The Silent Scream*, while giving credence through medical sources where and at what point in the pregnancy the procedure could have health impacts on the mother and be painful for the fetus.

On day 2, the discussion moves toward the history of abortion with the question: *What was it like when abortion was illegal?* For those who are inclined toward abortion bans, these sources, including newspaper evidence of various trials and deaths, give students a window into what it was like when abortion was illegal in the US during the 1930s-1970s. These sources could be supplemented with newspapers since *Dobbs*. Maternal and infant death rates should be presented to students and some of the hardest medical cases and unique incestuous and rape cases examined so students can appreciate that laws need to be written in a way to apply to *all* cases. Students could even be sent on a WebQuest to find their own source material so long as it came from a variety of perspectives and media outlets. In a world history class, this could be a cultural comparison.

On day 3, the discussion shifts toward morality, asking *Is abortion moral?* We saved this one for last for probably obvious reasons. To not ask the question would invalidate a huge argument in the religious right's playbook: the innocence of the unborn child. Asking the question allows the complex moral judgments at play in abortion to be hashed out too. *Is it morally right to force a minor to give birth? Or a rape victim? Or a mother of three who might die during pregnancy number four?* All of this should be on the table so that the "moral police" on all sides can see that it's a bit more complicated.

The goal of discussing these topics is not to resolve it but to hear and understand each other. At the end of the full inquiry, a good outcome would be that students are able to articulate multiple perspectives in the public debates and to honestly say and understand whose rights they are willing to squash if their policy perspective were upheld. Emphasis throughout should be placed on the greatest public good.

My personal opinions on abortion are probably obvious. I'm vehemently pro-choice in all cases. The death rates for women *and* infants speak for themselves. I probably wouldn't share my opinions with my students; I want them to come to their own understandings. But as their teacher, I want those understandings to be grounded in fact and the greatest public good. It does not hurt me to listen to anti-abortion arguments. Quite the contrary, it makes me understand the issues more deeply. I may have strong opinions, but the essence of our field is also learning to talk across difference. I am not scared of a little disagreement, and I'm certainly not scared to defend my opinion.

My opinion on abortion was shaped by the stories of my friends and my own horrible birth experience. Knowing all I went through physically and emotionally, I grew in my empathy for other women. You don't have to agree with me to see how personal experiences or stories of other people's real experiences with healthcare and pregnancy could deeply influence them. These private experiences must come out into the discourse for people to consider all the possible scenarios and make informed voting decisions.

Having a one-off conversation about abortion in government class is hard if medical history and abortion have not been discussed throughout the social studies courses. High school teachers fail to show the depth of women's second-class status, the way culture shamed women for male behaviors, and how little power women had over their bodies. Hell, marital rape became illegal only recently and remains un-aggressively prosecuted in some states.[28]

If teachers bring up abortion only in 20th-century history classes, it creates a false narrative that abortion is new. Teachers need to go far back enough to know about how common abortion was, how practices were known, and how the lack of real religious history has given us the illusion that *religion* is fueling the attacks on abortion rights.

For most of history, governments declined to rule on abortion, leaving these decisions to women in their private conversations with other women. The use of contraceptive and abortive measures is documented in the historic record as far back as can be traced and are elaborated on by the Greeks and Egyptians. Around the world, scriptural interpretations related to life allowed room for some form of abortion, even in the most rigged communities. Although the Quran does not directly address abortion at all, it clearly divided the development of the fetus into four categories, which most scholars interpreted to mean that abortion was legal up to a certain point.[29] The Islamic position on abortion is not monolithic and is complicated in some more conservative cultures by their harsh stance on "illegal pregnancies," or pregnancies out of wedlock—punishable by 100 lashes in some places! In the Jewish and Christian faiths, the scriptures made clear that abortion was allowed until the quickening, or until the mother could begin to feel the baby moving, which is around halfway to term.[30] As a result, Jewish women have been leading the charge in defense of their religious freedom and right to an abortion wherever it is under attack.

As conditions for women in giving birth began to improve, so increased the assault on their freedom to choose whether to become mothers. In the mid-1800s, governments became engaged in regulating contraception methods and abortions. They also passed laws that held men liable for women's poor behavior during pregnancy, reinforcing the patriarchal norm, when all around women were beginning to advocate for their rights.

Dragged in front of judges and juries in the first decades of the 1900s, women seeking abortions and their doctors accused of murder began to speak publicly about something that had previously been private.[31] These public conversations helped society understand the gray areas around abortion and the ways in which contraception and abortion allowed adult women to live full lives. The testimonies included women with terminal pregnancies, harried mothers who can't take on another kid, a traumatized rape victim, a woman who would have to quit her job, a girl who was separated from her lover, and a woman in an abusive relationship. They also highlight some of the major challenges our society faces today, specifically how to hold men accountable for causing pregnancy and how to hold men accountable to their children and ensure that they support women they impregnate. Even today, child support does not begin until *after* birth, so mothers are alone with their medical bills and preparing for the arrival of their baby.[32]

Students should learn about each of the major Supreme Court cases that paved the way to legalizing abortion in the US. *Griswold v. Connecticut*, for example, was groundbreaking, and yet the legal arguments were far from feminist. It's important to consider why these early courts moved on these issues and what changed their minds. Students should understand the way the court worked to protect privacy of not just women but adult couples: men.

Roe v. Wade is one of the few agreed-upon women's history topics mentioned in the 50 state standards and is therefore an essential piece of history. As a result, the 2022 *Dobbs v. Jackson* decision which struck down *Roe v. Wade* should also be discussed in schools. The right to privacy which it created not only expanded women's freedom over their bodies but also protected interracial and homosexual couples.[33] The nuances of the case, the unique conditions of the not one but two plaintiffs, would all help children understand the issue more deeply and the challenge of creating a one-size-fits-all policy on the issue.

Students need to learn the history of abortion and discuss it in a nonpartisan climate. Otherwise, how will they learn to navigate this highly politicized topic out in the real world? If they aren't allowed to try out their arguments, ask feminist, structural questions, and be proven wrong in a safe space, what other opportunities are we giving students to practice being citizens? How are we teaching them to find points of agreement across differences? And, most importantly, if abortion is too controversial to be discussed in a democratic classroom, what does that say about democracy? Abortion touches economics, it touches government, it touches history, it touches sociology, it touches psychology, it touches anthropology. It is deeply entrenched in every subject of the social studies. Teachers should be brave enough to teach it.

Breaker: Be Brave

Social studies teachers are trained to discuss controversial topics in the classroom—they just may not have been trained to teach these topics. They must work to extend their training on race and class to gender and sexuality. The principles for examination are the same. Teachers in the classroom have the potential, right now, to try to be the stop gate. They have the power to decide if the same old fallacies about women will be told and if girls get to learn their history.

When teachers patronize their students, they leave them unprepared and teach them cowardly history. They deny boys examples of how to be allies to women and girls the tools to be self-sufficient. They deny girls the stories of real-life women who lived through violence, survived, and were resilient. Teachers need to be honest about the darker sides of humanity in order to find solutions to sexism, which continues to haunt our modern world.

Topics like rape, abortion, sex, and sexuality are seen as controversial, a coincidence that leads to the erasure of important, interesting, and highly relevant women's history. Teachers must make choices about what to include in their curriculum; they can't teach all of history, so anytime history is important, interesting, and highly relevant to students' lives, it should top their list of selection. When they encounter controversial topics, secondary teachers must lean into the controversy because that's where learning happens.

To make students better, teachers must be brave. They must address controversy, and they must show that the other half of the population exists. Teaching inclusive history and managing difficult conversations—*this* is what social studies teachers are trained and certified to do. Social studies teachers, more than teachers of any other subject, are qualified and prepared to take this on.

Criticisms of teachers are not new, and that should be calming, not stressful. Teachers are not alone; there are millions of us. Criticisms should also fuel us because they are a reminder of how important the work of public education, social studies, and diversity education is. *What social studies and history teachers do is the most important job in the world*. And they are needed, now more than ever. Teachers are the most valuable assets in their community because they create community citizens. Even though there is a concerted effort to drive teachers into the culture wars, teachers should not cave. Teachers know that inclusive history allows them to reach all children in their classes. Politicians and laypeople can squabble, but teachers have a responsibility to all the students in the room—to their education. All of them. Not just the boys.

The attacks on the profession and teacher's professionalism are real but not insurmountable. They are intended to intimidate teachers into teaching whitewashed, weak, noncontroversial his-story—but that is not what social studies teachers do. School is where students *practice* being citizens, theorize about ideas, and test their hypotheses. We expertly guide students through conversations to reach deeper understandings on issues of gender, sexuality, class, race, multiculturalism, and patriotism so students will become more informed citizens, better consumers of media, more empathetic toward their neighbors, and better participants in our democracy. We don't tell them what to think—rather, we show them many ways of thinking. That's the job of a teacher. It's what we do.

The responsibility to teach diverse and inclusive material is on social studies teachers more than anyone else. The world their students will enter is half female. The students in their classrooms are half female. They must be brave and let their class reflect the world: women are half of humanity.

Blueprint: Critical Inquiry

In Chapter 3, I introduced the challenges of teaching women, gender, and sexuality in the secondary classroom since these topics are so politicized and feminism is a dirty word. There I introduced scholarship by Mardi Schmeichel about the ways teachers "skirt" around feminism when discussing these topics and how this may hinder their efforts to promote gender equality and feminism. Schmeichel is, in effect, arguing that women's progress is tied to the bravery of teachers to address these issues, yet teachers tend to do it in a gender-neutral way.

Scholars refer to these two camps more specifically as "liberal feminists" and "critical feminists." They differ in principle but perhaps not in object. Liberal feminists focus on diversifying spaces, school resources, and adding more women.[34] Critical feminists, by contrast, focus on the effect that the patriarchy and structural sexism have on people's lives and experiences. Critical feminists promote widespread structural change and attempt to dismantle the patriarchy specifically. Critical feminists are overtly feminist, while liberal feminists may be more covert. Based on the findings in Chapter 3 where we discussed the F word, it should surprise no one that liberal feminism has been the most successful in education.

At this fourth stage, the words feminism, sexism, misogyny, and the patriarchy should be on the table. Here students should be invited to examine the structural underpinnings that effect and create the events in history. Women's history does not occur in a vacuum. It happens in a society, one dominated by the patriarchy. There are loads of different feminist theories out there, but they all have two main goals in common. First, they want to point out the obvious and not-so-obvious ways that men and women are treated unequally. Second, they want changes to get rid of those inequalities. When it comes to the nitty-gritty details, feminist scholars have their differences. They argue about stuff like how to define "sex" and "gender" and how much change needs to happen in relationships between genders and what's the best way to make that change. The so-called liberal feminists support equal opportunities, while others focus on radically shifting the structures of society. Basically, there are different flavors of feminist scholarship, some critical and others not so much.[35]

Dividing Feminists

Social reformers were usually pitted against each other. There was first the division between women who supported the 15th Amendment granting black men the right to vote and those who did not. This initial division split universal suffrage forces in favor of incremental suffrage. This initial division split advocates like Frederick Douglass and Alice Stone from Susan B. Anthony and Elizabeth Cady Stanton. After two decades, the forces reconciled and rejoined. The American Woman Suffrage Association united with the National Woman Suffrage Association to form the National American Woman Suffrage Association (NAWSA). So much alphabet soup.

Divisions among women didn't stop there. NAWSA refused to support a younger, more radical crop of women. Those women, led by Alice Paul and Lucy Burns, broke off to form the National Women's Party (NWP). Both NAWSA and NWP failed to fully include their Black sisters, leading many Black women to form clubs to meet the needs of the Black communities. Nevertheless, some women like Ida B. Wells and Mary Church Terrell rode out the storms, voicing their protest frequently.

Suffrage was countered at every step by not only men and male politicians but *other women* like Molly Elliot Seawell, who wrote prolifically in opposition. Anti-suffragists antagonized the suffragists, causing some to take more moderate positions in order to persuade others to their side.

When Paul proposed the Equal Rights Amendment (ERA) in the years after the vote, women again divided. The ERA said simply, "Equality of rights under the law shall not be denied or abridged by the United States or by any state on account of sex." If passed, it would have led to sweeping changes in legal codes. Some women, like Carrie Chapman Catt, wanted to preserve women's privileges, like the privilege to not be drafted, and opted instead for the slower change of targeting individual discriminatory laws, like those that prevented women from opening bank accounts, denied them equal protection under the law, the ability to serve on juries, and so on. With the disruption of the Great Depression and World War II, women's advocacy took a back seat to major challenges.

By the 1960s, women were poised, with decades of higher-wage work experience and politization behind them, to demand more, but again they were divided. Title IX passed, granting women equal access to educational programs; a series of causes related to birth control swung in favor of women ending with *Roe v. Wade*, which granted women a right to abortion; and the ERA passed Congress. Leading feminists like Bella Abzug, Shirley Chisolm, and Gloria Steinem worked to pass the amendment. But like the anti-suffragists before them, women like Phyllis Schlafly stood up in opposition, fearing the amendment would deny women privileges and force women out of the domestic sphere.

These two camps still exist, and we need to be conscious of how these groups are pitted against one another to slow their progress. As hard as liberal feminists may try, it is difficult to segregate feminism from its critical, more radical roots. Feminism is fundamentally critical of society's treatment of women to varying degrees. In his piece, Stopford explained that, in understanding feminism, "students must learn to be critical of dominant modes of sociocultural ideology, and they must learn to see, and see through, the distorted self-representations of sociocultural ideology through which hegemony simultaneously fantasises itself, and hides behind."[36] In other words, society has its own view of gender, which is perhaps a distortion of our state of nature. Students need to learn to see that it doesn't have to be that way and that we can reimagine a society that is more gender-friendly. In Stopford's experience teaching feminist philosophy at university, teaching feminism was more difficult than other philosophical concepts, which is bizarre given some of the wild philosophies out there. He said, some students "get it" quickly, some are open while others are "hostile."[37] It's important that teachers teach feminism well, so that those primed to be hostile are at least willing to listen.

Critical Feminist Theory, or CFT, is just one approach among feminist theories. It's a theory that parallels its more controversial cousin, Critical Race Theory. The foundations of CFT and CRT are the same, although they vary quite a bit between scholars. CFT is a theoretical approach (not a pedagogic approach) to examining society or history. It suggests that men and women are equal and therefore should have equal opportunity and rights, but if you've paid attention to politics lately, you know it's more complicated than that. At the Feminist Stage of inclusion, the question is should teachers be liberal feminists or critical feminists? Which is more effective in instruction? Which will receive pushback? And, most importantly, since all feminists want change, which is the fastest path to success?

Should Teachers Follow a Liberal or Critical Feminist Approach?

As with all things women's history and women's studies, more research needs to be done on the success of these approaches in the secondary classroom. That said, there are some indicators in the field and evidence from outside feminist scholarship that tell us what best practice is in social studies education: inquiry. In short, in a social studies classroom, teachers should not deviate from inclusive pedagogies and the inquiry model. Both of these promote democracy, are student-centered, dismantle classroom hierarchies, and create engaged, critical thinkers. That answer is neither inherently liberal nor critical; instead, it creates a measure by which one can evaluate our choice of feminist approaches. Since both inclusive pedagogy and the inquiry model have already been hashed out, here I want to discuss the dangers of critical feminism and the tendency of practitioners to become lecture-y about feminism rather than allow feminist ideology to manifest. Liberal feminism *has already* been used successfully in the classroom and is in line with every recommendation thus far in the book. Here I want to discuss teaching critical feminism in ways that are still in line with inquiry. When one preaches about feminism, they create a new hierarchy instead of modeling curiosity and inclusivity.

As a framework, CFT focuses less on the stories of individual women but rather the structures that cause oppression. The goal is to "unlearn" the patriarchy.[38] Stopford explained that "any critical feminism must challenge hegemonic practices in both knowledge-making and education."[39] In other words, in social studies, critical feminism requires that we interrogate how we know what we know about women and gender and the system of educating girls and boys about gender. The word "challenge" is important here. When something is challenged in court, another word for that is "tested." Challenged does not mean that traditional gender roles and expectations are discarded and replaced with some "woke" approach. Challenged means that those traditional roles are questioned, scrutinized, and examined through multiple lenses, and ultimately learners decide if those standards did serve and continue to serve the people living under them. It should be a test, not an answer. It *should be* an inquiry.

Of the many feminist perspectives, one that occurs in scholarly literature about secondary teaching is the bell hooks[40] critical feminist approach.[41] In her book, *Feminism is for Everybody*, she argues that

1. People are socialized to adopt sexist ways of thinking.
2. Gendered hierarchies are established when gender differences give men power over women and other genders.
3. There is a patriarchal power structure in society based on male supremacy.

These tenants are reinforced by the work of many feminist scholars, including Gerda Learner.[42] In my own life experience, I have found these to be true in most cases and most environments. Yet, in the teaching of feminism, each should be examined on a case-by-case basis to help students raised within a patriarchy to understand the tenants and how they apply to the specific example in front of them. According to Stopford, students need to learn to "see the distortions of hegemony" and thus have to "perform a profound act of political imagination" given their worldview has likely endorsed the patriarchy.[43] Therefore, teaching these tenants should involve presenting them not as truths but rather as questions to examine or lenses through which to be curious.

Let's explore an example. One women's topic that many teachers hit is the arrest of Susan B. Anthony in 1872. She went with a group of women to register to vote, arguing that the Fourteenth Amendment guaranteed their vote under the due process clause. The inspectors of election allowed them to vote. The day of the presidential election, the women voted. They were later arrested. Anthony refused to leave her home until she was handcuffed, making a scene. She was taken to jail, but her lawyer, Henry R. Seldon, paid her bail for her. He said he couldn't bear to see a woman sleep in jail. Her trial made it to appeals and was attended by former president Millard Fillmore. She was not allowed to speak in her defense. Seldon defended her brilliantly. She was fined the cost of her carriage ride to prison. She never paid it.

Using hooks's tenants, let's be curious about the role of the patriarchy. Is it possible that people around Anthony, including her family, lawyer, and the court, were socialized to adopt sexist ways of thinking? Anthony's father insisted on her education and that of all the girls who worked at his mill. In many ways, he was a man ahead of his time. Anthony was surrounded by forward-thinking people, like the many abolitionists she worked with. But many of those abolitionists held sexist views of women. Perhaps the most well-known example was when a group of prominent female abolitionists traveled to London for the annual meeting and were not allowed seats.[44] Less than three years before, Anthony openly argued with her fellow abolitionists at the American Equal Rights Association annual meeting. She accused them of abandoning the cause of women for the Black man and accurately predicted that endorsement of the Fifteenth Amendment would set woman suffrage back decades. All of the actors in the courtroom itself were male, save Anthony. Anthony was not allowed to speak. The prosecutor argued, "She is not competent as a witness in her own behalf."[45] So yes, it's possible some people were sexist.

The second tenant asks students to consider whether, in this case, there is a gendered hierarchy that favors men over women. This, of course, has already been answered with the evidence of a male judge, jury, and lawyers, not to mention laws entirely authored by men. Is it possible for women to get a fair trial in this court? Seldon argued no. In his closing arguments, he stated, "The teachings of history, in regard to the condition of women under the care of these self-constituted protectors, [shows that men have not protected women's interests. Women have] in law no individual existence, and consequently no action [can] be brought by her to redress... grievous wrong."[46] He provided several examples from his career as a lawyer about women failing to get a good trial and claimed that if the courts and lawmakers were made up of women, the results in cases would be different. So, yes, there is a system in place where women are controlled by men.

Finally, is this power structure centered on the belief in male supremacy? It has clearly been proven that in court the answer is yes. In faith, in life?

These are trickier and require outside evidence. Catherine Beecher, sister of Harriet Beecher Stowe, was a well-known writer and educator. While a defender of women's education, Catherine Beecher is the epitome of internalized misogyny. In 1837, she wrote:

> It is the grand feature of the Divine economy, that there should be different stations of superiority and subordination, and it is impossible to annihilate this beneficent and immutable law… In this arrangement of the duties of life, Heaven has appointed to one sex the superior, and to the other the subordinate station, and this without any reference to the character or conduct of either. It is therefore as much for the dignity as it is for the interest of females, in all respects to conform to the duties of this relation.[47]

This passage reveals her belief that in both church and life "Heaven has appointed to one sex the superior." That is the definition of a belief in male supremacy. She is one person, one source, but an examination of this era would find that her beliefs, which she carried until her death in 1878, were widespread. There were exceptional people, like abolitionists Angelina Grimke and her spouse Theodore Weld, who rejected male supremacy in marriage by rejecting the marriage vow "to obey," but they are just that: exceptional.

Three for three, hooks's framework stands up against Anthony's 1872 trial. Given the amount of progress toward gender equality since 1872, this example is more palatable for students. It is easier for them to see that the norms of the era were constructed by that society and did not *have* to remain in place. This is part of a disillusionment process that Stopford refers to this as "counter[ing]-hegemonic claims."[48] In Anthony's time, the hegemony of men is obvious and obviously oppressive.

Using critical feminism in non-contemporary contexts is a powerful tool for making it palatable when applied to the present context. It is much easier for students to imagine that women in the 19th century lived under an oppressive set of laws and social customs, but teachers shouldn't generalize or oversimplify the history. When asked if women are still oppressed today, students often say, "Well they can vote, so, no." It's important that exploration of 19th-century women be grounded in theory and specifically call out *what* was oppressing to women. Otherwise, "the patriarchy" becomes the boogieman and a cop-out. Students may then say, "Well, in the 19th century, women couldn't vote, serve on juries or as lawyers, and were rarely voted into elected office. Today, while women can vote and serve on juries, they are still small minorities as lawyers and elected officials." Adopting a critical mindset, one then asks, well why? What vestiges of the 19th century remain?

Because women graduate college at higher numbers than men, why are they a minority among lawyers? What is it about law school that is more difficult to complete as women? Or perhaps it's the law profession? Why aren't women elected? What is keeping them out?

When teachers begin to ask these critical questions alongside their students and guide them through answering them with evidence and research, some students may still be in the fog of patriarchal illusion and struggle with the evidence. This is perhaps truer with discussions about gender and sexuality than any other subject because it is so deeply ingrained from a young age. Stopford described one scenario where he was teaching Butler's feminist theory about gender and a student demanded he use a scientific approach to understanding it. Stopford explains:

> I wanted to approach the situation more on his terms, in order to jostle loose some possibility of seeing things differently. I pointed out that these did not sound much like scientific facts to me. If scientific facts are anything at all, they are surely precise, technical and dependent on theory context for their meaning and intelligibility. To be scientific surely we would need biological detail, for example. We would need something on what 'males' and 'females' are. And then we'd need some (scientific?) theory that brings together this 'biological' description with gender terms. As expected, he wanted to draw upon chromosomal and hormonal detail. These are the scientific facts, and we can read off the generalist facts from these specifics. I encouraged him to look up some of these facts. He quickly found out that the science is more complicated than he had imagined: chromosomal profiles are not the binary affairs he expected; hormonal profiles don't map between sex and gender in the way that he had assumed. Indeed, there are even counter-hegemonic 'scientific facts' about sex and gender...[49]

The student did not rebut; instead, he stayed in a "kind of confused, irritated silence." He remained after class to ask the professor if he was playing "devil's advocate" and was "deeply unhappy" when Stopford made clear he was not. This interaction with the student hit Stopford deeply. He spends three paragraphs of his article reflecting on the moment. As a teacher, he experienced what I have many times, falling from the pedestal a student has built for me. He said, "I think he was hoping I was going to drop the game, and explain to him what was really wrong with Butler's view... He was certain Butler was wrong." But why? Why does a theorist *have* to be wrong? Stopford teaches lots of theories in his philosophy classes, but only with feminism do students come to him as this student did for "reassurance." He concludes,

"Other views are such that students rhetorically situate them as the devil's work... Why is that?"[50]

For many, the F word is disturbing because it is challenging the way things are. In Anthony's trial, the prosecutor could not have tried less. The entire argument, repeated over and over in court testimony, was this: Anthony voted and she was a woman. There is nothing complicated about it. He was certain. In fact, most hierarchies function on assumed supremacy until those assumptions can be challenged. Stopford explained:

> The issue of certainty is therefore a deep problem for feminist theory: feminism wants to take as contingent, and contest, what hegemony takes as certain. But given that certainty is the frame in which such contestations take place, feminist theory is always already undermined by hegemonic certainty.

As long as the hegemony exists outside the classroom, certainty that feminism is wrong will exist inside the classroom.

Critical feminism provides a means for consciousness-raising, making visible the invisible forces of the patriarchy that remain and hurt all of us. People benefit most when they are walked through the logic to understanding a perspective they've never been exposed to. The problem with critical feminism is that, presented out of context, without specific and narrow examples, it can be alienating to the very people who most need to understand it.

In Chapter 3, I explained that teachers who identify as feminists are more likely to teach women's topics. The researchers who conducted that study are leading the charge on continued gender research. Kaylene Stevens of Boston University and Christopher Martell of the University of Massachusetts Boston have published a number of more recent studies on the nuances of teaching about gender and race in the secondary classroom. In their 2018 study of six teachers who identified as feminists, they found that all the teachers worked toward promoting young women, creating safe spaces for female voices in their classrooms, and being mindful of equal participation from both genders.[51] Liberal feminist teachers emphasized the importance of exposing students to diverse perspectives, valued the students' right to express their opinions, and aimed to make the curriculum more inclusive of women. By contrast, it was the critical feminist teachers who focused on challenging their students' beliefs.

Teachers who identified as critical feminists were more inclined to develop lessons that focused on gender inequity, and not surprisingly women teachers were a bit bolder. For example, Jay created lessons that the researchers felt challenged his students to propose solutions for closing the wage gap.[52] However, it appeared that Jay primarily applied a critical feminist approach in his elective classes, while in his core history classes, like modern world history, he tended to primarily cover women's contributions without explicitly addressing the systemic advantages men have.

Another teacher, Alex, had a strong commitment to addressing racial issues translated into more gender-equitable practices. However, he acknowledged feeling more comfortable addressing race than gender. The researchers concluded that in his lesson on Lange's photography from the Great Depression, he could have delved deeper into the issues of poverty and inequity faced by women rather than solely featuring a prominent female photographer from that era. They added that Alex did incorporate lessons that critically examined structural inequities. For instance, he had students analyze images from both contemporary media and the 1950s to illustrate the enduring objectification of women.[53] Teachers like Alex, familiar with oppression though not gendered oppression, are on track toward gendered analysis and may just need a nudge and examples that help them do it.

According to Martell and Stevens, Tina and Michelle, two other teachers in their study, exemplified teachers whose beliefs and practices aligned most closely with the critical feminist framework.[54] Both expressed a strong commitment to challenging systemic male dominance and reducing sexism among their students. They viewed the curriculum and department through a different lens compared with some of their colleagues. Their goal was not solely to modify lessons to be more inclusive of women but also to create opportunities through class discussions and lessons that shed light on gender inequities. Michelle aimed to shift her students' tendency to blame victims of rape, while Tina designed lessons in which students testified before a mock Congress to improve conditions for women.

These types of lessons empowered women to have a voice and encouraged them to move beyond the role of victims by actively resisting existing power structures. For instance, Tina shared an experience where she altered a lesson to help a student struggling with the concept of male privilege, providing historical context from the 1950s to help the student understand the roots of gender stratification. Michelle also sought to influence her students' beliefs, as seen in her class discussion on a rape incident at a local college, where she engaged students in a blame-the-victim exercise to foster critical thinking about the responsibility for such incidents.

Challenging and questioning ideas are not the same as preaching ideas. Challenging questions in the classroom look like this:

◆ It's interesting you concluded that. Why?
◆ I can see that's a strong opinion you have. How do you think that view impacts women?

◆ I'm intrigued by that idea, but I also really value taking multiple viewpoints. Which groups would be most impacted by this view? Why?
◆ That seems like an informed decision. Is it backed by data?
◆ Those are strong ideas. Who is your source? Are they reliable on this topic?

Dabbling in critical feminism requires an artful teacher. In Chapter 4, I introduced inclusive pedagogies that help marginalized students from a variety of backgrounds to find their voice in the classroom. Wanting to "teach feminism" does not undo the importance of feminist pedagogies which de-centralize the teacher. It is important that the teacher support the students in their learning and research, not become the sole voice of the classroom. Students need to hear from many sources, which should include feminism, but feminism should not be the only voice they hear. Students need to learn to question things from a feminist lens and ultimately form their own conclusions.

I once met a man who was repulsed by my feminism. On further conversation, I learned that his mother was a "feminist." Feminism in his house looked like this: dad worked all day, paid for a housekeeper, and came home, cooked dinner, and did all the dishes. What did his mother do? Nothing. She sat there while everyone served her. She had weaponized feminism to make servants of men in her home. This man understandably needed a lot more convincing. It took a lot of examples, evidence, and data to teach him that his mother was the exception, not the rule, and to show him that most women have the complete opposite experience and that it is entirely endorsed by society. This guy could be in your class: remember him.

People don't know what they don't know, and many of our students have had very narrow experiences. Teaching about how systems, especially present systems, are designed to oppress women is complicated. I once taught a lesson plan about rape culture to high schoolers in which I "talked" and students listened. The entire lesson backfired—obviously. One of my favorite male students in the class complained that I was disconnected. I wasn't, he was, but I did very little to teach him about the society and social context around him. He was poor, living in a rural community. He looked around at the lake houses nearby and saw privilege he didn't have. He wasn't wrong. He looked at examples I provided and felt I was overreacting because here I was, his final social studies teacher, telling him things no one else had provided any context to. Imagine if the Ancient History teacher told him that Rome's entire founding was framed around not one but three rape stories—the original story of Western power was about rape. Would that, amplified by every other subject area in secondary classes, have made him more receptive? Probably.

Teacher-centered presentation not only is boring for students but also puts the teacher at risk of being accused of indoctrinating or preaching feminism. Scholars Martha Copp and Sherryl Kleinman point out, "If we give up on student-centered teaching methods—failing to practice what we teach— then students are less likely to actively engage with feminist ideas. They may see us as militant, shoving feminist messages down their throats."[55]

The problems with my lesson plan were many, which experience and research have taught me. Inquiry requires us all to be open to wherever the evidence leads us. The challenge for courts and teachers discussing rape is providing adequate context to the ways that boys and girls are conditioned in our society. The earliest creation stories and laws, that carried through to contemporary society, favored the silence of women. In every culture, women had to fight and continue to fight for their ability to speak for themselves in court and be judged by a jury of their peers. Therefore, they are deemed unreliable witnesses on their own behalf even when they have the legal right, because culture takes a long time to change. Social scripts are designed to give men the power to initiate and women the power to resist, a breeding ground for rape. Part of femininity is to be chaste, so women say no when they don't mean it, which makes it confusing when they do mean it. This context matters when deciding what to believe about rape culture.

Beyond the context, when teachers come in hot with a conclusion, they're not really modeling Enlightenment thinking, open-mindedness, or critical inquiry. So, the irony is that they're trying to wake students up while wearing pedagogical blinders. Teaching critical feminism must be done artfully. Schmeichel says "integrating women into social studies curriculum is not a neutral act."[56] This is a radical undertaking, and it will require a radical group of teachers: feminists. It requires teachers who are willing to look at the full context of the female experience and are brave enough to address controversy and challenge sexist ideas.

Resources for Critical Inquiry
Recommended Reading: Skill Building Books

Teachers need help navigating the challenging environment they are in. They need to build skills for talking across difference, and they need to develop thick skin that depersonalizes the culture wars brewing around them. While not a book, the podcast *Open for Debate* is funded by foundations hoping to fight polarization and improve civil discourse. I assign these in my classes, and I enjoy the way the host, John Donvan, mediates the discussion. Every episode, he proves that talking across difference is doable.

Teachers care. It's their greatest strength and greatest weakness. I had a hard time walking away from conflicts, and I see a lot of teachers struggling with it, too. I often recommend the book *The Subtle Art of Not Giving a F**** to my undergraduates. While the title is snarky, the book's ideas are profound. We need to apply the idea of scarcity to our time and energy. You have only so many things to care about today; is this thing you're stressing about worth your energy and time? If not, dismiss it and go back to being an all-star teacher.

Sample Inquiry: How Were Women and Black Men Pitted Against Each Other in Reconstruction?

It is downloadable on the Remedial Herstory Project's website.

How were women and Black men pitted against each other in Reconstruction?

In this inquiry, students will examine contrasting primary-source accounts and form their own conclusions about the role that racism played in the early women's suffrage movement. In the years after the American Civil War, abolitionists were united behind the goal of universal suffrage, which effectively would have enfranchised all women and Black men. Together they formed the American Equal Rights Association [AERA]. It eventually became clear that Washington did not yet have an appetite for women's suffrage but that Black male suffrage was palatable. So division among AERA members was sown. The following documents explore the debates that ensued.

Document A: Frederick Douglass on Women's Suffrage

Douglass was one of the few men and the only Black person present at the Seneca Falls Convention. He was a founding member of the American Equal Rights Association, and he gave this speech in 1888 reflecting on his experience.

Mrs. President, Ladies and Gentlemen:— I come to this platform with unusual diffidence. Although I have long been identified with the Woman's Suffrage movement, and have often spoken in its favor, I am somewhat at a loss to know what to say on this really great and uncommon occasion, where so much has been said.

When I look around on this assembly, and see the many able and eloquent women, full of the subject, ready to speak, and who only need the opportunity to impress this audience with their views… I do not feel like taking up more than a very small space of your time and attention, and shall not. **I would not, even now, presume to speak**, but for the circumstance of my early connection with the cause, and of having been called upon to do so… Men have very little business here as speakers, anyhow; and if they come here at all they should take back benches and wrap themselves in silence. For this is an International Council, not of men, but of women, and woman should have all the say in it. This is her day in court…

…When I ran away from slavery, it was for myself; when I advocated emancipation, it was for my people; but when I stood up for the rights of woman, self was out of the question, and I found a little nobility in the act.

…Man has been so long the king and woman the subject—man has been so long accustomed to command and woman to obey… thus has been piled up a mountain of iron against woman's enfranchisement.

The same thing confronted us in our conflicts with slavery… But neither the power of time nor the might of legislation has been able to keep life in that stupendous barbarism.

Frederick Douglass, Woman's Journal, *April 14, 1888.*

Source
1. Why is Douglass an appropriate speaker at Seneca Falls and future women's rights conventions?

Document
2. Why does Douglass think it is wrong that he is speaking at this event?
3. Does he think women's rights and slavery are the same? How so?

Document B: Divided Sisters

This book details the divisions over Reconstruction that pitted former allies of abolition and universal suffrage against each other and forced priorities. Susan B. Anthony was a prominent and passionate woman suffragist and abolitionist.

Frederick Douglass, at an 1866 meeting of the American Equal Rights Association. Their former ally appeared to back down from his earlier commitment to female suffrage, and was now saying that, while the ballot was "desirable" for women, it was "vital" for Black men. In response, Anthony declared, "I will cut off this right arm of mine before I will ever work or demand the ballot for the Negro and not the woman."

Wilson, Midge and Kathy Russel. Divided Sisters: Bridging The Gap Between Black Women and White Women. *Anchor, 1996. Retrieved from https://condor.depaul.edu/mwilson/divided/chptone.html.*

Document C: Susan B. Anthony

In 1869, Anthony defended her position in favor of woman suffrage in her suffrage newspaper The Revolution.

The Revolution criticizes, 'opposes' the fifteenth amendment, not for what it is, but for what it is not. Not because it enfranchises black men, but because it does not enfranchise all women, black and white. It is not the little good it proposes, but the greater evil it perpetuates that we deprecate.

It is not that in the abstract we do not rejoice that black men are to become equals of white men, but that we deplore the fact that two million (sic) black women, hitherto the political and social equals of the men by their side, are to become subjects, slaves of these men. Our protest is not that all men are lifted out of the degradation of disfranchisement, but that all women are left in. The Revolution and the National Women's Suffrage Association make women's suffrage their test of loyalty, not Negro suffrage, not Maine law or prohibition. Do you believe women should vote? Is the one and only question in our catechism.

Anthony, Susan B. The Revolution. October 7, 1869. Retrieved from http:// www.susanbanthonybirthplace.com/racism.html.

Source
1. Who is Susan B. Anthony?

Document
2. Put her argument into your own words.

Analysis
3. Do you interpret Anthony's comment to be elitist, anti-gradual enfranchisement, and/or racist? Why?

Document D: Sojourner Truth

Sojourner Truth escaped slavery and lived in Michigan. She changed her name to Sojourner Truth as a symbol of her freedom, Sojourner meaning a person who wanders. She became a powerful and outspoken voice for universal rights and suffrage. She delivered this speech at an Equal Rights Association convention in New York in 1867.

My friends, I am rejoiced that you are glad, but I don't know how you will feel when I get through. I come from another field - the country of the slave. They have got their liberty - so much good luck to have slavery partly destroyed; not entirely. I want it root and branch destroyed. Then we will all be free indeed. I feel that if I have to answer for the deeds done in my body just as much as man, I have a right to have as much as a man. There is a great stir about colored men getting their rights, but not a word about the colored women; and if colored men get their rights, and not colored women theirs, you see the colored men will be masters over the women, and it will be just as bad as it was before. So I am for keeping the thing going while things are stirring; because if we wait till it is still, it will take a great while to get it going again. White women are a great deal smarter, and know more than colored women, while colored women do not know scarcely anything.

They go out washing, which is about as high as a colored woman gets, and their men go about idle, strutting up and down; and when the women come home, they ask for their money and take it all, and then scold you because there is no food. I want you to consider on that chil'n. I call you chil'n; you are somebody's chil'n, and I am old enough to be mother of all that is here. I want women to have their rights. In the courts women have no right, no voice; nobody speaks for them. I wish woman to have her voice there among the pettifoggers. If it is not a fit place for women, it us unfit for men to be there.

...I used to work in the field and bind grain, keeping up with the cradler, but men doing no more, got twice as much pay... You have been having our rights so long, that you think, like a slave-holder, that you own us... There ought to be equal rights now more than ever, since colored people have got their freedom.

Truth, Sojourner. "Address to the First Annual Meeting of the American Equal Rights Association." New York City, May 9, 1867. Retrieved from Society for the Study of American Women Writers. Harriet Jacobs, Ed. https://www.lehigh.edu/~dek7/SSAWW/writTruthAddress.htm.

Source
1. Why would Truth be an appropriate speaker at an AERA convention and future women's rights conventions?

Document
2. Does she think women's rights and slavery are the same? How so?

Analysis
3. How is Truth's message different from Douglass, or are they the same?

Document E: Elizabeth Cady Stanton "Manhood Suffrage"

During the debates over the 15th Amendment, Stanton published these comments in the suffrage newspaper The Revolution. *Some historians have argued that she was attempting to use male logic against them.*

"Think of Patrick and Sambo [derogatory, meaning mixed-race] and Hans and Yung Tung who do not know the difference between a Monarchy and a Republic, who never read the Declaration of Independence or Webster's spelling book, making laws for Lydia Maria Child, Lucretia Mott or Fanny Kemble. Think of jurors drawn from these ranks to try young girls for the crime of infanticide."

Stanton, Elizabeth Cady. "Manhood Suffrage." The Revolution. Retrieved from http://www.susanbanthonybirthplace.com/racism.html.

Analysis
1. Do you interpret Stanton's comment to be elitist, anti-gradual enfranchisement, or racist? Why?

Document F: Minutes from the American Equal Rights Association Convention, 1869

Tensions were high in 1869 as debates over the 15th Amendment raged. Women felt abandoned in the quest for Universal Suffrage. The following are minutes from a debate in the AERA convention.

Mr. Foster: …I admire our talented president with all my heart, and love the woman. (Great laughter.) but I believe she has publicly repudiated the principles of the society.

Mrs. Stanton: I would like Mr. Foster to say in what way.

Mr. Foster: what are these principles? The equality of men – universal suffrage. These ladies stand at the head of a paper which has adopted its motto educated suffrage. I put myself on this platform as an enemy of educated suffrage, as an enemy of white suffrage, as an enemy of man suffrage, as an enemy of any kind of suffrage except universal suffrage. *The Revolution* lately had an article headed "That Infamous 15th Amendment."… The Massachusetts Abolitionists cannot cooperate with the society as it is now organized. If you choose to put officers here that ridicule the Negro, and pronounce the amendment infamous, why… I cannot work with you…

Henry B. Blackwell said: In regard to the criticisms of our officers, I will agree that many unwise things have been written in *The Revolution* by a gentleman who furnished part of the means by which that paper has been carried on. But that gentleman has withdrawn and you, who know the real opinions of Miss Anthony and Mrs. Stanton on the questions of Negro Suffrage, do not believe that they mean to create antagonism between the Negro and the woman question. If they did disbelieve in Negro suffrage, it would be no reason for excluding them… But I know that Miss. Anthony and Mrs. Stanton believe in the right of the Negro to vote…

Mr. Douglass: I came here more as a listener than to speak, and I have listened with a great deal of pleasure to the eloquent address… there is no name greater than that of Elizabeth Cady Stanton in the matter of women's rights and equal rights, but my sentiments are tinged a little against *The Revolution*. There was in the address to which I allude the employment of certain names such as "Sambo,"[derogatory, meaning mixed-race] and the gardener, and the boot black, and the daughters of Jefferson and Washington, and all the rest that I cannot coincide with. I have asked what difference there is between the daughters of Jefferson and Washington and other daughters. (Laughter.) I must say that I do not see how anyone can pretend that there is the same urgency and giving the ballot to woman as to the Negro. With us, the matter is a question of life and death, at least, and 15 states of the union. When women, because they are women, are hunted down through the cities of New York and New Orleans; when they are drag from their houses and hung up on lamp-posts; when their children are torn from their arms, and their brains dashed out upon the pavement; when they are objects of insult and outraged at every turn; When they are in danger of having their homes burnt down over their heads; when their children are not allowed to enter schools; then they will have an urgency to obtain the ballot equal to our own. (Great applause.)

A VOICE: is that not all true about black women?

Mr. Douglass: yes, yes, yes; it is true of the black woman, but not because she is a woman, but because she is black. (Applause.) Julia Ward Howe at the conclusion of her great speech delivered at the convention in Boston last year, said: "I am willing that the Negro shall get the ballot before me." (Applause.) Woman! Why, she has 10,000 modes of grappling with her difficulties. I believe that all the virtue of the world can take care of all the evil. I believe that all the intelligence can take care of all the ignorance. (Applause.) I am in favor of women's suffrage in order that we shall have all the virtue and vice confronted. Let me tell you that when there were a few houses in which the black man could have put his head, this woolly head of mine found a refuge in the house of Miss Elizabeth Cady Stanton, and if I had been blacker than 16 midnights, without a single star, it would have been the same. (Applause.)

Miss Anthony: the old anti-slavery school says women must stand back and wait until the Negroes shall be recognized. But we say, if you will not give the whole loaf of suffrage to the entire people, give it to the most intelligent first. (Applause.) if intelligence, justice, and morality are to have precedence in the Government, let the question of woman be brought up first and that of the Negro last. (Applause.) while I was canvassing the state with petitions and had them filled with names for our cause to the legislature, a man dared to say to me that the freedom of women was all a theory and not a practical thing. (Applause.) when Mr. Douglass mentioned the black man first and the woman last, if he had noticed he would have seen that it was the men that clapped and not the women. There is not the woman born who desires to eat the bread of dependence no matter whether it be from the hand of the father, husband, or brother; for anyone who does so eat her bread places herself in the power of the person from whom she takes it. (Applause.) Mr. Douglass talks about the wrongs of the Negro; but with all the outrageous that he to-day suffers, he would not exchange his sex and take the place of Elizabeth Cady Stanton. (Laughter and applause.)

Mr. Douglass: I want to know if granting you the right of suffrage will change the nature of our sexes? (Great laughter.)

Miss Anthony: it will change the pecuniary position of a woman; it will place her where she can earn her own bread. (Loud applause.) She will not then be driven to such employment only as man chooses for her.

Mrs. Norton said that Mr. Douglass' remarks left her to defend the government from the inferred inability to grapple with the two questions at once. It legislates upon many questions at one and at the same time, it has the power to decide the woman question and the Negro question at one and the same time. (Applause.)

Mrs. Lucy Stone: Mrs. Stanton will, of course, advocate for the presidents for her sex, and Mr. Douglass will strive for the first position for his, and both are perhaps right. If it be true that the government derives its authority from the constant of the governed, we are safe in trusting that principle to the other most. If one has a right to say that you can not read and therefore cannot vote, then it may be said that you are a woman and therefore cannot vote. We are lost if we turn away from the middle principle and argue for one class. I was once a teacher among fugitive slaves. There was one old man, and every tooth was gone, his hair was white, and his face was full of wrinkles, yet, day after day and hour after hour, he came up to the school house and tried with patients to learn to read, and by- and-by, when he had spelled out the first few verses of the first chapter of the gospel of St. John, he said to me, "now, I want to learn to write." I tried to make him satisfied with what he had acquired, but the old man said, "Mrs. Stone, somewhere in the wide world I have A son; I have not heard from him in 20 years; if I should hear from him, I want to write to him, so to take hold of my hand and teach me." I did, but before he had preceded in many lessons the angels came and gathered him up and bore him to his Father. Let no man speak of an educated Suffrage. The gentleman who addressed you claimed that the Negroes had the first right to the suffrage, and drew a picture which only his great word Dash power can do. He again in Massachusetts, when it had cast a majority in favor of Grant and Negro Suffrage, stood up on the platform and said that women had better wait for the Negro; that is, that both could not be carried, and that the Negro had better be the one. But I freely for gave him because he felt as he spoke. But woman suffrage is more imperative than his own; and I want to remind the audience that when he says what the Ku Klux's is dead all over the south, the Ku Klux Klan is here and the north in the shape of men, take away the children from the mother, and separate them as completely as if done on the block of the auctioneer. Over in New Jersey they have a law which says that any father – he might be the most brutal man that ever existed – any father, it says, whether he be under the age or not, maybe by his last, will and testament dispose of the custody of his child, born or to be born, and that such a disposition shall be good against all persons, and that the mother may not recover her child; and that law modified inform exists over every state in the union except in Kansas. Woman has an ocean of wrongs too deep for any plummet, and the Negro, too, has an ocean of wrongs that cannot be fathomed. There are two great oceans; in the one is the black man, and the other is the woman. But I think God for that XV. Amendment, and hope that it will be adopted in every state. I will be thankful in my soul if anybody can get out of the terrible pit. But I believe that the safety of the government would be more promoted by the admission of woman as an element of restoration in harmony than the Negro. I believe that the influence of woman will save the country before every other power. (Applause.) I see the signs of the times pointing to this consummation, and I believe that in some parts of the country women will vote for the President of the United States in 1872. (Applause.)

Buhle, Mari Jo and Paul Buhle. The Concise History of Woman Suffrage. *Chicago, University of Illinois Press, 2005.*

Source
1. Are minutes from a meeting a reliable primary source?

Document
2. For what reason does Stephen Foster want Susan B. Anthony and Elizabeth Cady Stanton to resign from the American Equal Rights Association?
3. For what reason does Douglass take offense to *The Revolution*?
4. Why does Douglass argue that Black men need the vote first?
5. Why does Anthony argue that educated women need the vote first?
6. Why does Douglass believe that Stanton is NOT racist?
7. Mrs. Norton and Lucy Stone make alternative arguments. Describe them in your own words.

Analysis
8. Look back through the document. At what did audience members laugh? Why?
9. Can laughter be a sign of a bit of tongue-in-cheek? Or do you think prejudice is on display here?

Overall Analysis
1. Of the arguments in this inquiry packet, which voice do you find most compelling? Why?
2. Would you consider any of the voices racist?
3. Would you consider any of the voices sexist?
4. The social barriers to woman suffrage were clearly greater than those to universal male suffrage. Do you think they should have been? Do Black men need the vote first?
5. Do you think it remains true that gender equality is harder to achieve than racial equality? Explain.

Notes

1 Nash, Crabtree, and Dunn, *History on Trial*, 23.
2 Beard, *Women and Power*, p.8.
3 Beard, *Women and Power*, p.8.
4 Rob Wolfe, "Edelblut OK'd as N.H. Education Commissioner," *Valley News*, March 23, 2017, https://www.vnews.com/Edelblut-Confirmed-By-Council-8844331
5 Ethan Dewitt, "As they Await State Guidance, Teachers Consider how Divisive Concepts Law will Affect lesson Plans," *The New Hampshire Bulletin*, July 12, 2021, https://newhampshirebulletin.com/2021/07/12/as-they-await-state-guidance-teachers-consider-how-divisive-concepts-law-will-affect-lesson-plans/
6 Sarah Gibson, "Majority of Sununu's Diversity and Inclusion Council Resigns," *New Hampshire Public Radio*, June 29, 2021, https://www.nhpr.org/nh-news/2021-06-29/majority-of-gov-sununus-diversity-and-inclusion-council-resigns
7 Dewitt, "As they Await State Guidance."
8 Dewitt, "As they Await State Guidance."
9 Peter Greene, "New Hampshire and Mom's for Liberty Pit Bounty on Teacher's Heads," *Forbes Magazine*, November 12, 2021, https://www.forbes.com/sites/petergreene/2021/11/12/new-hampshire-and-moms-for-liberty-put-bounty-on-teachers-heads/?sh=7f33e954a4bf
10 Margaret Smith Crocco, "The missing discourse about gender and sexuality in the social studies," *Theory into Practice*, 2001, 40(1), 70.
11 Zakhar Agranenko as quoted in Antony Beevor, "'They raped every German female from eight to 80'," May 1, 2002. https://www.theguardian.com/books/2002/may/01/news.features11

12 Natalya Gesse as quoted in Antony Beevor, "'They raped every German female from eight to 80'," May 1, 2002. https://www.theguardian.com/books/2002/may/01/news.features11

13 Miriam Gebhardt, *Crimes Unspoken: The Rape of German Women at the End of the Second World War* (Cambridge: Polity Press, 2017).

14 Anne Mah, "This Picture Tells a Tragic Story of What Happened to Women After D-Day," *Time Magazine*, June 6, 2018, https://time.com/5303229/women-after-d-day/

15 Hilary Mayell, "Genghis Khan a Prolific Lover, DNA Data Implies," *National Geographic*, February 14, 2003. https://www.nationalgeographic.com/news/2003/2/mongolia-genghis-khan-

16 Mayell, "Genghis Khan a Prolific Lover, DNA Data Implies."

17 Robert Strayer and Eric Nelson. 2016. *Ways of the World: A Global History with Sources*. 471–472.

18 Robin McKie, "We owe it all to superstud Genghis: Warlord Khan has 16m male relatives alive now, says study," *The Guardian*. March 2, 2003, https://www.theguardian.com/uk/2003/mar/02/science.research

19 Mayell, "Genghis Khan a Prolific Lover, DNA Data Implies."

20 Harriet A. Jacobs, *Incidents in the life of a slave girl: written by herself.* Cambridge, Mass: Harvard University Press, 2000.

21 Alexander, Kerri Lee. "Recy Taylor" National Women's History Museum. 2020. www.womenshistory.org/education-resources/biographies/recy-taylor

22 McGuire, *The Dark End of the Street*, 49.

23 Alexander, Kerri Lee. "Recy Taylor" National Women's History Museum. 2020. www.womenshistory.org/education-resources/biographies/recy-taylor

24 Danielle L McGuire, *At the Dark End of the Street: Black Women Rape and Resistance - a New History of the Civil Rights Movement from Rosa Parks to the Rise of Black Power* (New York: Vintage Books, 2011), 64.

25 Danielle McGuire, "More Than A Seat On The Bus," We're History. December 1, 2015, http://werehistory.org/rosa-parks/

26 "Jo Ann Robinson A Heroine of the Montgomery Bus Boycott," National Museum of African American History and Culture, n.d. https://nmaahc.si.edu/explore/stories/jo-ann-robinson-heroine-montgomery-bus-boycott

27 I built a lesson plan about Montgomery, which is available for free at www.remedialherstory.com. It was one of my first contributions to the sites collection and is now accompanied by many more on the civil rights movement.

28 Amanda Kippert, "Can He Rape Me if We're Married?: Marital rape is a very real—and very illegal—offense," March 15, 2023, https://www.domesticshelters.org/articles/identifying-abuse/can-he-rape-me-if-we-re-married

29 Abdulrahman Al-Matary and Jaffar Ali, "Controversies and considerations regarding the termination of pregnancy for Foetal Anomalies in Islam," BMC Med Ethics 15, 10 (2014). https://doi.org/10.1186/1472-6939-15-10

30 National Council for Jewish Women, "Judaism and Abortion," National Council for Jewish Women, April 2019, https://www.ncjw.org/wp-content/uploads/2019/05/Judaism-and-Abortion-FINAL.pdf

31 Alicia Gutierrez-Romine, *From Back Alley to the Border: Criminal Abortion in California, 1920–1969* (Lincoln: University of Nebraska Press, 2020). 3.

32 Mariel Padilla, "Americans support extending child support payments to pregnancy, survey finds: 'If we're thinking of a fetus as an actual person with rights, then a whole bunch of other stuff has to change,' said Chris Ellis, the co-director of the Bucknell Institute for Public Policy," July 12, 2022, https://19thnews.org/2022/07/child-support-payments-pregnancy-conception-survey/

33 Jasmine Aguilera, "What Will Happen to Same-Sex Marriage Around the Country if Obergefell Falls," December 14, 2022. https://time.com/6240497/same-sex-marriage-rights-us-obergefell/

34 Stevens & Martell, "Feminist Social Studies Teachers," 2–3.

35 Joanne Martin, "Feminist Theory and Critical Theory: Unexplored Synergies," *Organizational Behavior, Stanford Graduate School of Business*, Working Paper No. 1758, February 2002, 2.

36 Stopford, "Teaching feminism," 1205.

37 Stopford, "Teaching feminism," 1205.

38 Stevens & Martell, "Feminist Social Studies Teachers," 2.

39 Stopford, "Teaching feminism," 1208.

40 hooks preferred to have her pen name lowercase to focus on the message in her writing rather than herself.

41 bell hooks, *Feminism is for Everybody* (Cambridge, MA: South End Press, 2000).

42 Gerda Lerner, *The creation of patriarchy*, (Oxford: Oxford University Press, 1986).

43 Stopford, "Teaching feminism," 1210.

44 Elizabeth Cady Stanton, Susan B. Anthony, and Matilda Joselyn Gage, eds., *History of Woman Suffrage, Vol. 1* (New York: Fowler and Wells, 1881), 53–54, 61–62.

45 "Argument for the Defense Concerning Legal Issues in the case of *United States vs Susan B. Anthony*," University of Missouri at Kansas City Law School, http://law2.umkc.edu/faculty/projects/ftrials/anthony/defargument.html

46 "Testimony in the Case of the United States vs Susan B. Anthony," University of.
Missouri at Kansas City Law School, http://law2.umkc.edu/faculty/projects/ftrials/anthony/trialtestimony.html

47 Catherine Beecher, "An Essay on Slavery and Abolitionism, in Reference to the Duty of American Females," Philadelphia: Henry Perkins, 1837. 96.

48 Stopford, "Teaching feminism," 1210.

49 Stopford, "Teaching feminism," 1214–1215.

50 Stopford, "Teaching feminism," 1215.

51 Stevens & Martell, "Feminist Social Studies Teachers," 8.

52 Stevens & Martell, "Feminist Social Studies Teachers," 10.

53 Stevens & Martell, "Feminist Social Studies Teachers," 10.

54 Stevens & Martell, "Feminist Social Studies Teachers," 11.

55 Martha Copp and Sherryl Kleinman, "Practicing What We Teach: Feminist Strategies for Teaching about Sexism," Feminist Teacher 18, no. 2 (2008): 101–24. http://www.jstor.org/stable/40546059

56 Schmeichel, "Skirting around critical feminist rationales for teaching women in social studies," 4.

6

Strategies and Guidelines to Bypass the Sexists

Most teachers are in the early phases of Phase Theory. Some are in the Feminist Phase, trying to do justice to and diversify the female perspectives they include. Therefore, integrated history is still ahead of them. In this chapter, I will provide tools for integrating women better; however, it's important to first hash out that almost every tool an educator would turn to in order to integrate women's history is tainted by sexism and disregard for the real and diverse experiences of women in those times and places. *How can educators teach what they never learned?* The answer lies in examining those tools as barriers to women's inclusion, beginning to use them strategically, and acknowledging their weaknesses. Textbooks, if they mention women, relegate them to the margins. The standards provide little consensus on which women should be taught and name women at a small fraction of the rate they name men. Teacher education programs do not require women's history. And if all of that wasn't frustrating enough, the social studies in general are devalued and provided little funding and support, which makes reform efforts feel impossible. Educators need to understand these barriers so they can systematically tackle each of them.

Before jumping into these challenges, we must have a systematic process for creating strong curriculum design. This process should have guidelines and frameworks and be informed by experts. It's important to question the processes for developing curriculum and textbook content. As I progressed in my career, I became rapidly disillusioned that experts were steering the ship.

DOI: 10.4324/9781003472889-7

Changing the System

Background: Process Matters

When I began my career, I dutifully taught to all the standards. I systematically went through the state framework and checked off each item as I knew I met them. I trusted the process. What I didn't know was that third-party organizations had given our standards an F when they were immediately drawn up in 2006. As time went on and society shifted, the standards did not. Our state had a rule that required the standards to be revised and revisited every ten years. The ten-year anniversary came and went.

Then, in 2017, I was serving my profession as a board member of the New Hampshire Council for the Social Studies (NHCSS) when suddenly we were caught off-guard. Another board member informed us that the state's commissioner of education had begun to revise our outdated 2006 standards. This important process came, surprisingly, as an aside comment. That's how the state's largest organization of experts on, and teachers of, social studies education found out that the standards that are so central to our curricula were being updated. And updated without our input.

Numerous outreach attempts to the commissioner's office proved frustrating at first but thankfully became promising if ultimately fruitless too. Through our liaison with the New Hampshire Historical Society, we found out the date and time when the committee was to convene, and, independently, several of us attended. To the commissioner's credit, we were welcomed. But from that point forwards, it became evident that too little attention was going to be placed on the most important areas of curriculum development. In fact, it was the worst process I've ever experienced.

First there was the funding. The only funds the commissioner appropriated were paid to the chair he appointed. Oddly, the chair was a former English teacher with what appeared to be limited leadership experience, and none of it connected to the social studies leaders who were key stakeholders in social studies across the state. The NHCSS and New Hampshire Historical Society were not officially invited, and no advertisements went out to others who might see themselves as vested in the quality of the committee's work. On top of this, the project was given only a couple of months, in which no formal process was developed on how to achieve a finished product. As might be predicted from all of this, the many long hours that devoted committee members such as myself spent resulted in something like spinning wheels, lost in time and space.

By all accounts, it was chaotic. At the outset, I was the only person on the economics subcommittee. Had I wanted to, because I had complete power,

I could have shaped these standards according to whim. Of course, because I don't have a degree in economics, I reached out to my many connections—but what about the chairs on subcommittees that might not have been as connected as I? The results showed the lack of depth of expertise: Where were the professors and teachers? Where were the organizations and institutions? Some professionals who had volunteered were so flabbergasted they used terms that suggested the Department of Education was putting lipstick on a pig of standards. Not surprisingly, when outsiders finally reviewed the committee's original work in its entirety, it failed.

It is worth considering the absent stakeholders. Whole fields were underrepresented: no one from any of the economics, political science, geography, sociology, psychology, or anthropology departments in any of New Hampshire's institutions of higher education was present. Whole peoples were absent: no one from New Hampshire's Black Heritage Trail was present, nor was anyone from the Manchester Chapter of the NAACP education subcommittee; no one represented New Hampshire's various Indigenous organizations and museums. Granted New Hampshire is an overwhelmingly white state, with only about 7 percent of the population identifying otherwise, not a single person of color was in the room. And, of course, not a single expert on women's studies or women's history was present, even though women comprise half the state's history and half of the students who would be shaped by the standards. How on earth could this committee form adequate and inclusive standards for the social studies?

Because no efforts were made to get the right people at the table, all the wrong people were guaranteed a spot: self-proclaimed experts who were legends only in their minds. Expertise should have been defined at the start, and the experts should have been purposefully invited from day 1. The committee should have included individuals from state-wide organizations, certified teachers with master's degrees and a decade or more of teaching experience, who had been promoted to Department Head or served the state in some other service capacity, or university professors with terminal degrees and actual expertise in the social studies subjects and pedagogy. Some of these requirements would have excluded me at the time—and that makes sense. But there I was, greener than I would have liked to have been, aspiring to be more, but already a professional, yet surrounded mostly by amateurs, some fresh out of their undergraduate commencement exercises.

Our leader did not guide the group of novices very well, I found. We were not given guidance in any scholarly research or theories on best practices in social studies education. While we did review various state standards, we were never given a framework to analyze them or select which of the frameworks from the other states was best. We never reviewed assessments of our current standards by national organizations. The result of all of this was a committee that essentially applied personal assessments of the standards, willy-nilly. And because no one on the committee had been vetted for bias or qualification, it devolved into an unprofessional mess, literally.

I finally left the committee because the process was so unbelievably bad. Fortunately, the freedom afforded to local school boards and schools by the State of New Hampshire allowed me to lobby my school to adopt frameworks that I argued were better than what was emerging from the committee. Well-conceived processes had resulted in the C3 (College, Career, and Civic Life) Standards, sponsored by the National Council for the Social Studies (NCSS). New York State had adopted them in large part because that processes had been funded, planned, and followed. And the deliverables of New Hampshire's committee? As of 2023, New Hampshire was still in the process of revising its standards, a deficit that led many principals, superintendents, and concerned teachers and parents to ask for action to come from outside their government. An ad hoc committee of concerned organizations, on which I served, had recently released "guidelines" for administrators on what to do about the social studies, but these acknowledge the absence of worthy state standards. The guidelines were built collaboratively among professionals who paid attention to both the disciplines that comprise the social studies and the diversity of people who made the past, live in the present, and shape the future.

I share this story so citizens, parents, and school professionals remember that not all processes for establishing school curriculum are done well. Just because a state issues standards or curriculum does not mean it is untainted, unbiased, or well produced. It's important to follow the money and know which organizations are funding curriculum. Do they have political leanings? If a project was unfunded, how can one guarantee that these volunteers put their best foot forward? What sort of oversight was put in place?

Process matters.

For women, the process has systematically denied them a place in the curriculum. Examine the textbooks, standards, curriculum, and professional development tools used in the classroom. Were women the authors of these resources? Were women's history and gender studies scholars consulted? As the rapidly growing field of gender studies produces new research on women, gender, and sexuality, are texts revised to reflect it?

Barriers: Teacher's Tool Kit
Textbooks
Symbolic of the way women are not treated equally in history classes at large, textbooks provide a way to analyze that exclusion in print. Novice teachers often turn to these texts to help them know what to teach when standards are vague, so if women aren't there, it creates a massive barrier to inclusion.

Further, if teachers make an effort to include women but the text mentions them at a ratio of 1 to 4, it could undermine that effort.

Interestingly, adding the voices, achievements, and issues that affect over half of the population to the history texts has become politicized, even deemed unpatriotic. When pre-World War II historian Arthur Schlesinger Sr. dared to include a chapter titled "The Role of Women in American History" in his book, he was ridiculed for being a historical thief promoting both "un-American" and "unpatriotic" sentiments. His staffers went so far as to say that his work was "treason-tainted."[1] Fortunately, he was influential enough to ride out these critiques.

Since Schlesinger's time, more and more scholars have called for the inclusion of women's voices. Although that sounds encouraging on the surface, women are often categorized by what they protested for, and few are noted for their achievements in fields dominated by men.[2] The mention of women is progress, but it continues the trend of mentioning women only when they fit into male definitions of leaders. It "counts" women when they enter into the man's world. This can no longer be.

For many schools, textbooks drive their curriculum. Textbooks help teachers and provide them with guidance from current historians on what should be taught. With changing philosophies and the overwhelming amount of information that could be known, textbooks are used more in history than in other subjects.[3] However, textbooks fail to teach critical thinking, because they provide an "omniscient voice," which leaves students with the false sense that there is a single narrative or set of facts about what happened in history.

In one of my training textbooks, Theresa M. McCormick wrote an article titled "Generating Effective Teaching through Primary Sources," in which she explained that many professional organizations, including the American Historical Association (AHA) and the NCSS, all recommended the alternative of primary sources to "facilitate inquiry" and "expose students to multiple perspectives on great issues past and present."[4] More than textbooks, primary sources get students to use the higher-level thinking skills of history: analysis, interpretation, and evaluation. They include more voices and empower students.

Not all teachers have the flexibility to teach to current practice, however; many are prescribed their curriculum, and each day is outlined for them. Students read page after page of dense, boring textbook content and memorize the narrative it provides. Textbooks therefore have incredible power.

As is often the case, textbooks follow social movements. In the 1960s and 1970s, women and their allies began analyzing history textbooks for their coverage of women's history. Despite the emerging research, textbooks fell far short of providing substantive coverage of women and their diverse stories.

In 1971, J. Trecker critiqued US history textbooks and found that even in areas where plenty of records existed on women's history, little was in the textbooks.[5] A huge reason for the exclusion was the texts' emphasis on male-dominated subjects such as politics, diplomacy, and the military. She noted that in cases where men and women collaborated to achieve something significant, only the man's contributions were mentioned, such as with regard to frontier life. Topics drawn from the women's sphere were entirely absent.

In 1986, Tetreault reexamined newer samples of textbooks using a feminist framework for integration to assess the quality of women's history instruction.[6] She found that women were included when they supported the mission of white men, such as exploration or war, and at least one woman was consistently mentioned in texts under topics related to reforms.[7] Those reformers who cared for people in unfortunate circumstances got special and consistent attention.[8] She thought it strange that while scholars don't spend much time on first ladies, American textbooks do. First ladies appeared in images with their husbands.[9] Tetreault said these textbooks conveyed a subtle message, by whom and how they chose to include women, that women had a place.[10]

The systematic and intimate oppression of women was briefly noted in some of the books, although they attributed female oppression to neutral topics like cultural norms, removing blame from specific laws.[11] Tetreault found that the work women did to battle their own oppression was spread out with little narrative connection between major events, which could prevent students from connecting the work of early reformers to later reformers.[12] And most failed to adequately address the cause and effect of the women's emphasis on constitutional amendments and access to education.[13] Information about the role that women's clubs played in self-improvement was presented in only two of the texts, and only one included Black women's clubs.[14] Abortion and birth control were discussed in some of the texts that Tetreault examined. The single text that acknowledged Margaret Sanger by name failed to emphasize the effect of access to birth control on society and women's status but rather focused on Sanger's arrests, stating that birth control continues to be problematic.[15]

In relation to work, most texts discussed women's traditional domestic work and their pursuit of nontraditional jobs outside of the home but failed to do so in all eras. The colonial era, for example, is emphasized in all texts as well as the rise of women working outside the home during the Industrial Revolution and World War II.[16] Some mentioned that industrialization relieved women of having to produce things in the home that they otherwise could not get, but only one acknowledged that the hours per week that a woman worked in 1920 matched those prior to the Industrial Revolution, which delegitimized these claims.[17] On average, women worked 51 hours a week.

However, bearing and raising children are barely mentioned in the majority of texts; therefore, substantive discussion of what domestic work entailed is absent.[18] Students were given only abstract reasons for why women sought work outside the home, and none of those abstract reasons included conditions that women controlled or motivations women might have had.[19] Legislation related to sex discrimination in the workforce was mentioned but presented in ways that almost challenged the legitimacy of the legislation. Some texts went so far as to challenge whether women should fight to uphold their constitutional rights![20]

Tetreault also found that the textbooks failed to acknowledge that women's history has been omitted from the textbooks. There was no discussion of how the various points of emphasis in the public sphere have fundamentally and systematically excluded women. Students were not guided in any way to understand that the exclusion of women is only half the story.[21] The failure of texts to include substantive information on the impacts of race, ethnicity, and social class on women's experiences leaves middle-class women as the norm and virtually excludes minority groups.[22] Like history, herstory was whitewashed. This does a disservice not only to women but to all people. It distorts their views of the past and present realities. When women today discuss their challenges, they are presented out of the context of millennia of women struggling with the same issues.

What impression did these texts leave students with? Tetreault claimed that because the curriculum included women's activities in the public spheres only when they either championed male activities or broadened women's supporting role within the family, it left students with the impression that these were the only public activities for women that were acceptable.[23] The texts propagated the sexist notion that women's virtue lies in self-sacrifice.[24]

In 1997, probably owing to the great work of people like Tetreault, the AHA created criteria for evaluating history textbooks to emphasize key focuses in the field of history.[25] They said the texts must

- ◆ Reinforce high-quality history by empowering students to do history
- ◆ Teach critical thinking and how to understand bias
- ◆ Provide continuous chronological content showing continuity and change over time
- ◆ Reflect current scholarship and be peer-reviewed
- ◆ Include the factual experiences of diverse people[26]

Writing in 2006, Kay Chick was critical of the AHA's guidelines because they failed to be specific. She said since the AHA has called for gender balance, they must be held accountable for defining it. If they are calling for a 50/50 split in the gender representations of historical figures, textbook publishers have yet to meet that goal.[27] The AHA updated their guidelines in 2018, but they remain nonspecific, with no outline for an appropriate ratio.

Since 2006, more editions and revision of texts have been done. More women's history and research have emerged, and the national dialogue and culture have become more open to women's experiences and attitudes. The #MeToo movement brought much discussion of the lives of women into the public discourse. *How much have these cultural shifts impacted the coverage and narrative related to women in textbooks?*

Not much. In 2020, my advanced placement (AP) US history students and I examined three textbooks that had been revised for the updated exam. We found that, on average, they named, pictured, and offered primary sources by women once for every four times they did so for men.[28] In her own review of the literature on the failure of textbooks to include women, Kathryn E. Engebretson wrote in 2014, "As many social studies teachers use textbooks in their teaching, this underrepresentation and limited view of gender constrains the potential of teaching multiple perspectives of women, and teachers are thus charged with modifying inadequate materials."[29] Teachers, untrained and uneducated on these topics, should not be on their own, primarily responsible for finding women's history to integrate.

Standards

State standards are another clear area where we see the devaluing of the social sciences and the ineptitude of their expectations for cultural competence related to women. The National Women's History Museum (NWHM), in their study on the standards, explained that the standards for social studies on a national level are "wildly different… The universe of possible content and topics overlaid by political, cultural, and ideological perspectives resulted in individualized state standards."[30] Having variation between states is somewhat reasonable because state and local histories should impact historical instruction to give students a deep contextual understanding of their local culture and systems. It would make sense that East and West Coast schools emphasize different Indigenous communities as well as English and Spanish settlements. *But why would the size and scope of the curriculum be so vastly different? How is it that two states can have no set standards at all, and some have as few as three pages of instruction for teachers?*

One study explored the social studies standards in the 50 states. They found:

Forty-eight states and the District of Columbia have established academic standards to address academic achievement in history, the social sciences, or social studies. The sole exceptions are Iowa and Rhode Island which allow local jurisdictions to set the history/social studies curriculum. Any apparent consensus ends there, however, as most states interpret the nature and meaning of educational standards in radically different ways. Documents can range from slim (3 pages) to epic (580 pages), with lengths everywhere in between.[31]

The same variations are not found in other subjects.

National and state social studies standards provide a top-down opportunity to create widespread change and open the door to include women. Unfortunately, this is a route unlikely to produce many gains. States notoriously underfund the social studies and provide little professional development for them. While preference for localized instruction allows for teacher freedom and empowers teachers to jump on current hot topics, it leaves room for cyclical prejudices to remain in our instruction—such as the exclusion of women—and does not provide the structure for our instruction to match contemporary issues and ever-changing views on history. These variations are doubly felt when examining the way the standards portray women. The limited mention of women in the state standards was so dire that the NWHM wrote a report titled "Where are the women?"[32] Scholars there analyzed the state standards in all 50 states as well as the District of Columbia and concluded that

> women's experiences and stories are not well integrated into US state history standards. The lack of representation and context in state-level materials presupposes that women's history is even less represented at the classroom level. This implies that women's history is not important.[33]

Perhaps one of the main reasons women are not easily recallable is that there is little consensus on which women are worthy of mention. In their study, the NWHM found that 178 women were named in state standards but only if their names achieved national or regional prominence. There seemed to be little consistency regarding which women should be taught, as only 15 women were named more than ten times. A lack of consensus leads to a lack of repetition, and a lack of repetition leads to few people remembering women's names.

Not surprisingly, the NWHM found that women were sparse because of the "historiographical framework" preference for "male-oriented exceptional leadership while over-emphasizing women's domestic roles."[34] More than half of the standards emphasized women in their domestic roles, and the rest focused on women who protested for a cause, with wealthier white women getting greater attention. The focus on domestic roles neglects the economic necessity of those roles being fulfilled and can belittle the labor.

Overall, the NWHM concluded that the standards failed to adequately represent and explain the roles of women in history and society. The standards are outdated and do not reflect a womankind consistent with the current lives of women: diverse, active, and very much participants in society, not protesters of it. Americans have been encouraging girls to pursue careers in the STEM (science, technology, engineering, and mathematics) fields, to take leadership positions in business, and to run for office, yet there are few historical examples of women engaging in these activities in our history standards. Even rarer is a demonstrative example of a woman both being a mother with domestic duties and having a career of note. The challenge of this balance is one that seems to be uniquely female. The NWHM explained:

> Women's history studies historical events, topics, people, and subjects from a woman's perspective. It understands that culture affects experience and that women's historical experiences differed from men's. Women's history contextualizes women within the social, political, legal, and cultural systems of their times. History that does not acknowledge women's situations as well as their activities and accomplishments is, by definition, not a full history. We found that women's topics are often an addendum to the main storyline. Women are frequently included in lists of marginalized groups as a reminder to teachers that when covering a broad topic, they should also include the experiences of women among others.[35]

In New Hampshire, for example, the framework itself is a blessing and curse. It is one of the larger sets of state history standards—a whopping 106 pages. It is organized into ten themes with suggestions of topics that can be covered in those themes. At its best, it gives teachers flexibility in how topics are covered. At its worst, it is too vague to be useful and outdated, having last been updated in 2006 and entirely ignoring major shifts in law and culture around LGBTQ rights and others issues. One of the themes, "Patterns of Social and Political Interaction," gives specific license for teachers to discuss the "changing role of women." In the section on world history, students are encouraged to "analyze the impact of the agricultural revolution on humans using examples, e.g., the role of women."[36] What this standard is referring to is how more agriculture led to surplus food, which created better living conditions, which led to more people surviving infancy, which led to women having greater child-rearing responsibilities. Historians point to the agricultural revolution as the dawn of civilization and the beginning of the "traditional role" for women. Left out is evidence that women likely discovered agriculture and that the pagan religions of the time worshipped goddesses often superior to male gods. In the entire 106-page, 27,637-word document, the word *woman* appears seven times, and, more importantly, it references women in their *changing role*, withholding a myriad of other things women did and accomplished.

If we only learned the women's history in the state standards, it's not a stretch to suggest that women participated only in domestic duties and protests. If the entire history for half of humanity can be summarized in one sentence, teachers aren't giving the topic its due diligence. This narrative has many unintended consequences, foremost among them that it informs students that *women are summarize-able*. Women's history has its own patterns, for the same reasons that our collective history has patterns, and we are doomed to repeat them because women don't know the patterns or the historical solutions people have used to combat them.

Outside of the individual state standards, the closest thing to a social studies governing body, the NCSS, has a very open-ended framework for the social studies that does not in any way inhibit teachers from teaching women's history, but it also doesn't encourage or guide them toward a gendered history. Many states have opted to offer their own standards rather than follow those issues by NCSS, and thus the standards become a "mere suggestion."[37] Social studies frameworks are unlike those in other subjects because the acquisition of knowledge is only a piece of the triad. Students need to know information that is subject-specific, and the social studies incorporate seven disciplines (history, geography, political science, economics, psychology, sociology, and anthropology). Students also need to develop skills, which is why the NCSS recently embraced the C3 Framework, which better incorporates social studies skills development into the curriculum. Finally, there are themes—generally agreed-upon understandings that we want students to know. The NCSS themes are vague to allow for school choice and local control. This ambiguity by default leaves teachers to interpret their meaning, which likely leaves teachers to default to traditional interpretations.[38]

NCSS standards fail to guide teachers toward women's history; in fact, what little guidance they offer on content is gender-biased. Similar to findings about how textbooks become less inclusive from elementary to secondary classes, the NCSS standards do as well. Naming of historical women decreases in the standards by middle and high school where it includes only white and mythological women![39] (Table 6.1).

In her analysis, Katheryn E. Engebretson wrote, "With three non-fictional females named within the middle grades section and none in the high school section, it is clear that females in this document are given a near zero status as important figures throughout history."[40] She ridicules the NCSS for trying to "incorporate current research" and utterly failing to do so.[41] Not only does the high school list entirely exclude women, the women selected for middle school

Table 6.1 Female and Male Key Figures in NCSS Standards

	Female	Male
Elementary	Marian Anderson Jr. Helen Keller Sacajawea Amelia Earhart	Martin Luther King Franklin Delano Roosevelt Nelson Mandela Franklin Chang-Dias
Middle	Grimke Sisters Harriet Beecher Stowe Artemis	Lewis and Clark Abraham Lincoln Frederick Douglass John Brown Frank Lloyd Wright Zeus George Washington Saddam Hussein
High School		Marco Polo Keith Ellison Thomas Jefferson Abraham Lincoln George Washington Mao Zedong Deng Xiaoping Hu Jintao John F. Kennedy Daniel Shays Nat Turner

Source: Eckert's table with data from Kathryn E. Engebretson, "Another missed opportunity: Gender in the national curriculum standards for social studies," *Social Studies Research and Practice*, 9(3), 2014, 26–27.

are women who took stands against oppression and became notable in within a male-dominated political landscape. The list leaves no space for women's diversity and the lives and accomplishments of women who excelled within the women's sphere. Of course, all are white, and, Engebretson added, "this document presents an image of the world as one where women simply do not matter as much as men and the figured, or typical, world presented is one of gender imbalance."[42] Women are half of humanity, not zero.

Engebretson also analyzed the impacts of the men selected for study and concluded that they promoted a narrow definition of masculinity: politically powerful, advancing the world politically and economically, while personal character assessments are not included. She wrote,

> This limited view of what important men do is as disturbing and paralleled by women only being lauded when performing the acts of politically important men. This perpetuates a narrow vision of masculinity and pigeon-holes men into only being valuable contributors to history when they have achieved certain political advancements.[43]

As Margaret Smith Crocco found, this promotion of gender stereotypes in school is dysfunctional and harmful to adolescent development.[44] Promoting these strong and stoic men as repressors of emotion, independent, and competitors inhibits young men's sense of personhood. We should all be concerned.

Stoic men and absent women present students with a fictional worldview and leaves them unprepared for a world of women leaders, thinkers, and problem solvers.

Teacher Education Programs

Vague frameworks, as well as no frameworks, have the following effect: teachers teach the topics they learned, and they didn't learn women's history. Worse, teacher education programs and training texts promote gender biases! Texts designed for preservice teachers have the outstanding privilege of training future teachers, but in the decades since the feminist movement, little has changed in the way these texts prepare undergraduate and graduate students for their future careers in the classroom. These texts were found to not only have gender bias but promote a damaging gender bias. Researchers wrote, "Foundation texts provide slightly more than 7% of content to gender issues, including the experiences and contributions of females, and methods texts average little more than 1%."[45] This is deeply concerning given the amount of research and advocacy work that has been done to date.

The biggest barrier to teaching women's history is teachers' lack of coursework on women's studies and pedagogies that effect gender equality. Those of us who took mainstream routes to teacher certification never studied women's history. How are we supposed to teach it? If you examine where women's history is taught, you learn that it isn't a component of history—it's a different subject entirely: women's studies or gender studies. Although the skill set and learning objectives are the same, the subjects are taught separately. What message does that send? That there is HISTORY and then *women's history*? Women's studies are predominantly taught by women to women, and men, either intentionally or unintentionally, are often not in the room. In effect, learning about women's experience in history is something only women do. These enlightened women then find themselves alone in a world of people who learned only his-story. Male family members and colleagues in particular have little sense of the history of women's experience.

Some colleges have worked to integrate these courses. I am from New England, so in 2021, I examined the history curriculums of some of the top universities in the region: Harvard, MIT, Williams, Yale, Brown, Dartmouth, and Amherst. Most still had a segregated major for women's studies. I was curious about whether any schools required a course in women's history or gender studies for graduation with a generic history major. None did. So then I was curious about how many of the optional classes were about women, gender, or sexuality. I scrolled through the course offerings and found that while interesting classes in these areas were offered, it was a meager percentage of the offerings—and I was being generous. If the course title or description mentioned women, gender, or sexuality, I counted it. If the course title or description referenced any woman, families, feminist theory, witches, women, or LGBTQ+ movement, I counted it. In all cases besides Amherst, courses about women were less than 10 percent of the offered curriculum. Now, this assessment has serious flaws. First and foremost, some schools have integrated women's history into their courses, so a class might actually highlight important women, but that just wasn't reflected in the title or course description. For example, a course could be titled "European History" but the professor highlights women's experiences alongside the traditionally male-dominated curriculum. So, without taking all of these courses, I am left with my own experience of having been educated at a time after this supposed "integration" took place. Only one of my college-level history classes featured any required reading written by a woman, and none featured a woman in any significant sense.

Teachers are desperate for professional development on teaching gender and race history. In Martell and Steven's 2018 study, nearly 70 percent of teachers said they wanted professional development.[46] They concluded that the "maleness and Whiteness of social studies... is so entrenched in our schools that the teachers in this study, despite desire to more often teach about race and gender, have been hesitant to go against traditional curriculum."[47] And their study was done in "progressive" Massachusetts. *What does the rest of the country look like?*

Devaluing the Social Studies

Teaching women's history might be doable if schools would put funding toward professional development for social studies teachers. But, sadly, social studies classes are the least funded, least tested, and therefore the least valued of the four core subjects in the majority of school systems. In the early 1990s, students spent 9.5 hours a week in social studies courses. A decade later, that time was cut by 2 hours.[48] In a 2011 survey, 37 percent of teachers said they had seen the social studies—like other less valued subjects—being crowded out by testing for math and English.[49] The Brookings Institute claimed that "the country's accountability systems have generally placed social studies conspicuously lower in the hierarchy of academic achievement, superseded by math, literacy, and science."[50] Some states, such as Texas, even cut the graduation requirements for social studies from four to three classes.[51] Some believe that social studies can be integrated with English and literature. Schools claim they have covered topics when students have read about them, but literary exercises do not constitute the development of social studies analysis skills.

In most fields, professional development is widely accepted as beneficial, but in the social studies, this is hard to come by. The marginalization of the subject has made opportunities for professional development sparse.[52]

In Iowa, a state assessment of social studies instruction reported that fewer than half of teachers had received professional development specific to the field in the prior three years. When professional development was specific to grade levels taught, those who taught high school were more likely to have had professional development than those in the elementary school, where only 12.9 percent had received content-area instruction in the prior three years.[53] Regardless of grade levels taught, teachers across the state said the opportunities for professional development were "too few." When asked whether they would participate in professional development in their subject area if offered, the plurality said yes, but many said other subjects were of greater importance.[54] Not surprisingly, in fewer than half of the states, social studies teachers said they were familiar with the state frameworks for the subject and were prepared to teach to them—not exactly a recipe for success in teaching social studies content or skills.

Social studies has the least professional development dedicated to it because it is the "least important" as dictated by standardized testing and the new emphasis on STEM as well as having no clear national standards. It is in this laissez-faire tumult that women's history is lost. It comes down to the wills of individual teachers, administrators, or even uneducated school boards to decide what is taught, which is a recipe for failure. Women's studies are bound to the social studies, and the social studies are on the chopping block. National Education Association (NEA) President Lily Eskelsen García said, "It's our job to bring back the arts and Social Studies and world languages and whatever it is our students need to leave behind the corrupting, unconscionable testing culture of blame and punish by test scores and move forward with an education that opens their minds to the infinite possibilities of their lives."[55] Margit McGuire, director of teacher education at Seattle University and a social studies specialist, said that this treatment of social studies education "doesn't foster a very sophisticated treatment of the subject matter."[56]

The difference in coverage from elementary to high school is profound. Elementary schools have seen social studies cut almost entirely, the rationale being that these topics will be covered in middle or high school and that developing foundational reading skills is more important. I was once teaching a high school class about the Korean War and explained to my students that the peace agreement divided Korea along the 38th parallel. Not a single student in the room knew what that meant, as social studies mapping skills had been lost in their educational experience. I had to shift gears and do a mini-lesson on longitude and latitude before I could continue. This is just one example of the many skills and understandings my students were missing when they arrived in my high school classroom. In the school district I taught in, social studies were taught in the elementary school on Mondays and Wednesdays for 45 minutes, and even those two periods got cut because federal holidays regularly fall on Mondays. One social studies teacher in the elementary school told me that, because of snow days and afternoon assemblies, she hadn't taught her class in a month. These are the undocumented ways in which educators experience systemic devaluing of the social studies.

A massive volume of literature exists on the effect of not testing social studies. The consensus is that it is not scrutinized, and thus little professional development is concentrated on the subject. In all my years of teaching, not one school-wide professional development course was taught by or focused on the needs of social studies educators (or science, for that matter). A great deal was focused on literacy and math.

As a result of the way in which funding and values are dictated by standardized testing, I have pragmatically become a proponent of state testing for the social studies. Tests such as AP exams demand and enforce social studies skills like primary-source analysis and evaluation that, if modified for a general audience, could serve as a possible test to improve the treatment of social studies.

Without training and professional development, the social studies lag in their quality and relevance. The lack of investment in the social studies means that few companies produce high-quality materials or trainings for the subject. Teachers can get obsessed with projects that lack purposeful skill development. They can overfocus on certain content or even become lecture-driven, emphasizing memorization over critical thinking. Teachers take it upon themselves to reform and improve the content to make it relevant, rigorous, and timely without the benefits of research and peer review.

Teachers do not have access to adequate professional development to remain current on the abundant women's scholarship emerging, and they therefore regurgitate little and poor-quality women's history. The failure of our own educations, the disparity and lack of guidance in some state standards, and the overall sense that the social studies can be skipped if we run out of time lead to the subject not getting revised. As a result, women's voices remain a vast minority.

Breakers: Revised Tool Kits

Textbooks

Even the most recent textbooks fail to include women's voices in a robust sense. In an effort to include women and minorities, many have moved toward not using a single textbook but instead relying on diverse primary and secondary sources to let students do the work of a historian. Primary sources can be found for free online, and primary-source collections are purchasable through academic organizations.

The Remedial Herstory Project has a robust website designed for the secondary classroom. For every era of US and world history, we have chapters and primary sources as well as inquiry-based lesson plans like those found in this book. All of our work is peer-reviewed through an internal review process with our network of women's historians. Educators can also find other women's groups and museums that have cataloged women's primary source material. The NWHM, The Girl Museum, the California Women's History Museum, the Women in the American Story website from the New York Historical Society, and the Texas Women's History Project, just to name a few, have primary material about women archives and are easy to find.

Online tools are ever-changing, but a few great ones to find primary source material include the following:

- ◆ US History
  - ◆ Internet Archive
  - ◆ Library of Congress
  - ◆ Gilder Lehrman Institute
  - ◆ Digital Public Library of America
- ◆ World History
  - ◆ Internet Archive
  - ◆ Project Guttenberg
  - ◆ The Avalon Project from Yale University
  - ◆ Source Guides from Fordham University

All these sources will allow teachers to draw materials from across the globe on groups that have been marginalized in the curriculum, including women.

Standards

State standards demonstrate a lack of consensus or effort put into determining which women are essential for all students to know. The variety of women named in the 50 state standards in the United States shifts dramatically from state to state. *How can history teachers begin to address women's history if there is no semblance of consensus on which women should be taught?*

Too much pressure falls directly on teachers, when the whole system of teacher preparation is to blame. Women's historians must demand to be invited to serve on boards and committees working to revise state standards. Local governments need to look for models of standards that include women and encourage the revitalizing of history education. Similarly, state and federal governments need to look for models of standards that allow for local topics and selection while demanding high-level social studies skills as well as models that are inclusive of the diverse histories of women and minorities.

While cultural values and state standards remain in flux, teachers must go on whatever consensus already exists and integrate women and women's themes into the curriculum they are already teaching. The NWHM's study identified the few women who regularly appeared in the state standards:

◆ Rosa Parks
◆ Susan B. Anthony
◆ Harriet Tubman
◆ Elizabeth Cady Stanton
◆ Sojourner Truth
◆ Abigail Adams
◆ Harriet Beecher Stowe
◆ Jane Addams
◆ Norma McCorvey (Jane Roe)
◆ Ida B. Wells-Barnett
◆ Eleanor Roosevelt
◆ Sacagawea
◆ Phillis Wheatly
◆ Mercy Otis Warren
◆ Anne Hutchinson[57]

Certainly, these are not the only women, but they set a minimum standard for women who must be taught in schools.

In 2021, I spoke at an event about the lack of inclusion of women in the social studies curriculum. The event was cosponsored by a slew of national women's history organizations and included Alex Cuenca, a board member from the NCSS. Regarding the barriers to getting women into history curriculum, he said, "Although standards are standards, in reality, they're all pretty vague. How you interpret these standards and what you decide to include and exclude is a powerful political choice. And I ask you to exercise that agency and not shy away from issues critical to women's humanity."[58] There are few higher authorities in the social studies who can stress the importance of including women.

Women's historians, male and female, have been researching and writing for decades. New books come out every day. The scholarship is there. The primary sources are there. The NCSS focuses its standards on the skills of the historian, which can be practiced regardless of the gender of a teacher's primary source! Those standards leave the content to the states, and most states fail to have comprehensive content standards. Teachers can exploit this failure and teach women's history. If states *do* have comprehensive standards, can they seriously claim that Harriet Tubman and Clara Barton were not notable parts of Civil War history? That Eleanor Roosevelt and the WAVES (Women Accepted for Volunteer Emergency Service) were not central to the World War II era?

I think one of the reasons states have utterly failed to produce inclusive standards is that it's really difficult! And so much social history is currently being written. History standards in general are challenging because a historical figure that is significant varies by region. Realizing the breadth of the challenge in revising state standards, the Remedial Herstory Project decided to replace individual standards related to women's history with one standard. A special thank you to Dr. Alicia Gutierrez-Romine, Dr. Barbara Tischler, and Michelle Stonis, who collaborated with me on this.

> Students critically analyze the social, political, cultural, and economic lives and interactions of diverse groups of women, including the ways they profoundly influenced, and were influenced by, the historical past in every time period.

However, this "standard" is in many ways insufficient to dismantle some of the fallacies about women's history I have come to recognize and have heard from many history teachers. So, a caveat would be that teachers need to be cautious about the following traps. Consider these "anti-standards" but lies that teachers should not pass on:

- *All women…* Instead, there is no single "women's story."
- *In x time, women did x job.* Instead, "women's work" varied considerably by class, race, region, rural and urban.
- *Back then, women had no rights.* Instead, women had rights and privileges in every society, they just differed from those available to men and those women may have today.

And while that helps make clear the goal, it doesn't do anything practical for teachers. Who are these women they are supposed to be incorporating? What women's groups, movements, and topics should they include? Funnily enough, much of the literature I have read on the importance of social history skirts around, providing a tangible list that educators could use. If you want a teacher to teach about women, give them a list of names and topics.

Thus, through my work with the Remedial Herstory Project, I led a team of historians to create a spreadsheet of women from every era and region of world history. Once the parameters were established, we sent it out to our network of historians to help fill in the gaps. The results are not an exhaustive list, and it is certainly not supposed to represent "standards" of what teachers *have* to teach. The list merely represents a starting point for educators with women they *could* include for every unit they might teach in a history class. An effort was made to incorporate women from every race, region, and class and include the lives of queer people for every era. This document is regularly updated and available on the Remedial Herstory Project website.

Selected women were added because their stories overlap content already taught in social studies classes, although they may be lesser-known women. For example, Lozen was an Apache woman who fought alongside Geronimo against the US Army during the period of westward expansion. Or Mary Anna Custis Lee because her husband, Robert E. Lee, was so important to understanding the Civil War. Other women are included expressly because they *do not* parallel traditional history topics and *should be included*. For example, Olympe de Gouges, who wrote the women's declaration of rights during the French Revolution and was executed for it, burying the struggles of women in that era against the patriarchy. Or Margaret Sanger, who founded Planned Parenthood and is probably left out for obvious reasons and nevertheless has defined the 20th and, so far, the 21st century. She should be taught in history classes. Names of women like Angela, whom little is known about other than she was on the 1619 ship of enslaved people who landed in Virginia, are included because her presence in the Americas is important and the lack of information about her also speaks to her status and life.

Women are placed in the era in which they most influenced American history. Women who cross multiple eras can be found in the era in which they first had an impact. For example, Eleanor Roosevelt is important to both the period of her husband's administration but also the Cold War era for her work in the UN. She appears only in the first era.

Why did we decide on a list of women? Dr. Camilla Townsend shifted my view on this during an interview we did for my podcast. She shared that when so little is known about women's lives, knowing one woman well can illuminate the possible life experiences of other women whose documents were not archived, whose story was left unrecorded, and whose personal reflections are lost. Contrasting different women's experiences and ideas gives us windows into the range of challenges, interests, and opinions of women in a given time.

It is my sincere hope that someone will take the time to critique this list and let us know how mistaken we were to leave someone important out.

Professional Development

No assigned book in my graduate or undergraduate experience was specific to the lives and experiences of women, yet such books exist and should be requisite in any humanities or social science program and across all of the seven social studies fields. Teachers *should* be responsible for only a small part of this effort, but sadly in the present landscape, it feels entirely on their own initiative. The issue is systemic. History education programs must either require integrated courses that involve the lives and complex histories of women or else require graduates to take a segregated women's history course. And, frankly, this should be true for all marginalized groups.

Knowing that professional development will not likely be provided or funded, educators must seek free professional development on women's history independently, and this *does* exist. The Remedial Herstory Project, The NWHM, state humanities councils, and local historical societies all offer free trainings and talks about women. These groups have done a wonderful job of offering teacher trainings and adding women's experiences to our narrative.

Blueprint: Reimagining Periodization

I'm sure there are many people reading who are thinking about how both overwhelming and divisive it is to take the human experience and say that we need to separate it out into black, white, Asian, indigenous, female, male, rich, poor, abled, disabled: aren't we all just human? *History is our story, so can't we just tell the average human experience story without parceling it up among every single group?* Yes. That is the dream. But most teachers are at the stage of compensatory or bi-focal history.

The problem is the long history of history excluding so many people in the story. An average would be the sum of all of our experiences, divided by the number of people. If you take only the white, male, elite people and average their stories and call it the human experience, you are lying. A mathematician would call fraud.

It's kind of like when people say "All Lives Matter" instead of acknowledging the historical and perpetual devaluing of Black lives. Of course, all lives matter, but those who champion that political perspective are missing the damn point. Once we take time to respect and honor Black humans in our lives and in our past and correct structures that continue to discriminate, *then* and only then can we say all lives truly matter.

When someone says "just teach history," it's the same as someone saying all lives matter. What they're saying is teach white, male, elite, history: his-story. They are not asking for the average human experience. They don't want to know what it was like for all of us; they want to know what it was like for less than 5% of us. History is not yet all of ours. Most of us, poor people, people of color, people with disabilities—and yes women—have been left out. This concept should not be a male-versus-female, white-versus-people of color, upper class-versus-lower class, abled-versus-disabled thing. People of all genders, races, classes, and any other division you want to include will benefit from reevaluating where the average standpoint is.

Sadly, we are in the middle of the reevaluation process, and secondary educators are only at the beginning. Teachers need to compensate, add women's contributions, and appreciate the broader female experience before there can be an integrated history. To get there, it is helpful to look at histories that are just about women to see how their periodization differs from traditional periodization and begin to weave these narratives together.

Shifting Periodization

Holistic, integrated history will involve a reconsideration of periods, which really hasn't happened at all in schools or texts.[59] Women are inserted yes, but the structure in which those women are trying to fit is entirely male-designed and following the history of the male experience. Traditional periodization of history, for example, was very political and therefore male-dominated. But for women, the timelines are a bit different. A merger of that acknowledges these differences would be helpful.

So, what was traditional periodization? In 1996, Garry Nash and Charlotte Crabtree led a four-year research effort to produce national content standards for history with the National Center for History in the Schools at the University of California, Los Angeles funded by the National Endowment for the Humanities and the U.S. Department of Education. As previously mentioned, these standards lit up the culture wars for being too multicultural, yet they barely included women.[60] These standards offered guidance for a male-centered periodization that many other curriculums parallel to some extent.

The AP World History exam followed nine periods. The following are the periods designated for both World and US History courses.

World History
◆ Era 1: The Beginnings of Human Society
◆ Era 2: Early Civilizations and the Emergence of Pastoral Peoples, 4000–1000 BCE
◆ Era 3: Classical Traditions, Major Religions, and Giant Empires, 1000 BCE–300 CE
◆ Era 4: Expanding Zones of Exchange and Encounter, 300–1000 CE
◆ Era 5: Intensified Hemispheric Interactions, 1000–1500 CE
◆ Era 6: Emergence of the First Global Age, 1450–1770
◆ Era 7: An Age of Revolutions, 1750–1914
◆ Era 8: A Half-Century of Crisis and Achievement, 1900–1945
◆ Era 9: The 20th Century Since 1945: Promises and Paradoxes

US History
- ◆ Era 1: Three Worlds Meet (Beginnings to 1620)
- ◆ Era 2: Colonization and Settlement (1585–1763)
- ◆ Era 3: Revolution and the New Nation (1754–1820s)
- ◆ Era 4: Expansion and Reform (1801–1861)
- ◆ Era 5: Civil War and Reconstruction (1850–1877)
- ◆ Era 6: The Development of the Industrial United States (1870–1900)
- ◆ Era 7: The Emergence of Modern America (1890–1930)
- ◆ Era 8: The Great Depression and World War II (1929–1945)
- ◆ Era 9: Postwar United States (1945–early 1970s)
- ◆ Era 10: Contemporary United States (1968–present)

The problem with this periodization is that the many significant transformations and turning points for women's lives happened in the middle of these periods. The titles of the periods are also problematic as they center issues which are white, male, and elite, fragmenting major themes in women's history. In world history, the Age of Revolutions had a mixed, if not negative, impact on the status of women in society, so the word revolution applies in a military sense, but not in relation to social change. In US history the unionization and strikes of the Lowell Mill girls are significant to the year 1836, but if industrialization is only discussed between 1870 and 1900 they will be erased. Women's suffrage spans 1848 to 1920 in the US and all the way to 1944 for French "revolutionaries," a timeline that would be chopped up in the eras outlined here.

Wave Model Debunked

It is common to hear reference to the "waves theory" of women's history, essentially three distinct periods of women's history and feminist activity. This theory is problematic for several reasons, but foremost is that it leaves out feminist activities in ancient and medieval history. The famous waves of feminism have been debunked as a tool for periodizing women's history since they are not inclusive of most women's experiences and dictated by early feminist historians. The wave model went something like this:

Wave 1: First-Wave Suffrage Activism
Wave 2: Second Wave Triggered by the Betty Friedan's *Feminine Mystique*
Wave 3: Third Wave Triggered by the Anita Hill hearing

The problem with this model is that it does not account for the diversity of women's experiences. The "model is based exclusively on middle-class white women's feminist activities" instead of a more complex periodization including class, sexuality, and race. These waves do not reflect the waves of feminist activism in other groups. Aruga explains, "We need a large picture of women's and gender history, with its complexity explained simply and clearly."[61] In a crucial piece of literature for anyone attempting to understand and then teach women's history, "The Big Tent of U.S. Women's and Gender History," Cornelia H. Dayton and Lisa Levenstein show how the waves just do not reflect the intersectional, Eckert test-passing, understanding of women's history that scholars in the field now have. They write:

> Nearly every U.S. history textbook and survey course discusses the growth of feminism… This master narrative bears very little resemblance to historians' current reconceptualizations of the trajectory of feminist politics… The image of nineteenth- and twentieth-century feminism as a white middle-class, northeastern movement dominated by a few famous figures rarely appears in current scholarship. A range of authors has uncovered an incredibly diverse group of feminist activists who hailed from all classes, races, and sexual orientations and were located in all parts of the country. Without ignoring the racism embedded in some white women's organizing, scholars are also increasingly exploring how feminists resisted hierarchies based on gender, class, race, and sexuality, forging effective, albeit often painful, coalitions. These women campaigned for legal equality and for maternity leave, child care, reproductive rights, employment equity, social welfare services, protection from domestic and sexual violence, racial equality, economic justice, and sexual freedom. The breadth of the issues pursued by different groups of women and the longue durée of their organizing has led the field largely to cast aside the idea of first, second, and third "waves" of feminist activism. Particularly because some of the most important organizing by non-white and working-class women does not fit this periodization, the wave model does not account for the multiclass, multiracial movement that historians have uncovered.[62]

This is true in most areas. They explore the way gender ideologies impacted imperialism and white women's roles in colonization, which oppressed other women, as well as emerging transnational feminism which places the American movements inside a global movement for women.

New Periodization

So, what will work? First and foremost, my hope is that teachers will question the periods and begin to see the ways in which the turning points may not work for all groups. Second, I hope teachers question the titles and look for period titles that better reflect the experiences of all groups. By questioning, we can collectively improve and expand the periods taught in schools.

World History

The best place to look for structured guidance on *new* periodization is to read surveys from women historians. For world history, this is incredibly difficult as few surveys of women's world history really exist. Often one will see a collection of biographies attempting to pass as a survey, like "the history of the world in 10 women" or something to that effect. Biographies do help tell women's history. *Who Cooked the Last Supper: The Women's History of the World* by Rosalind Miles does strive to be a survey, as does her sequel, *The Women's History of the Modern World: How Radicals, Rebels, and Everywomen Revolutionized the Last 200 Years*. Her books are Western-centric, assert debunked theories, and are a bit slanted. There are more neutral sources. In a two-volume work, *Women in World History: Readings from Prehistory to 1500* and *1500 to the Present*, Sarah Shaver Hughes and Brady Hughes didn't write a history but instead compiled collections of essays related to women and gender in periods. They chose an approach that may resonate with some world history teachers, which was to use geography as a way of creating themes. Their organization is as follows:

1. Prehistoric Women
2. The Women of Ancient Egypt
3. India
4. Greece
5. China
6. Women in the Late Roman Republic
7. Western Europe
8. The Middle East
9. China and Japan
10. Africa
11. Southeast Asia
12. The Americas

In Volume II, they keep the geographic themes but move them to subthemes under time frames.

I. 1500–1800
   1. China and Japan
   2. The Middle East
   3. India

4. Europe
5. Gender in the European Colonization of the Americas
6. African Women in a New Era of Commerce and State Building

II. 1800–present
1. Western Europe
2. Africa
3. The Symbol of the Veil in Modern Islam
4. India
5. Seeking Liberation of New East Asian Societies
6. The Americas

Finally, Bonnie G. Smith, a Distinguished Professor of History at Rutgers University, wrote a modern world history text titled *Women in World History*. She uses the following periodization:

1. Productive and Reproductive Lives, c. 1450–1600
2. Early Modern Structures of Power
3. Imagining Their World, 1450–1600
4. Productive Life across a Connected Globe, 1600–1750
5. Populations, Ideas, and the Industrious Revolution, 1600–1800
6. Revolts, Revolutions and States, 1650–1830
7. Industrial Work and the Local/Global Economy, 1750–1880
8. Modernizing Women and the Nation, 1830–1900
9. Expanding Empires, 1870–1914
10. Global Warfare, 1914–1945
11. Decolonizing the World, Decolonizing Women
12. At the Vanguard of Change: Women's Globalization

The consulting team of scholars who helped with the Remedial Herstory Project's online textbook decided on the following chapter outline:

1. to 15,000 BCE: Before Gendered Constructs
2. to 15,000 BCE: Great Goddesses?
3. 10,000 BCE: The Agricultural Revolution: A great mistake?
4. 4000–1000 BCE: Domesticating Women in the First City-States
5. 800–400 BCE: Founding Myths and Women's Place
6. 800–300 BCE: Asian Philosophies and Women's Place
7. 100 BCE–100 CE: Women and the Roman Empire
8. 100 BCE–100 CE: Women and the Han Empire
9. 0: One Male God over Women

10. 100–500: Women Travelers and Merchants on the Silk Road
11. 500–900: The Age of Queens and Empresses
12. 700–1200: The Golden Age of Islam
13. 900–1500: Women in Feudal Europe and Japan
14. 900–1200: Women Crusaders and Stabilizers
15. 1200–1400: Pastoral and Mongol Women
16. 1300–1500: Renaissance and Ottoman Women Thinkers
17. 1000–1600: Gender Dynamics in New Worlds
18. 1000–1600: Women Explorers and Leaders
19. 1500–1600: Women and the Reformation
20. 1500–1800: Virgin Encounters in the New World
21. 1600–1850: Gender, Sexuality and the Slave Trade
22. 1700–1850: The Enlightenment and Women
23. 1700–1850: Cloistered Women in Asia
24. 1850–1950: Women's Industrial Revolution
25. 1850–1950: Women's Lives under Imperialism
26. 1900–1930: Women's Worlds in Collision
27. 1930–1950: Women and the Global War
28. 1950–1990: Decolonization
29. 1950–1990: Transnational Feminism

US History

For US history, there are more attempts at a survey. In *Women's America: Refocusing the Past* by Linda K. Kerber, Jane Sherron De Hart, Cornelia Hughes Dayton, and Judy Tzu-Chun Wu, all university professors, they use the following periods:

1. Early America: 1600–1820
2. America Many Frontiers: 1820–1880
3. Modern America: 1880–1920
4. Stormy America: 1920–1945
5. A Global Transformation: 1945–present
6. 21st century, an old battle reformed and begun anew

Susan Ware, professor emeritus from Harvard University, in her "very short introduction" for Oxford titled *American Women's History*, uses the following periods:

1. In the beginning: North America's women to 1750
2. Freedoms ferment, 1750–1848

3. The challenges of citizenship, 1848–1920
4. Modern American women, 1920–present

Finally, perhaps my favorite of these choices because it includes primary sources is *Through Women's Eyes: An American History* by Ellen Carol DuBois and Lynn Dumenil, professors of history at UCLA and UC Berkeley, respectively. They structure their survey as follows:

1. America in the world, to 1650
2. Colonial worlds, 1607–1750
3. Mothers and daughters of the Revolution, 1750–1800
4. Pedestal, loom, and auction block, 1800–1860
5. Shifting boundaries: expansion, reform, and Civil War, 1840–1865
6. Reconstructing women's lives North and South, 1865–1900
7. Women in an expanding nation: consolidation of the West, mass immigration, and the crisis of the 1890s
8. Power and politics: women in the Progressive Era, 1900–1920
9. Change and continuity: women in prosperity, Depression, and war, 1920–1945
10. Beyond the feminine mystique: women's lives, 1945–1965
11. Modern feminism and American society, 1965–1980
12. U.S. women in a global age, 1980–present

What I like about these titles and dates is that they align with major turning points for women, and the titles reflect the diversity of the female experience, especially in the chapter, "Beyond the feminine mystique."

The Remedial Herstory Project's textbook has the following periodization:

1. Early North American Women
2. Women's Cultural Encounters
3. Women's Colonial Life
4. Women's American Revolution
5. Republican Motherhood
6. Native Women Forced West
7. Abolition is Women's Ticket
8. Women and the West
9. Women and the Civil War
10. Women and Reconstruction
11. The Rise of National American Woman Suffrage Association (NAWSA) and National Association of Colored Women's Clubs (NACWC)
12. Women and Expansion

13. Women Laborers and Activists
14. Progressive Women
15. Women and World War I
16. Woman Suffrage
17. The New Woman
18. Women and the Depression
19. Women and World War II
20. Post War Women
21. Women and the Civil Rights Movement
22. Women and the Cold War
23. Reproductive Justice and Working Women
24. The Feminist Era
25. Women and LGBTQ+
26. The Modern Era

These various examples show that there isn't one way to do it but that women-centered titles may yield a different focus. I hope by highlighting the few examples that exist, practitioners can use their training and expertise to better examine traditional periodization.

The final phase is weaving these histories together with a periodization that reflects the lives and experiences of men and women. According to Tetreault, history can be examined using a holistic and integrated gendered approach after all those earlier stages are achieved.[63] She proposed the following questions to dissect the curriculum:

◆ Are the private as well as the public aspects of history presented as a continuum in women's and men's experiences?
◆ How is gender asymmetry linked to economic systems, family organizations, marriage, ritual, and political systems?
◆ How can we compare women and men in all aspects of their lives to reveal gender as a crucial historical determinant?
◆ How did the variables of race, ethnicity, social class, marital status, and sexual preference affect women's and men's experiences in history?
◆ How can we expand our conceptualization of historical time to a pluralistic one that conceives of three levels of history: structures, trends, and events? How can we unify approaches and types of knowledge of all social sciences and history as a means of investigating specific problems in relational history?

By doing this, students will discover a more inclusive social history that reflects humanity.

Resources for Integrating Women
Recommended Reading: Scholarly Sources

To examine how to best reimagine and teach holistic and inclusive history, check out the scholars who informed this book most: Margaret Smith Crocco, Mary Kay Thompson Tetreault, Christopher Martell, Kaylene Stevens, Nel Noddings, and Mardi Schmeichel among others. You can find their articles in scholarly databases and cited in the bibliography.

Sample Inquiry: Were the Dahomey Amazons Powerful?

This final inquiry was added to show the ways that teachers can bring in women's history even when there are limits to available primary material. In this inquiry, the bulk of the source material about African women is from European men. Bas-relief sculptures are included to give students a Dahomey source's description of these women warriors. Students are tasked with considering these perspectives and how reliable the sources are for fully understanding the women they observed. It is downloadable on the Remedial Herstory Project's website. A special thank you to Dr. Melissa Blair, who collaborated with me on this lesson plan as a reviewer.

Were the Dahomey Amazons powerful?

Students will analyze primary and secondary sources to more deeply understand the Dahomey warrior women. Given the mythology, intrigue, and distortions of the historical material available, is it possible to know how powerful the Dahomey warriors were?

Background: Dahomey Amazons or Mino Women

The Dahomey Amazons… were a Fon [one of the largest West African ethnic groups] all-female military regiment of the Kingdom of Dahomey. Western observers and historians named them due to their similarity to the mythical Amazons of ancient Anatolia… European merchants recorded their presence… The group referenced as Mino, meaning "Our Mothers," came from the male army of Dahomey…

Dahomey became increasingly warmongering. [The King] recruited both men and women soldiers, from foreign captives, though women soldiers were also recruited from free Dahomean women, some enrolled as young as eight years old. Some women in Fon society became soldiers voluntarily, while others were involuntarily enrolled if their husbands or fathers complained to the king about their behavior. Membership among the Mino was supposed to hone any aggressive character traits for war. During their membership, they were not allowed to have children or be part of married life (though they were legally married to the king). Many of them were virgins.

The regiment had a semi-sacred status, intertwined with the Fon belief in Vodun. The Mino trained with intense physical exercise. They learned survival skills and indifference to pain and death... The Mino were also wealthy and held high status. The Mino took a prominent role in the Grand Council, debating the kingdom's policy...

[T]he Annual Customs of Dahomey included a parade and review of the troops, and the troops swore an oath to the king. The celebrations on the 27th day of the Annual Customs consisted of a mock battle in which the Amazons attacked a "fort" and "captured" the slaves within, a custom recorded by the priest Francesco Borghero in his diaries. The women soldiers were rigorously trained and given uniforms... These documented reports also indicated that the women soldiers suffered several defeats. The women soldiers were said to be structured in parallel with the army, with a center wing (the king's bodyguards) flanked on both sides, each under separate commanders. Some accounts note that each male soldier had a female warrior counterpart...

The women's army consisted of many regiments: huntresses, riflewomen, reapers, archers, and gunners... [T]he Dahomean female warriors were armed with Winchester rifles, clubs, and knives. Units were under female command. The Dahomey Kingdom was often at war with its neighbors, and captives were needed for the Middle Passage [the slave trade]. The Dahomey women soldiers fought in slave raids... European intrusion into West Africa gained pace during the latter half of the 19th century with the 1884 Berlin Conference...

African American Registry Editors. "The Dahomey Amazon Women, a story." African American Registry. n.d. https://aaregistry.org/story/the-dahomey-amazons-a-brief-story/.

Hypothesis 1: Were the Dahomey Amazons powerful?

Document A: Victorious Mino Warrior in Battle

In the 1700s, King Agaja commissioned the decorating of palace walls with murals and bas-reliefs. They are some of the most beautiful pieces of surviving art in West Africa. The king honored the Dahomean army in high esteem and honored them with several depictions on the palace walls. Here an Amazon carries off a captive from battle.

Source: Susan Middleton, ©1994 J. Paul Getty Trust, published in Piqué, Francesca, and Leslie H. Rainer. 1999. Palace Sculptures of Abomey: History Told on Walls. Conservation and Cultural Heritage. Los Angeles, CA: Getty Conservation Institute and the J. Paul Getty Museum. http://hdl.handle.net/10020/gci_pubs/palace_abomey.

Guiding Questions
1. How would you describe the Mino, or Amazon, warrior woman depicted here?
2. How does she compare with the conquered victim?

Document B: Dahomey Mino Warrior Using Torture

In another bas-relief, an Amazon is depicted torturing a conquered Ketou warrior. The victim's stomach is being split open and filled with earth.

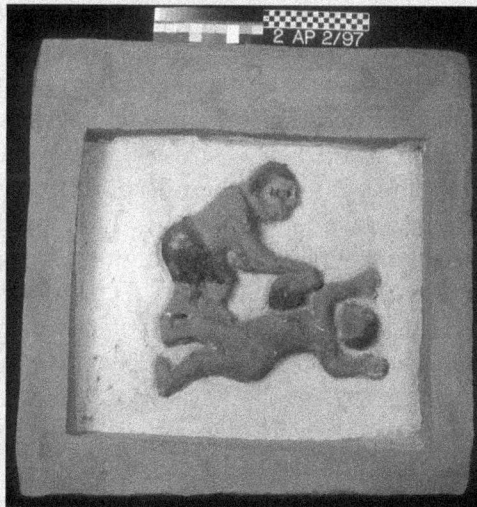

Source: Susan Middleton, ©1997 J. Paul Getty Trust, published in Piqué, Francesca, and Leslie H. Rainer. 1999. Palace Sculptures of Abomey: History Told on Walls. Conservation and Cultural Heritage. Los Angeles, CA: Getty Conservation Institute and the J. Paul Getty Museum. http://hdl.handle.net/10020/gci_pubs/ palace_abomey.

Guiding Questions
3. How would you describe the Mino, or Amazon, warrior woman depicted here?
4. Why would the king include examples of torture?

Hypothesis 2: Were the Dahomey Amazons powerful?

Document C: Amazons Depicted by Englishmen

Frederick Forbes traveled to West Africa as an officer for the British Royal Navy and published his journal in 1851. He was sent to the kingdom to persuade the King to suppress Dahomey's involvement with the slave trade. As Britain had banned the slave trade, Forbes worked to bring to the public's attention the slave hunts practiced by the Dahomey. This is one of his sketches of a Mino or Amazon warrior next to his description of the Amazons.

The amazons are not supposed to marry, and, by their own statement, they have changed their sex. "We are men," say they, "not women." All dress alike, diet alike, and male and female emulate each other: what the males do, the amazons will endeavour to surpass. They all take great care of their arms, polish the barrels, and, except when on duty, keep them in covers. There is no duty at the palace, except when the king is in public, and then a guard of amazons protect the royal person, and, on review, he is guarded by the males; but outside the palace is always a strong detachment of males ready for service. The amazons are in barracks within the palace enclosure, and under the care of the eunuchs and the camboodee or treasurer. In every action (with males and females), there is some reference to cutting off heads.

[T]he palace, or the grand Fetish houses…The royal wives and their slaves, I presume from the jealousy of their despotic lord, are considered too sacred for man to gaze upon; and on meeting any of these sable beauties on the road, a bell warns the wayfarer to turn off, or stand against a wall while they pass. The king has thousands of wives… If one of the wives of the king, or a high officer's, commits adultery, the culprits are summarily beheaded; and the skull of one of the Agaou's wives is at present exposed in the square of the palace of Agrimgomeh, in Abomey. But if adultery be committed by parties of lower rank, they are sold Marriages. If a man seduces a girl, the law obliges marriage, and the payment of eighty heads of cowries to the parent or master, on pain of becoming himself a slave. In marriage there is no ceremony, except where the king confers the wife, in which instance the maiden presents her future lord with a glass of rum.

Forbes, Frederick. "Seh-Dong-Hong-Beh, leader of the en:Dahomey Amazons." *Dahomey of the Dahomans*. 1851. (being the journals of two missions to the king of Dahomey, and residence at his capital), 23–24. Retrieved from https://archive.org/details/dahomeydahomansb00forb/page/n41/mode/2up.

Guiding Questions

5. How does he describe the Amazon warrior women?
6. Why might this British officer have a different perspective on the Amazons than the Dahomey themselves? How might that impact this account?

Document D: Dahomey As It Is

Alfred Skertchly left England in 1871 to collect zoological specimens on the West Coast of Africa. He traveled to Abomey, the capital of Dahomey, to train the King on the use of new weapons. He expected to stay for eight days but was held as an unwilling yet well-treated guest. This is his account of the Amazons.

One of the most singular institutions of Dahomey is the female army, or Amazons, as they have been called. When these soldieresses were first introduced into the country is unknown…

Who has not heard of the ferocious actions of a drunken woman; and do not the daily papers bear witness to the fact that, once roused, a woman will perpetrate far greater cruelty than a man? Did not the petroleuses of Paris wander about like she-demons of the nether world? What spectacle is more calculated to inspire horror than a savage and brutal woman in a passion? and when we imagine such to be besprinkled with the blood of the slain, and perhaps carrying the gory head of some decapitated victim, one may cease to wonder at the dread with which these female warriors were, and still are, looked upon by the surrounding nations…

[I]t would… be a happy release from their relatives if all the old maids could be enlisted, and trained to vent their feline spite and mischief-making propensities on the enemies of the country, instead of their neighbours. At any rate, they would be removed out of the way of the sycophantic parasites, who invariably hover round them, should they be possessed of any property, in the hope of cajoling them out of it. Instances are not by any means rare, of females who have donned the soldier's uniform, and fought bravely side by side, not taking into consideration such heroines as Joan of Arc, Margaret of Anjou, Boadicea, and a host of others… As for physical endurance, do not scores of charwomen and laundresses drag out a life of literal slavery…

Nevertheless, there can be no doubt that the Amazonian army of Dahomey is one of the causes of its slow decadence... Dahomey will have to be classed among the nations that have been.

Skertchly, J. Alfred. "Dahomey as it Is." London: Legare Street Press, 2021. First published in 1884 by Chapman and Hall, 454–459.

Guiding Questions
7. Underline words used to describe the Amazon warriors. Overall, how would you say they are viewed?
8. How might differences in culture impact his account?

Final Hypothesis: Were the Dahomey Amazons powerful?

Before writing your final hypothesis, explore online secondary sources about the Dahomey warriors. The Smithsonian has a great article by Mike Dash. Consider how these portrayals compare with the primary accounts of these women.

Notes

1 Nash, Crabtree, and Dunn, *History on Trial*, 22.
2 National Women's History Museum. "Where are the women?" https://www.womenshistory.org/social-studies-standards
3 Loewen, *Lies*, 2.
4 Theresa M. McCormick, "Generating Effective Teaching through Primary Sources," in *Social Studies and Diversity Education*, ed. Elizabeth Heilman (New York: Routledge, 2010), 90.
5 Trecker, J. "Women in United States History High School Textbooks." Social Education, 1971, 35,248–335.
6 Tetreault, "Integrating Women's History," 218.
7 Tetreault, "Integrating Women's History," 218.
8 Tetreault, "Integrating Women's History," 220.
9 Tetreault, "Integrating Women's History," 218–220.
10 Tetreault, "Integrating Women's History," 221.
11 Tetreault, "Integrating Women's History," 222–223.
12 Tetreault, "Integrating Women's History," 224.
13 Tetreault, "Integrating Women's History," 229.
14 Tetreault, "Integrating Women's History," 237.
15 Tetreault, "Integrating Women's History," 237.
16 Tetreault, "Integrating Women's History," 231.
17 Tetreault, "Integrating Women's History," 226.

18 Tetreault, "Integrating Women's History," 227.
19 Tetreault, "Integrating Women's History," 232.
20 Tetreault, "Integrating Women's History," 233.
21 Tetreault, "Integrating Women's History," 230.
22 Tetreault, "Integrating Women's History," 240.
23 Scheiner-Fisher, "The Inclusion Of Women's History In The Secondary Social Studies Classroom," 25.
24 Scheiner-Fisher, "The Inclusion Of Women's History In The Secondary Social Studies Classroom," 25.
25 American Historical Association, "Guidelines for the Preparation, Evaluation, and Selection of History Textbooks," American Historical Association, last modified June 2018, https://www.historians.org/jobs-and-professional-development/statements-standards-and-guidelines-of-the-discipline/guidelines-for-the-preparation-evaluation-and-selection-of-history-textbooks
26 American Historical Association, "Guidelines for the Preparation, Evaluation, and Selection of History Textbooks."
27 Mary K. Chick, " "Gender Balance in K-12 American History Textbooks," *Social Studies Research and Practice.* no.1(3): 2006, https://pdfs.semanticscholar.org/fcc4/9f161fc48561e1ac1adef4a45c1775105811.pdf, 285.
28 We examined *The American Promise, America's History*, and *The Enduring Vision*.
29 Kathryn E. Engebretson, "Another missed opportunity: Gender in the national curriculum standards for social studies," *Social Studies Research and Practice*, 9(3), 2014, 23.
30 National Women's History Museum. "Where are the women?" https://www.womenshistory.org/social-studies-standards
31 Daisy Martin, Maldonado, Saúl & Schneider, Jack & Smith, Mark, A Report on the State of History Education State Policies and National Programs Second Edition. 2011. 10.13140/RG.2.2.12801.40802, 12.
32 The studies methods were reliable and consistent, they explained, "Project staff highlighted every standard that referred to a woman or a topic associated with women. Each standard was copied into a database. Researchers—following guidance from the Museum's advisory council of scholars, public historians, and educators—reviewed the database entries to ensure that the selected standards met the project's definitions of history about women. In the final step, researchers counted the number of times that women's names and key terms occurred within the standards." National Women's History Museum. "Where are the women?" https://www.womenshistory.org/social-studies-standards

33 National Women's History Museum. "Where are the women?" https://www.womenshistory.org/social-studies-standards

34 Elizabeth L. Maurer, et al, "Where are the women?" National Women's History Museum, 2018, https://www.womenshistory.org/social-studies-standards

35 Elizabeth L. Maurer, et al, "Where are the women?"

36 New Hampshire Department of Education, "K-12 Social Studies. New Hampshire Curriculum Framework," New Hampshire Department of Education, June 2006, https://www.education.nh.gov/sites/g/files/ehbemt326/files/inline-documents/standards-socialstudies-framework.pdf

37 Kathryn E. Engebretson, "Another missed opportunity: Gender in the national curriculum standards for social studies," *Social Studies Research and Practice*, 9(3), 2014, 26.

38 Martell and Stevens, "Perceptions of Teaching Race and Gender: Results of a Survey of Social Studies Teachers," 283.

39 Kathryn E. Engebretson, "Another missed opportunity: Gender in the national curriculum standards for social studies," *Social Studies Research and Practice*, 9(3), 2014, 27.

40 Kathryn E. Engebretson, "Another missed opportunity: Gender in the national curriculum standards for social studies," *Social Studies Research and Practice*, 9(3), 2014, 27.

41 Kathryn E. Engebretson, "Another missed opportunity: Gender in the national curriculum standards for social studies," *Social Studies Research and Practice*, 9(3), 2014, 28.

42 Kathryn E. Engebretson, "Another missed opportunity: Gender in the national curriculum standards for social studies," *Social Studies Research and Practice*, 9(3), 2014, 29.

43 Kathryn E. Engebretson, "Another missed opportunity: Gender in the national curriculum standards for social studies," *Social Studies Research and Practice*, 9(3), 2014, 29.

44 Crocco, "The missing discourse about gender and sexuality in the social studies,"67.

45 Karen Zittleman and David Sadker, "Gender Bias in Teacher Education Texts: New (and Old) Lessons," Journal of Teacher Education 53, no. 2 (March 2002): 168–80. https://doi.org/10.1177/0022487102053002008, 178.

46 Martell and Stevens, "Perceptions of Teaching Race and Gender: Results of a Survey of Social Studies Teachers," 283.

47 Martell and Stevens, "Perceptions of Teaching Race and Gender: Results of a Survey of Social Studies Teachers," 284.

48 Jen Kalaidis, "Bring Back Social Studies: The amount of time public-school kids spend learning about government and civics is shrinking," *The*

Atlantic, https://www.theatlantic.com/education/archive/2013/09/bring-back-social-studies/279891/

49 Tim Walker, "Testing Obsession and the Disappearing Curriculum" NEA Today, September 2, 2014, http://neatoday.org/2014/09/02/the-testing-obsession-and-the-disappearing-curriculum-2/

50 Michael Hansen and Diana Quintero, "The state of the nation's social studies educators," Monday, July 3, 2017 retrieved from https://www.brookings.edu/blog/brown-center-chalkboard/2017/07/03/the-state-of-the-nations-social-studies-educators/

51 Tim Walker, "Testing Obsession and the Disappearing Curriculum."

52 Christopher C. Martell, Ed., *Social Studies Teacher Education: Critical Issues and Current Perspectives*. IAP: Charlotte, NC. 2018.

53 Iowa Department of Education, "Social Studies: A Call to Action," November 16, 2015, https://www.educateiowa.gov/sites/files/ed/documents/Social%20Studies%20report_11-16-15%20FINAL.pdf

54 Iowa Department of Education, "Social Studies."

55 Tim Walker, "Testing Obsession and the Disappearing Curriculum."

56 Tim Walker, "Testing Obsession and the Disappearing Curriculum."

57 Elizabeth L. Maurer, et al, "Where are the women?"

58 Alex Cuenca, "UNLADYLIKE2020 and American Masters Present: Where Are the Women? Summit," American Masters PBS, February 13, 2021, https://www.youtube.com/watch?v=6geLUaGBJ8I&lc=UgwQrYuWEQ0fPqFCbep4AaABAg

59 Natsuki Aruga, "Can We Have a Total American History? A Comment on the Achievements of Women's and Gender History," *Journal of American History*, 2012, 99, 818–821. 10.1093/jahist/jas465.

60 Kathryn E. Engebretson, "Another missed opportunity: Gender in the national curriculum standards for social studies," *Social Studies Research and Practice*, 9(3), 2014, 23.

61 Natsuki Aruga, "Can we have a total American history? A comment on the achievements of women's and gender history," *The Journal of American History* 99, no. 3 (2012): 818–21. http://www.jstor.org/stable/44308392, 819.

62 Cornelia H. Dayton and Lisa Levenstein, "The Big Tent of U.S. Women's and Gender History: A State of the Field," *The Journal of American History* 99, no. 3 (2012): 807–808. http://www.jstor.org/stable/44308391

63 Tetreault, "Integrating Women's History," 216.

Conclusion

Those who tell the stories also hold the power.

—Plato

I played the game: I joined good-old-boys clubs and coached sports, and I can hang with the guys in the social studies department, debating whatever historical topic the hour called upon. I was a well-behaved teacher. To my knowledge, I am the first woman to hold my job: Coordinator of Social Studies Education at Plymouth State University. I am now responsible for preparing the next generation of social studies teachers to serve my state. It took 100 years of preparing future history teachers at the institution for this to happen. It's not to say that women professors had not supported students on their path or that women teachers have not successfully graduated the program, but women were not seen coaching and leading them. In essence, the sense I had when I completed my degree here was that to be a good social studies teacher, I had to think and act like a male one. My strength, my students' strengths, is that they think and act like themselves.

Today, thousands of educators are using the resources I have made with teams of scholars through the Remedial Herstory Project. This means that hundreds of thousands of young people are growing up in a culture that boldly claims that women are just as deserving of historical study. I now play a major role in preparing and certifying new teachers to ensure that they know women are half of us and are prepared with the resources needed to teach an inclusive history as well as the skills to implement it.

DOI: 10.4324/9781003472889-8

Still, the old guard of male social studies teachers isn't sure what do with me or the Remedial Herstory Project. A collaborator on our project told me that when she tells her male colleagues about the project, "they've seemed put off, esp[ecially] male colleagues. I think they are assuming it's a radical feminist movement versus the practical approach of incorporating women into the historical narrative."[1] In December 2023, we had a vendor booth at the National Council for the Social Studies conference, where we handed out our resources to teachers. These lessons were funded by the Library of Congress and reviewed by experts. This group of teachers who all worked in the same school district was mingling through the vendor hall. The group was all women, except one man. The women gawked at the t-shirts we had for sale, which read "Her-story is Half of His-story," and decided to listen in to our elevator pitch. They all bought shirts and took copies of plans. The guy stood back awkwardly about five feet. When our Director of Professional Development called out the awkwardness of the situation by addressing him personally with "Men are allowed here too," he made a face and stepped further back. I watched the whole thing from behind my laptop. What was going through his mind? Here's a guy who has made *social* studies his career. That means teaching about social issues, causes, and the society around his classroom. Does he not get that women are half of that—more than half actually? We have to get over this sense of loss at a system that was so prejudiced at start.

Whole, complete history is the goal. Women, all women, should be seen and heard in history just as men of varying races, cultures, and economic backgrounds are now given that privilege. For women especially, women who dare should be contrasted with their counterparts who conform to help the next generation navigate the unique pressures that women experience. Teachers need to notice the blanks left by the absence of certain groups of people from historical study. Women's history is not immune to the racial and class-based biases of history. Teachers must look for those absences and fill them.

Not all men react like that guy—in fact, *most* don't. Most stop and ask thoughtful questions. Most leave with more ideas about what they could do to rethink their curriculum. I'll never forget when I did professional development work with a department, and two older male teachers whom I had pegged as the ones I needed to convince said, "I love what you're doing."

The systematic approach to adding women to the curriculum outlined by the Phase Theory will help teachers grow in their understanding of women's history and reduce mistakes. Teachers of all genders should be the proponents of including women in history. Men have greater social freedom to do so—and thus the majority of social studies should use that social capital toward producing equal role models for their male and female students.

Teachers should research and study themes of history left out from their own educations: medicine, religion, and home economics. They should research groups that fought for the climate and for peace. In these different themes, rich primary material is present, and so are women. Teachers may find they are inspired by this history differently.

To move from Compensatory to Bi-Focal history, teachers must look for women's diversity and allow women to have the same complexity of perspective the men in history have. The Eckert Test can be a rough guideline for what this looks like in a classroom. Women shouldn't be tokenized, forced to speak for all women.

Although women are virtually absent from the textbooks, standards, and teacher education programs, the tools are there to teach about women. It is unfair to ask teachers to redo their degree, but it is not unfair to ask them to continue their education. One cannot separate women from the story of humanity; to do so denies girls an equal education. Because of the widespread support for the inquiry model of instruction, the weak standards and bad textbooks are not actually a barrier to teaching women's history. Students should be analyzing primary source material in our classes in order to better understand facts and information, and as a bonus, women are in the primary material! Teachers can become the barrier to teaching women's history if they fail to use their talent as educators and historians. Instead, they should use texts and standards as tools, or guidelines for subjects and themes, but not as the be-all and end-all in your classroom.

Teaching women's history is ultimately the responsibility of teachers. They are accountable to the young people in their classes every day. The strategies outlined in this book help teachers find women's history and include it in their curriculum. Teachers must be brave, change what they've always done, and tackle topics that society, through a double standard, has deemed too controversial or unworthy of study. The full integration of women in society hinges on their full integration in the classes that teach the next generation about society. Teachers are the crucial key to undoing male centrism in social studies.

Note

1 Kristin Brown, personal communication, January 11, 2024.

Bibliography

"Claudia Goldin wins the Nobel prize in economics: Her work has overturned assumptions about gender equality," *The Economist*, October 9, 2023, https://www.economist.com/finance-and-economics/2023/10/09/claudia-goldin-wins-the-nobel-prize-in-economics

"Discussion of Women's Political Clubs and Their Suppression, October 29–30 1793." *Liberty, Equality, Fraternity: Exploring The French Revolution.* https://revolution.chnm.org/d/294

"Empress Lu." Traditional East Asia. n.d. http://projects.leadr.msu.edu/traditionaleastasia/exhibits/show/badass-female-rulers/empress-lu

"Jo Ann Robinson A Heroine of the Montgomery Bus Boycott." National Museum of African American History and Culture. n.d. https://nmaahc.si.edu/explore/stories/jo-ann-robinson-heroine-montgomery-bus-boycott

"Testimony in the Case of the United States vs Susan B. Anthony." University of Missouri at Kansas City Law School. http://law2.umkc.edu/faculty/projects/ftrials/anthony/trialtestimony.html

"The French Civil Code" Liberty, Equality, Fraternity: Exploring The French Revolution. 1804. https://revolution.chnm.org/d/509

Aguilera, Jasmine. "What Will Happen to Same-Sex Marriage Around the Country if Obergefell Falls." December 14, 2022. https://time.com/6240497/same-sex-marriage-rights-us-obergefell/

Al-Matary, Abdulrahman and Jaffar Ali. "Controversies and considerations regarding the termination of pregnancy for Foetal Anomalies in Islam." *BMC Med Ethics* 15 (2014): 10. https://doi.org/10.1186/1472-6939-15-10

Alexander, Kerri Lee. "Recy Taylor." *National Women's History Museum* 2020. www.womenshistory.org/education-resources/biographies/recy-taylor

Allegretto, Sylvia. "The teacher pay penalty has hit a new high: Trends in teacher wages and compensation through 2021." *EPI.* August 16, 2022, https://www.epi.org/publication/teacher-pay-penalty-2022/

Allison, R. W. "Let Women Be Silent in the Churches (1 Cor. 14.33b-36): What Did Paul Really Say, and What Did It Mean?" *Journal for the Study of the New Testament* 10, no. 32 (1988): 27–60. https://doi.org/10.1177/0142064X8801003203

American Historical Association. "Guidelines for the Preparation, Evaluation, and Selection of History Textbooks."

American Historical Association. "Guidelines for the Preparation, Evaluation, and Selection of History Textbooks." *American Historical Association.* June 2018. https://www.historians.org/jobs-and-professional-development/statements-standards-and-guidelines-of-the-discipline/guidelines-for-the-preparation-evaluation-and-selection-of-history-textbooks

Armstrong, Karen. *Islam: A Short History.* Waterville: Thorndike, 2002.

Armstrong, Karen. *Jerusalem: One City, Three Faiths.* 1st Ballantine Books ed. New York, Ballantine Books, 1997.

Aruga, Natsuki. "Can We Have a Total American History? A Comment on the Achievements of Women's and Gender History." The *Journal of American History* 99, no. 3 (2012): 818–821. http://www.jstor.org/stable/44308392

Banovic, Rebecca. "Does Albert Einstein's first wife Mileva Maric deserve credit for some of his work?" *Independent.* June 13, 2018. https://www.independent.co.uk/news/long_reads/mileva-maric-albert-einsten-physics-science-history-women-a8396411.html

Barrigner, Whitney, Lauren Brand, and Nichloas Kryczka. "No such thing as a bad question?" *Perspectives on History* 61: 6, September 2023.

Bassi, Marina, Mateo Diaz, Mercedes, Blumberg, Rae, and Reynoso, Ana Failing to notice? Uneven teachers' attention to boys and girls in the classroom. *IZA Journal of Labor Economics* (2018): 7. https://doi.org/10.1186/s40172-018-0069-4

Basu, Aparna. "Women's History in India: An Historiographical Survey." in: Offen K., Pierson R.R., and Rendall J. (Eds.), *Writing Women's History.* Palgrave Macmillan, London, 1991. https://doi.org/10.1007/978-1-349-21512-6_10

Beard, Mary Ritter. *Woman's Work in Municipalities.* New York: Appleton, 1915. https://lccn.loc.gov/15007484

Beard, Mary. *Women & Power: A Manifesto.* London: Profile Books, 2017.

Bechdel, Alison. "Bechdel Test." Bechdel Test. n.d., http://bechdeltest.com/

Beecher, Catherine. *An Essay on Slavery and Abolitionism, in Reference to the Duty of American Females.* Philadelphia: Henry Perkins, 1837. 96–107.

Beevor, Antony. "They raped every German female from eight to 80." *The Guardian.* May 1, 2002. https://www.theguardian.com/books/2002/may/01/news.features11

Berkin, Carol, Margaret S. Crocco, and Barbara Winslow Ed. *Clio in the Classroom: A Guide for Teaching U.S. Women's History.* Oxford: Oxford University Press, 2009.

Berry, Daina Ramey and Leslie M Harris. *Sexuality and Slavery: Reclaiming Intimate Histories in the Americas.* Athens Georgia: University of Georgia Press, 2018.

Black, Jeremy et. al., trans. *The Literature of Ancient Sumer*. Oxford University Press, 2006.

Bowels, Nellie. "Jordan Peterson, Custodian of the Patriarchy: He says there's a crisis in masculinity. Why won't women — all these wives and witches — Just behave? *The New York Times*. May 18, 2018. https://www.nytimes.com/2018/05/18/style/jordan-peterson-12-rules-for-life.html

Britannica, T. Editors of Encyclopaedia. "Gaohou." *Encyclopedia Britannica*, October 19, 2015. https://www.britannica.com/biography/Gaohou

British Library Editors. "Women in Medieval Society." British Library. https://www.bl.uk/the-middle-ages/articles/women-in-medieval-society

Broadbridge, Anne F. *Women and the Making of the Mongol Empire*. Cambridge: Cambridge University Press, 2018.

Brooks, Lisa. *Our Beloved Kin: A New History of King Philip's War*. Yale University Press, 2018. https://doi.org/10.2307/j.ctt1z27jbr

Brown, Peter. "The Silk Road in Late Antiquity" in: Victor H. Mair, and Jane Hickman (Ed.). *Reconfiguring the Silk Road*. University of Pennsylvania Press, 2014.

Buddhist Studies. "Ananda," Early Disciples of the Buddha. n.d. http://www.buddhanet.net/e-learning/history/db_04.htm

Burk, Martha. "D-Day: 150,000 Men — and One Woman." *Huffington Post*. December 6, 2017, https://www.huffpost.com/entry/d-day-150000-men---and-on_b_5452941

Caiazza, Amy. "Does Women's Representation in Elected Office Lead to Women-Friendly Policy? Analysis of State-Level Data," *Women & Politics* 26, no. 1, (2004): 35–70. https://doi.org/10.1300/J014v26n01_03

Carroll, James. "Who Was Mary Magdalene? From the writing of the New Testament to the filming of The Da Vinci Code, her image has been repeatedly conscripted, contorted and contradicted," *Smithsonian*, June, 2006, https://www.smithsonianmag.com/history/who-was-mary-magdalene-119565482/

Cartwright, Mark. "The Daily Life of Medieval Nuns." *World History Encyclopedia*. December 19, 2018. https://www.worldhistory.org/article/1298/the-daily-life-of-medieval-nuns/

Catalyst, "Quick Take: Women in Academia," January 23, 2020, https://www.catalyst.org/research/women-in-academia/

Center for Disease Control. "Suicide Data and Statistics." *Center for Disease Control*. May 11, 2023. https://www.cdc.gov/suicide/suicide-data-statistics.html

Center for American Progress. "The Basic Facts About Women in Poverty: Women, especially women of color, in the United States are more likely to live in poverty than men, and they need robust, targeted solutions to ensure their long-term economic security." *Center for American Progress*.

August 3, 2020. https://www.americanprogress.org/article/basic-facts-women-poverty/

Chick, Mary K. " "Gender Balance in K-12 American History Textbooks," *Social Studies Research and Practice* 1, no. 3 (2006). https://pdfs.semantic scholar.org/fcc4/9f161fc48561e1ac1adef4a45c1775105811.pdf

Chin, Kathleen, Amelia Wendt, Ian M Bennett, and Amritha Bhat. "Suicide and Maternal Mortality." *Current Psychiatry Reports* 24, no. 4 (2022): 239–275. https://doi.org/10.1007/s11920-022-01334-3

Chowdhury, Jennifer. "Woman of Impact: Reshma Saujani." *In Style*. November 1, 2023. https://www.instyle.com/reshma-saujani-moms-first-woman-of-impact-8385201

Collins, Gail. *America's Women: Four Hundred Years of Dolls Drudges Helpmates and Heroines*. New York: William Morrow, 2003.

Comnena, Anna, and Marcelle Thuebaux, trans., ed. *The Writings of Medieval Women*, vol. 14. New York: Garland Library of Medieval Literature, 1987. http://www.womeninworldhistory.com/dalassena.html

Copp, Martha, and Sheryl Kleinman. "Practicing What We Teach: Feminist Strategies for Teaching about Sexism." *Feminist Teacher* 18, no. 2 (2008): 101–124. http://www.jstor.org/stable/40546059

Crocco, M. S. The missing discourse about gender and sexuality in the social studies. *Theory into Practice* 40(1) (2001): 65–71.

Crocco, M. S. "Gender and Sexuality in the Social Studies" in L. S. Levstik, and C. A. Tyson (Eds.). *Handbook of research in social studies education* (pp. 172–196). New York, NY: Routledge, 2008.

Cuenca, Alex. "UNLADYLIKE2020 and American Masters Present: Where Are the Women? Summit." American Masters PBS, February 13, 2021, https://www.youtube.com/watch?v=6geLUaGBJ8I&lc=UgwQrYuWE Q0fPqFCbep4AaABAg

Das, Andrew. "U.S. Women's Players and U.S. Soccer Settle Equal Pay Lawsuit." *New York Times*. May 22, 2022. https://www.nytimes.com/2022/02/22/sports/soccer/us-womens-soccer-equal-pay.html

David, Wolman. "The Once-Classified Tale of Juanita Moody," Smithsonian Magazine, March 2021. https://www.smithsonianmag.com/history/juanita-moody-woman-helped-avert-nuclear-war-180976993/

Davis, Dernoral. "A Contested Presence: Free Black People in Antebellum Mississippi, 1820–1860."Mississippi Historical Society. May 2000. https://www.mshistorynow.mdah.ms.gov/issue/a-contested-presence-free-blacks-in-antebellum-mississippi-18201860

Dayton, Cornelia H., and Lisa Levenstein. "The Big Tent of U.S. Women's and Gender History: A State of the Field." *The Journal of American History* 99, no. 3 (2012): 793–817. http://www.jstor.org/stable/44308391

Dewitt, Ethan. "As they Await State Guidance, Teachers Consider how Divisive Concepts Law will Affect lesson Plans," *The New Hampshire Bulletin.* July 12, 2021. https://newhampshirebulletin.com/2021/07/12/as-they-await-state-guidance-teachers-consider-how-divisive-concepts-law-will-affect-lesson-plans/

Dickson, EJ, Adam Rawnsley, and Stefania Matache. "Andrew Tate Built an Empire on Bullshit: Here's the real story." *The Rolling Stone*, March 15, 2023. https://www.rollingstone.com/culture/culture-features/andrew-tate-empire-real-story-1234696706/

Domen, Ilona, Daan Scheepers, Belle Derks, and Ruth Van Veelen. "It's a man's world, right? How women's opinions about gender inequality affect physiological responses in men." *Group Processes & Intergroup Relations* 25 (2022): 703–726. https://doi.org/10.1177/13684302211042669

Doucet, Lyse. "The women reporters determined to cover World War Two." BBC. June 5, 2014. https://www.bbc.com/news/magazine-27677889

Eller, Cynthia. *The Myth of Matriarchal Prehistory: Why an Invented Past Won't Give Women a Future.* Beacon Press: Boston, 2000, pp. 3–104.

Encyclopaedia Britanica Editors. "St. Hildegard." *Encyclopedia Britannica.* September 14, 2022. https://www.britannica.com/biography/Saint-Hildegard

Encyclopaedia Britannica Editors. "Ban Zhao". *Encyclopedia Britannica.* January 1, 2022. https://www.britannica.com/biography/Ban-Zhao

Encyclopaedia Britannica Editors. "Gaohou." *Encyclopedia Britannica.* October 19, 2015. https://www.britannica.com/biography/Gaohou

Engebretson, Kathryn E. Another missed opportunity: Gender in the national curriculum standards for social studies. *Social Studies Research and Practice* 9, no, 3 (2014): 21–34.

Eubanks, Andrew. "Brunhilda of Austrasia." *World History Encyclopedia.* June 23, 2022. https://www.worldhistory.org/Brunhilda_of_Austrasia/

Fingerhut, Hannah. "In both parties, men and women differ over whether women still face obstacles to progress." PEW Research Center. August 16, 2016, https://www.pewresearch.org/fact-tank/2016/08/16/in-both-parties-men-and-women-differ-over-whether-women-still-face-bstacles-to-progress/

Frances Willard House Museum. "Introduction." Truth-Telling: Frances Willard and Ida B. Wells, n.d.-a https://scalar.usc.edu/works/willard-and-wells/introduction?path=index

Frances Willard House Museum. "The WCTU and Lynching, 1893." Truth-Telling: Frances Willard and Ida B. Wells. n.d.-b https://scalar.usc.edu/works/willard-and-wells/1893-wctu-anti-lynching-resolution?path=timeline

Franke-Ruta, Garance. "When America Was Female." *The Atlantic*. March 5, 2013. https://www.theatlantic.com/politics/archive/2013/03/when-america-was-female/273672/

Gajanan, Majita. "The USWNT Seeks Nearly $67 Million in Damages In Equal Pay Lawsuit Against U.S. Soccer. Here's What to Know About the Case." *Time Magazine*. February 21, 2020. https://time.com/5653250/uswnt-equal-pay-lawsuit/

Galton, Francis. "Vox populi," *Nature* 75 (1949): 450–451.

Gebhardt, Miriam. *Crimes Unspoken: The Rape of German Women at the End of the Second World War*. Cambridge: Polity Press, 2017.

Geiger, A.W. and Kim Parker. "For Women's History Month, a look at gender gains – and gaps – in the U.S." *PEW Research Center*. March 15, 2018. https://www.pewresearch.org/fact-tank/2018/03/15/for-womens-history-month-a-look-at-gender-gains-and-gaps-in-the-u-s/

Gibson, Sarah. "Majority of Sununu's Diversity and Inclusion Council Resigns." *New Hampshire Public Radio*. June 29, 2021. https://www.nhpr.org/nh-news/2021-06-29/majority-of-gov-sununus-diversity-and-inclusion-council-resigns

Gottschalk, S. "Mary Baker Eddy." *Encyclopedia Britannica*, July 12, 2022. https://www.britannica.com/biography/Mary-Baker-Eddy

Graham, Matthew C., Allison Ivey, Nicholette DeRosia, and Makseem Skorodinsky. Education for Whom? *The Writing is on the Walls, Equity & Excellence in Education* 53, no. 4 (2020): 551–568. https://doi.org/10.1080/10665684.2020.1791765

Greene, Peter. "New Hampshire and Mom's for Liberty Pit Bounty on Teacher's Heads." *Forbes Magazine*. November 12, 2021. https://www.forbes.com/sites/petergreene/2021/11/12/new-hampshire-and-moms-for-liberty-put-bounty-on-teachers-heads/?sh=7f33e954a4bf

Gross, Jenny. "Andrew Tate Is Released From Jail and Placed Under House Arrest." *The New York Times*. April 3, 2023. https://www.nytimes.com/2023/04/03/world/europe/andrew-tate-house-arrest-romania.html?login=smartlock&auth=login-smartlock

Gruss, Laura Tobias, and Daniel Schmitt. "The evolution of the human pelvis: changing adaptations to bipedalism, obstetrics and thermoregulation." *Philosophical Transactions of the Royal Society of London. Series B, Biological Sciences* 370, no. 1663 (2015): 20140063. https://doi.org/10.1098/rstb.2014.0063

Gurcheik, Kathy. "Availability, Use of Paternity Leave Remains Rare in U.S." *SHRM: Better Workplaces Better World*. August 16, 2019. https://www.shrm.org/resourcesandtools/hr-topics/behavioral-competencies/global-and-cultural-effectiveness/pages/availability-use-of-paternity-leave-remains-rare-in-us.aspx

Gutierrez-Romine, Alicia. *From Back Alley to the Border: Criminal Abortion in California, 1920–1969.* Lincoln: University of Nebraska Press, 2020.

Haeri, Shahla. *The Unforgettable Queens of Islam.* New York: Cambridge University Press, 2020.

Hansen, Michael and Diana Quintero. "The state of the nation's social studies educators," *Monday.* July 3, 2017. Retrieved from https://www.brookings.edu/blog/brown-center-chalkboard/2017/07/03/the-state-of-the-nations-social-studies-educators/

Hansen, Michael, "Elizabeth Mann Levesque, Jon Valant, and Diana Quintero. "2018 Brown Center Report on American Education: Understanding the social studies teacher workforce." June 27, 2018, retrieved from https://www.brookings.edu/research/2018-brown-center-report-on-american-education-understanding-the-social-studies-teacher-workforce/

Hartmann, Heidi, Ariane Hegewisch, Barbara Gault, Gina Chirillo, and Jennifer Clark. "Five Ways to Win an Argument about the Gender Wage Gap (Updated 2019)." *Institute for Women's Policy Research.* September 11, 2019. https://iwpr.org/publications/five-ways-to-win-an-argument-about-the-gender-wage-gap/

Heffernan, T. *The Passion of Perpetua and Felicity.* Oxford: Oxford University Press, 2012.

Hegewisch, Ariane and Adiam Tesfaselassie. "The Gender Wage Gap by Occupation 2018." *The Institute for Women's Policy Research.* April 2, 2019. https://iwpr.org/publications/gender-wage-gap-occupation-2018/

Hodson, Gordon, Megan Earle, and Maureen A. Craig. "Privilege lost: How dominant groups react to shifts in cultural primacy and power." *Group Processes & Intergroup Relations* 25, no. 3 (2022): 625–641.

Holland, Brynn. "The 'Father of Modern Gynecology' Performed Shocking Experiments on Slaves: He was a medical trailblazer, but at what cost?" *History.com.* December 4, 2018, https://www.history.com/news/the-father-of-modern-gynecology-performed-shocking-experiments-on-slaves

Holland, Brynn. "The Extraordinary Secret Life of Dr. James Barry: How—and why—did a groundbreaking physician pass as the opposite sex for more than 50 years?" January 17, 2019, https://www.history.com/news/the-extraordinary-secret-life-of-dr-james-barry

hooks, bell. *Feminism is for everybody.* New York: Routledge, 2020.

Hughes, Bettany. "Why Were Women Written Out Of History? An Interview With Bettany Hughes," *English Hertiage,* February 29, 2016, http://blog.english-heritage.org.uk/women-written-history-interview-bettany-hughes/

Hughes, H. Stewart. *History as Art and as Science.* Harper & Rowe, 1964.

Hunt, Lynn. *History: Why it Matters.* Cambridge: Polity Press, 2018.

Iowa Department of Education. "Social Studies: A Call to Action." November 16, 2015. https://www.educateiowa.gov/sites/files/ed/documents/Social%20Studies%20report_11-16-15%20FINAL.pdf

Jacobs, Harriet A. *Incidents in the life of a slave girl: written by herself.* Cambridge, Mass: Harvard University Press, 2000.

Kadari, Tamar. "Hagar: Midrash and Aggadah, Shalvi/Hyman." *Encyclopedia of Jewish Women*, December 31, 1999. Jewish Women's Archive. https://jwa.org/encyclopedia/article/hagar-midrash-and-aggadah

Kalaidis, Jen. "Bring Back Social Studies: The amount of time public-school kids spend learning about government and civics is shrinking." *The Atlantic.* September 2013. https://www.theatlantic.com/education/archive/2013/09/bring-back-social-studies/279891/

Kansas Historical Society. "Carrie Nation." *Kansas Historical Society, Kansaspedia.* August 2017. https://www.kshs.org/kansapedia/carry-a-nation/15502

Katz, Brigit. "Claudette Colvin, Who Was Arrested for Refusing to Give Up Her Bus Seat in 1955, Is Fighting to Clear Her Record: The civil rights pioneer pushed back against segregation nine months before Rosa Parks' landmark protest but has long been overlooked," *Smithsonian Magazine*, October 28, 2021, https://www.smithsonianmag.com/smart-news/claudette-colvin-who-was-arrested-for-refusing-to-give-up-her-bus-seat-in-1955-is-fighting-to-clear-her-record-180978959/

Kelley, Meghan. "The Good Life of Anna Comnena: First Female Historian and Byzantine Princess," *The Histories* 7, no. 2 (2019): 3. https://digitalcommons.lasalle.edu/the_histories/vol7/iss2/3

Kershaw, Alex, *The Bedford Boys: One American Town's Ultimate D-Day Sacrifice.* Waterville, Me.: Thorndike Press, 2003.

Khan, Andrew and Rebecca Onion. "Is History Written About Men, by Men?" *Slate.* January 6, 2016. http://www.slate.com/articles/news_and_politics/history/2016/01/popular_history_why_are_so_many_history_books_about_men_by_men.html

Klein, Susan S. Ed. *Handbook for Achieving Gender Equity through Education.* Mahwah, NJ: Larence Erlbaum Associates, 1985.

Kleinman, Sherryl, and Martha Copp. "Denying Social Harm: Students' Resistance to Lessons about Inequality." *Teaching Sociology* 37, no. 3 (2009): 283–293. http://www.jstor.org/stable/25594011

Kuiper, Kathleen. "Olympe de Gouges." *Encyclopedia Britannica.* October 30, 2022. https://www.britannica.com/biography/Olympe-de-Gouges

Lather, P. Critical frames in educational research: Feminist and post-structural perspectives. *Theory into Practice* 31, no. 2 (1992): 87–99.

Lee, Yuen Ting. "Ban Zhao: Scholar of Han Dynasty China." *World History Connected.* 2012. https://worldhistoryconnected.press.uillinois.edu/9.1/lee.html

Lerner, Gerda. "The Majority Finds Its Past, Oxford: Oxford University Press, 1979, Smith-Rosenberg, C., The New Woman and the New History," *Feminist Studies*. 3, no. 1 and 2 (1975): 185–191.

Lerner, Gerda. *The Creation of Patriarchy*. New York, NY: Oxford University Press, 1986.

Lewis, Jone Johnson. "The Woman's Bible and Elizabeth Cady Stanton on Genesis." *ThoughtCo*. https://www.thoughtco.com/the-womans-bible-excerpt-3530448

Lewis, Jone Johnson. "Biography of Anna Comnena, the First Female Historian," *Thought Co*, May 15, 2019a, https://www.thoughtco.com/anna-comnena-facts-3529667

Lewis, Jone Johnson. "Mercy Otis Warren," *Thought Co.*, February 4, 2019b, https://www.thoughtco.com/mercy-otis-warren-biography-3530669

Livingston, Gretchen. "Stay-at-home moms and dads account for about one-in-five U.S. parents," *PEW Research Center*, September 24, 2018, https://www.pewresearch.org/fact-tank/2018/09/24/stay-at-home-moms-and-dads-account-for-about-one-in-five-u-s-parents/

Lockyer, Bridget and Abigail Tazzymant. "'Victims of History': challenging students' perceptions of women in history." 2016. Teaching History (165): 8 Historical Association 2016 0040-0610.

Loewen, James. *Lies My Teacher Told Me*. New York, NY: New Press, 2018.

Long, Brandon. "Is Jordan Peterson Right About Agreeable Women? (No)," *Medium*. February 14, 2019. https://medium.com/slightly-educated/is-jordan-peterson-right-about-agreeable-women-no-d30eb6f319e

LumenLearning. "GenderDifferencesintheClassroom." *EducationalPsychology*. n.d. https://courses.lumenlearning.com/suny-educationalpsychology/chapter/gender-differences-in-the-classroom/

MacDonald, Janis L. "The Need for Contextual ReVision: Mercy Otis Warren, A Case in Point." *Yale Journal of Law & Feminism* 5, no. 1, Article 7 (1992): 186–187. http://digitalcommons.law.yale.edu/yjlf/vol5/iss1/7

Mah, Anne. "This Picture Tells a Tragic Story of What Happened to Women After D-Day." *Time Magazine*. June 6, 2018. https://time.com/5303229/women-after-d-day/

Marcotte, Amanda. "Nancy Reagan's anti-feminism might be her most lasting legacy." *Salon*. March 7, 2016. https://www.salon.com/2016/03/07/nancy_reagans_anti_feminism_might_be_her_most_lasting_legacy/

Mark, Harrison W. "Women's March on Versailles." *World History Encyclopedia*. June 28, 2022a. https://www.worldhistory.org/Women's_March_on_Versailles/

Mark, Joshua J. "Hildegard of Bingen." *Ancient History Encyclopedia*. May 30, 2019. https://www.ancient.eu/Hildegard_of_Bingen/

Mark, Joshua J. "Ten Women of the Protestant Reformation." *World History Encyclopedia*. March 17, 2022b. https://www.worldhistory.org/article/1964/ten-women-of-the-protestant-reformation/

Martell, Christopher C., and Kaylene M. Stevens. "Perceptions of Teaching Race and Gender: Results of a Survey of Social Studies Teachers." *The High School Journal* 101, no. 4 (2018): 274–299. https://www.jstor.org/stable/26785824

Martell, Christopher C., Ed. *Social Studies Teacher Education: Critical Issues and Current Perspectives*. IAP: Charlotte, NC. 2018.

Martin, Daisy, Maldonado, Saúl, Schneider, Jack, and Smith, Mark. (2011). A Report on the State of History Education State Policies and National Programs Second Edition. 10.13140/RG.2.2.12801.40802.

Martin, Joanne. "Feminist Theory and Critical Theory: Unexplored Synergies." *Organizational Behavior, Stanford Graduate School of Business*. Working Paper No. 1758, February 2002.

Mary Baker Eddy Library Editors. "The Life of Mary Baker Eddy." *Mary Baker Eddy Library*. n.d., https://www.marybakereddylibrary.org/mary-baker-eddy/the-life-of-mary-baker-eddy/

Maurer, Elizabeth L. et al. "Where are the women?" *National Women's History Museum*. 2018. https://www.womenshistory.org/social-studies-standards

Mayell, Hilary. "Genghis Khan a Prolific Lover, DNA Data Implies." *National Geographic*. February 14, 2003. https://www.nationalgeographic.com/news/2003/2/mongolia-genghis-khan-

McCaig, Amy. "Psychologists explain why 'America isn't ready for female president." *Rice University: News and Media Relations*. March 20, 2018. https://news.rice.edu/2018/03/20/psychologists-explain-why-america-isnt-ready-for-female-president/

McCormick, Theresa M. "Generating Effective Teaching through Primary Sources." in: Elizabeth Heilman (ed.). *Social Studies and Diversity Education*. New York: Routledge, 2010.

McDonald, Hollie, "Social Politics of Seventeenth Century London Coffee Houses: An Exploration of Class and Gender." *Honors Projects*. 208, 2013. http://scholarworks.gvsu.edu/honorsprojects/208

McGrath, Mary. "Opinion: Are Americans ready for a female president? Yes. In fact they might prefer one." November 24, 2019. http://www/latimes.com/opinion/story/2019-11-24/elect-woman-president-warren

McGuire, Danielle L. *At the Dark End of the Street: Black Women Rape and Resistance - a New History of the Civil Rights Movement from Rosa Parks to the Rise of Black Power*. New York: Vintage Books, 2011.

McGuire, Danielle. "More Than A Seat On The Bus." *We're History*. December 1, 2015, http://werehistory.org/rosa-parks/

McGuire, John Thomas. "'The Most Unjust Piece of Legislation': Section 213 of the Economy Act of 1932 and Feminism During the New Deal." *Journal of Policy History* 20, no. 4 (January 4, 2008): 516–541. https://doi.org/10.1353/jph.0.0026

McKie, Robin. "We owe it all to superstud Genghis: Warlord Khan has 16m male relatives alive now, says study." *The Guardian*. March 2, 2003. https://www.theguardian.com/uk/2003/mar/02/science.research

Melzian, Harley No. 31, Artists Victory Exhibit in miniature. Ever Ready Label Corp., 1943, Library of Virginia.

Meyer, Elizabeth J. "Sex, Gender, and Education Research: The Case for Transgender Studies in Education." *Educational Researcher* 51, no. 5 (June, 2022): 315–323. https://doi.org/10.3102/0013189X211048870

Michaels, Debra. "Mercy Otis Warren." *National Women's History Museum*. 2015. https://www.womenshistory.org/education-resources/biographies/mercy-otis-warren

Miles, Rosalind. *Women's History of the Modern World: How Radicals, Rebels, and Every Woman Revolutionized the Last 200 Years*. New York: William Morrow, 2021.

Miles, Rosalind. *Women's History of the World*. London: Paladin/Grafton Books, 1989.

Mobe, Tshiamo. "10 Women Scientists Leading the Fight Against the Climate Crisis: These incredible women in STEM fields are working towards a greener future." *Global Citizen*. April 11, 2022. https://www.globalcitizen.org/en/content/women-scientists-climate-change-solutions-stem/#:~:text=The%20Reuters%20Hot%20List%20of,reaching%20implications%20of%20climate%20change

Moscucci, Ornella. *The Science of Woman: Gynaecology and Gender in England, 1800-1929*. Cambridge: Cambridge University Press, 1990.

Mumford, Mily. "Dr. James Barry and Recognizing Trans Stories in the History of Science." *Westcoast Women in Engineering and Science*. August 17, 2021. https://www.sfu.ca/wwest/WWEST_blog/dr--james-barry-and-recognizing-trans-stories-in-the-history-of-.html

Mundy, Liza. *Code Girls: The Untold Story of the American Women Code Breakers of World War II*, First ed. New York: Hachette Books, 2017.

Murphy, Jocelyn Nichole. "The role of women in film: Supporting the men -- An analysis of how culture influences the changing discourse on gender representations in film." *Journalism Undergraduate Honors Theses*. 2, 2015. http://scholarworks.uark.edu/jouruht/

Mursell, Ian. "Giving Birth was One Big Battle." *Mexicolore*. Accessed March 18, 2024. https://www.mexicolore.co.uk/aztecs/aztec-life/giving-birth-was-fighting-a-battle

Nash, Gary B., Charlotte Crabtree, and Russ E. Dunn. *History on Trial: Culture Wars and the Teaching of the Past*. New York, NY: Alfred A. Knopf, 1997.

National Council for Jewish Women. "Judaism and Abortion." *National Council for Jewish Women*. April 2019. https://www.ncjw.org/wp-content/uploads/2019/05/Judaism-and-Abortion-FINAL.pdf

National Council for the Social Studies. *The College, Career, and Civic Life (C3) Framework for the Social Studies*. Silver Spring, MD: NCSS, 2017.

National Park Service Editors. "Quaker Influence." *National Park Service*. April 6, 2020. https://www.nps.gov/wori/learn/historyculture/quaker-influence.htm#:~:text=Followers%20of%20Fox%2C%20Quakers%2C%20believed,with%20God%20and%20the%20Bible

National Parks Service Editors, "Grimke Sisters," *National Parks Service*, February 26, 2015, https://www.nps.gov/wori/learn/historyculture/grimke-sisters.htm

New Hampshire Curriculum Framework," *New Hampshire Department of Education*, June 2006, https://www.education.nh.gov/sites/g/files/ehbemt326/files/inline-documents/standards-socialstudies-framework.pdf

Newport, Frank, David Moore, and Lydia Saad. "Long-Term Gallup Poll Trends: A Portrait of American Public Opinion Through the Century." December 20, 1999, http://news.gallup.com/poll/3400/longterm-gallup-poll-trends-portrait-american-public-opinion.aspx

Newton, Isaac. Letter to Robert Hooke. February, 1675.

Noddings, Nell. Social studies and feminism. *Theory & Research in Social Education* 20, no. 3 (1992): 230–241.

Noddings, Nell. The care tradition: Beyond "add women and stir". *Theory into Practice* 40, no. 1 (2001): 29–34.

Noyce, John. "Hildegard of Bingen and her Visions of the Divine Feminine," *Academia*, 2013, https://www.academia.edu/5406213/Hildegard_of_Bingen_and_her_Visions_of_the_Divine_Feminine

Offen, Karen. "On the French Origin of the Words Feminism and Feminist." *Gender Issues* 8 (1988): 45–51. https://doi.org/10.1007/BF02685596

Only a Teacher Editors. "Charlotte Forten." *PBS*. n.d. https://www.pbs.org/onlyateacher/charlotte.html

O'Reilly, Marie, Andrea Ó Súilleabháin, and Thania Paffenholz, "Chapter 03 Women's Participation And A Better Understanding Of The Political, Reimagining Peacemaking: Women's Roles in Peace Processes," *UN Women*, 2015, https://wps.unwomen.org/participation/

Organization for Economic Co-Operation and Development. "Employment: Time spent in paid and unpaid work, by sex." *OEDC*. 2022. https://stats.oecd.org/index.aspx?queryid=54757

Osmont, Marie-Louise. *The Normandy Diary of Marie-Louise Osmont*. New York: Random House, 1994.

Padilla, Mariel. "Americans support extending child support payments to pregnancy, survey finds: 'If we're thinking of a fetus as an actual person with rights, then a whole bunch of other stuff has to change,' said Chris Ellis, the co-director of the Bucknell Institute for Public Policy." *19th News*. July 12, 2022. https://19thnews.org/2022/07/child-support-payments-pregnancy-conception-survey/

Phelen, John. "Harvard Study: 'Gender Wage Gap' Explained Entirely by Work Choices of Men and Women: The 'gender wage gap' is as real as unicorns and has been killed more times than Michael Myers." *Foundation for Economic Education*. December 10, 2018, https://fee.org/articles/harvard-study-gender-pay-gap-explained-entirely-by-work-choices-of-men-and-women/?gclid=CjwKCAjw26H3BRB2EiwAy32zhZKsF45zDh2P22RHSXgHrfc-hthCcA1Xh1hyUhN3A9XFwvx9XP6u6hoCXokQAvD_BwE

Pondiscio, Robert. "The Not-So Great Society." *Heritage*. April 15, 2020. https://www.heritage.org/curricula-resource-initiative/research/the-not-so-great-society

Prifogle, Emily and Karin Wulf. "Why Women Also Know History." *Journal of Women's History* 32, no. 2 (2020): 113–117. https://doi.org/10.1353/jowh.2020.0014,113

Reddy, Helen, and Ray Burton. "I Am Woman," *I Don't Know How to Love Him*, Capital Records. 1972, Record.

Reeves, Richard V., and Isabel V. Sawhill. "Men's Lib." *The New York Times*. November 14, 2015. https://www.nytimes.com/2015/11/15/opinion/sunday/mens-lib.html?_r=0

Reeves, Richard V. *Of Boys and Men: Why the Modern Male Is Struggling, Why It Matters, and What to Do About It Washington*, D.C.: Brookings Institution Press, 2022.

Rich, Motoko. "'The Tale of Genji' Is More Than 1,000 Years Old. What Explains Its Lasting Appeal?: The book is often described as the world's first novel and a touchstone of Japanese literature. But some of its themes, including its take on gender and power, have echoed over centuries." *The New York Times*. April 20, 2023. https://www.nytimes.com/2023/04/15/books/tale-of-genji-japan-women.html

Rinard, Judith E. *Book of Flight*. New York: Firefly Books, 2001.

Rodsky, Eve. *Fair Play: Fair Play: A Game-Changing Solution for When You Have Too Much to Do (and More Life to Live)*. New York: Putnam and Sons, 2021.

Roosevelt, Eleanor. "Eleanor Roosevelt's 'My Day,' 6/7/1944: sacrifice on D-Day." *White House Historical Association.* 2020. https://www.white housechistory.org/eleanor-roosevelts-my-day-6-7-1944

Ruether, Rosemary Radford. "Sexism and Misogyny in the Christian Tradition: Liberating Alternatives." *Buddhist-Christian Studies* 34 (2014): 83–94. http://www.jstor.org/stable/24801355

Sadker, Myra, and Sadker, David. *Failing at Fairness: How America's Schools Cheat Girls.* New York, NY: Simon and Schuster, 2010.

Saracino, Jessica. "The Effect of Socioeconomic Status on the Number of Women in State Legislatures." *Public Purpose: An Interdisciplinary Journal American University's Graduate School of Public Affairs* 6, no. 1 (Spring 2008). https://www.american.edu/spa/publicpurpose/upload/the-effect-of-socioeconomic-status-on-the-number-of-women-in-state-legislatures. pdf, 125.

Scheiner-Fisher, Cicely. "The Inclusion of Women's History In The Secondary Social Studies Classroom." *Electronic Theses and Dissertations.* University of Central Florida, 2013.

Schmeichel, Mardi. "Skirting around critical feminist rationales for teaching women in social studies." *Theory & Research in Social Education* 43(1), 2015, 1–27.

Schochet, Leila. "The Child Care Crisis Is Keeping Women Out of the Workforce," Center for American Progress. March 28, 2019, https://www.americanprogress.org/issues/early-childhood/reports/2019/03/28/467488/child-care-crisis-keeping-women-workforce/

Shepard, A. and Walker, G. Gender, change and periodisation. *Gender and History* 20, no. 3 (2008): 453–462. ISSN 0953-5233.

Shocker, J. B. A case for using images to teach women's history. *The History Teacher* 47, no. 3 (2014): 421–450.

Shocker, J. B., and Woyshner, C. Representing African American women in U.S. history textbooks. *The Social Studies* 104, no. 1 (2013): 23–31.

Singer, Alan. "How the NCSS Sold Out Social Studies and History." *History News Network.* December 16, 2014. https://historynewsnetwork.org/article/157845

Smialek, Jeanna. "Claudia Goldin Wins Nobel in Economics for Studying Women in the Work Force: Her research uncovered the reasons for gender gaps in labor force participation and earnings. She is the third woman to win the prize." *The New York Times.* October 11, 2023. https://www.nytimes.com/2023/10/09/business/economy/claudia-goldin-nobel-prize-economics.html#:~:text=The%20Nobel%20Memorial%20Prize%20in,progress%20in%20the%20work%20force

Smith, William Raymond. *History As Argument: Three Patriot Historians Of The American Revolution.* The Hague: Mouton & Co., 1966.

Snellgrove, David Llewelyn, Donald S. Lopez, Frank E. Reynolds, Hajime Nakamura, Giuseppe Tucci, and Joseph M. Kitagawa. "Buddhism." *Encyclopedia Britannica*. August 23, 2022, https://www.britannica.com/topic/Buddhism

Stanton, Elizabeth Cady, Susan B. Anthony, and Matilda Joselyn Gage, eds. *History of Woman Suffrage*, Vol. 1. New York: Fowler and Wells, 1881.

Steinem, Gloria, Meenakshi Mukherjee, and Ira Pande. "A Conversation with Gloria Steinem." *India International Centre Quarterly* 34, no. 2 (2007): 90–105. http://www.jstor.org/stable/23006309

Steinem, Gloria. "The Importance of Work," *Outrageous Acts and Everyday Rebellions*, 3rd Edition. New York, NY: Henry Holt and Company, 2019.

Stevens, Kaylene M., and Martell, Christopher C. Feminist Social Studies Teachers: The Role of Teachers' Backgrounds and Beliefs in Shaping Gender-Equitable Practices. *Journal of Social Studies Research* (2018). https://doi.org/10.1016/j.jssr.2018.02.002

Stevens, Kaylene M., and Martell, Christopher C. An avenue for challenging sexism: Examining the high school sociology classroom. *Journal of Social Science Education* 15, no. 1 (2016): 63–73.

Stollberg-Rilinger, Barbara. *Maria Theresa: The Habsburg Empress in Her Time*. Princeton: Princeton University Press, 2021.

Stopford, Richard. "Teaching feminism: Problems of critical claims and student certainty." *Philosophy and Social Criticism* 46, no. 10 (2020): 1203–1224.

Strayer, Robert and E. Nelson. *Ways of The World*. 3rd ed. Boston: Bedford/St. Martin's, 2016.

Taie, Soheyla and Laurie Lewis. "Characteristics of 2020–21 Public and Private K–12 School Teachers in the United States: Results From the National Teacher and Principal Survey." The National Center for Education Statistics at IES. First Look. December 13, 2022. https://nces.ed.gov/pubs2022/2022113.pdf

Tetreault, Mary Kay Thompson. "Integrating Women's History." *The History Teacher* 19, no. 2 (February, 1986).

Townsend, Robert B. "What The Data Reveals About Women Historians." *Perspectives on History*. May 1, 2010. https://www.historians.org/publications-and-directories/perspectives-on-history/may-2010/what-the-data-reveals-about-women-historians

Trecker, J. "Women in United States History High School Textbooks." *Social Education* 1971, 35, 248–335.

Trickey, Erick. "The Woman Whose Words Inflamed the American Revolution." *Smithsonian Magazine*. June 20, 2017. https://www.smithsonianmag.com/history/woman-whose-words-inflamed-american-revolution-180963765/

Twain, Mark. *Christian Science: With Notes Containing Corrections to Date.* New York: Harper, 1907. Retrieved from Gutenberg Press. https://www.gutenberg.org/files/3187/3187-h/3187-h.htm#link2H_PREF

Ulrich, Laurel Thatcher. *Well-Behaved Women Seldom Make History,* 1st ed. New York: Alfred A. Knopf, 2007.

UN Women Editors. "The world is failing girls and women, according to new UN report." *UN Women.* September 7, 2023. https://www.unwomen.org/en/news-stories/press-release/2023/09/press-release-the-world-is-failing-girls-and-women-according-to-new-un-report

UN Women Editors. "Visualizing the data: Women's representation in society." *UN Women.* February 25, 2020. https://www.unwomen.org/en/digital-library/multimedia/2020/2/infographic-visualizing-the-data-womens-representation

Van Ess, Hans. "Praise and Slander: The Evocation of Empress Lü in the Shiji and the Hanshu." NAN NU -- Men, *Women & Gender in Early & Imperial China* 8, no. 2 (September 2006): 221–254. https://doi.org/10.1163/156852606779969824

Vann, Richard T. "Historiography: Women's History." *Encyclopedia Britannica.* January 17, 2020. https://www.britannica.com/topic/historiography

Varner, Ann. "March: Women's History Month." *University of Missouri Kansas City Women's Center.* March 5, 2018. https://info.umkc.edu/womenc/2018/03/05/march-womens-history-month/

Voorhees, Amy B. "Mary Baker Eddy, the Woman Question, and Christian Salvation: Finding a Consistent Connection by Broadening the Boundaries of Feminist Scholarship." *Journal of Feminist Studies in Religion* 28, no. 2 (Fall 2012), 5–25. https://www.jstor.org/stable/10.2979/jfemistudreli.28.2.5

Walker, Tim. "Testing Obsession and the Disappearing Curriculum." *NEA Today.* September 2, 2014. http://neatoday.org/2014/09/02/the-testing-obsession-and-the-disappearing-curriculum-2/

Wallner, Peter A. *Faith on Trial: Mary Baker Eddy, Christian Science and the First Amendment.* Concord, NH: Plaidswede Publishing, 2014.

Watson, Emma. "Gender Equality is Your Issue Too." *UN Women.* September 20, 2014. https://www.unwomen.org/en/news/stories/2014/9/emma-watson-gender-equality-is-your-issue-too

Weatherford, Jack. *The Secret History of the Mongol Queens: How the Daughters of Genghis Khan Rescued His Empire.* New York: Crown Publishing Group, 2010.

Whipps, Judy. "Sarah Grimké (1792—1873) and Angelina Grimké Weld (1805—1879)." *Internet Archive of Philosophy.* n.d. https://iep.utm.edu/grimke/

White, Gillian B. "Why Daycare Workers Are So Poor, Even Though Daycare Costs So Much: They can't even afford child care for their own kids." *The Atlantic*. November 5, 2015. https://www.theatlantic.com/business/archive/2015/11/childcare-workers-cant-afford-childcare/414496/

Will, Madeline. "Misogynist Influencer Andrew Tate Has Captured Boys' Attention. What Teachers Need to Know." *Education Week*. February 2, 2023. https://www.edweek.org/leadership/misogynist-influencer-andrew-tate-has-captured-boys-attention-what-teachers-need-to-know/2023/02

Women and the American Story. "Life Story: Weetamoo (c.1635-1676)." *New York Historical Society*. October 16, 2020. https://wams.nyhistory.org/early-encounters/english-colonies/weetamoo/

Wolf, Michelle. "Nice Lady." Performance at the Apollo. 2018. Retrieved from: The Female Lead. *YouTube*. Uploaded on September 3, 2023. https://www.youtube.com/watch?v=HRA8LsMNqTQ

Wolfe, Rob. "Edelblut OK'd as N.H. Education Commissioner." *Valley News*. March 23, 2017. https://www.vnews.com/Edelblut-Confirmed-By-Council-8844331

Woolf, Virginia. *A Room of One's Own*. New York NY: Harcourt Brace and Company, 1929.

Worrall, Simon. "Meet the 'Difficult' Women Who Wrote Their Own Rules." *National Geographic*. May 12, 2018. https://www.nationalgeographic.com/culture/article/meet-the-_difficult-women-who-wrote-their-own-rules

Yang, Xinying, Qiu, Hongfeng, and Zhu, Ranran. "Bargaining with patriarchy or converting men into pro-feminists: social-mediated frame alignment in feminist connective activism." *Feminist Media Studies* (2022): 1–19. https://doi.org/10.1080/14680777.2022.2075909

Zhao, Ban, and Nancy Swan, trans. *Lessons for Women*, c.IV. n.d.

Zinn, Howard. *A People's History of the United States*. New York: Harper & Row, 2003.

Zippia. "High School Coach Demographics And Statistics In The Us." *Zippia*. July 21, 2023. https://www.zippia.com/high-school-coach-jobs/demographics/

Zittleman, Karen, and David Sadker. "Gender Bias in Teacher Education Texts: New (and Old) Lessons." *Journal of Teacher Education* 53, no. 2 (March 2002): 168–180. https://doi.org/10.1177/0022487102053002008

For Product Safety Concerns and Information please contact our EU
representative GPSR@taylorandfrancis.com
Taylor & Francis Verlag GmbH, Kaufingerstraße 24, 80331 München, Germany

* 9 7 8 1 0 3 2 6 9 3 1 1 8 *